Trails of the

Sawtooth and White Cloud Mountains
by Margaret Fuller

8/12/04

Third Edition

Cover photo: Washington Lake. *Photo by Margaret Fuller*

Finger of Fate (Sawtooth Mountains)

Trails of the
Sawtooth and White Cloud Mountains

by Margaret Fuller

Third Edition

Signpost Books

Trails of the Sawtooth and White Cloud Mountains
Third Edition
© Copyright 1998, by Margaret Fuller
ISBN 0-913140-49-X

Other Signpost Books by Margaret Fuller

Trails of the Frank Church — River of No Return Wilderness

Trails of Western Idaho

Also by Margaret Fuller

Mountains: A Natural History and Hiking Guide

Forest Fires: An Introduction to Wildland Fire Behavior,
   Management, Firefighting, and Prevention

SIGNPOST BOOKS
8912 192nd St. SW
Edmonds, WA 98026

For Ryan, Christopher, and Sierra

Foreword

By Cecil D. Andrus
former Governor of Idaho

The Sawtooth National Recreation Area in the center of Idaho is one of those rare spots that remain little traveled and serenely remote, even though it is adjacent to popular vacation destinations. I know it well for I have spent many hours in its soul-satisfying confines.

Only a few miles from the popular Sun Valley area, the Sawtooth National Recreation Area provides access to wild backcountry for thousands of visitors every year.

My efforts to preserve this region when I was first governor of Idaho are some of my most satisfying accomplishments. Therefore, it was with the greatest pleasure that I saw Margaret Fuller produce the Area's first comprehensive guide in 1979. In writing it, Margaret compiled descriptions of all the trails she had hiked with her family in the Sawtooth, White Cloud and Boulder Mountains - the Sawtooth NRA's three rugged ranges.

Now she has revised and expanded *Trails of the Sawtooth and White Cloud Mountains*. Those who travel only by motorized vehicle won't benefit as much from the new edition as those who travel by foot or on horseback. But this is the perfect reference and trail companion for those who explore this section of the Idaho backcountry.

On the following pages, Margaret details many Idaho trails in the Sawtooth – White Cloud – Boulder Mountain area, an additon of more than two dozen hikes to the original book. They are grouped according to the lake, stream or other starting point from which they fan out into the wilderness.

For each trail she lists mileages from the starting point and also mileages to that starting point from the access. She notes elevation gains and the highest point and estimates the time required to complete the hike.

Her book includes also a general discussion about the area, a listing of campgrounds, and a history of the region, going back to early mining days.

Pettit Lake

It describes vegetation that will be found and lists wild animals that may be sighted. It tells how to obtain services of packers and guides. It offers advice on equipment, supplies, and methods of guarding against over-exertion. The would-be hiker is provided with safety precautions and first-aid suggestions.

I you've never tried an Idaho mountain trail, this book provides valuable information. If you've tried many trails but would like to experience some new ones, this book is likely to give you some ideas of where you could go.

It is my hope that this guide will continue to encourage visitors to the Sawtooth NRA to try the less-used trails and campsites and to disperse the public enjoyment throughout the Area.

This region is special to me. I hope this revision of Margaret's guide will help you share the very special Idaho experiences in store for visitors to the Sawtooth National Recreation Area. It's a worthwhile addition to literature on how to enjoy Idaho's unique quality of life.

Cecil D. Andrus

ACKNOWLEDGEMENTS

I would like to thank all those who helped me with the revision of this book, including Mose Shrum, supervisory forest technician for the Sawtooth National Recreation Area and Jim Dorr of his staff. A special thanks goes to Mary Ann Cameron for editing and Cliff Cameron for remaining my publisher for so many years. The most important were friends and members of my family who over many years have hiked with me to help me with my books. Without the help of my husband Wayne, my daughters Leslie Fuller Magryta and Hilary Fuller Renner, and my sons Doug, Neal and Stuart Fuller I could never have written this book or revised it. I would also especially like to thank former Idaho governor Cecil Andrus for writing the foreword.

The first edition of this book would not have been possible without the help and encouragement of Donna Parsons, director of the Snake River Regional Studies Center at the College of Idaho; Louise Marshall, publisher of *Signpost Magazine* and founder of Signpost Books; and Dave Lee, the first chief wilderness ranger for the SNRA.

I would also like to thank those who have helped me over the years with the book and with publicity for it, such as *The Idaho Statesman*, Albertson College of Idaho, Lou Florence, the Idaho Lung Association and the many organizations who have invited me to give slide shows for their members. I would also like to thank my customers, new and old, such as Backwoods Mountain Sports, Chapter 1, Chateau Drug, and the Elephants Perch in Ketchum; Ex Libris and the Sun Valley Gift Shop in Sun Valley; McCoy Tackle, Smiley Creek Lodge, the Sawtooth Interpretive Association, Riverwear Sports, River 1, and The Sawtooth Hotel in Stanley; the Sunbeam Store at Sunbeam; Twin Peaks Sports, the Village Square, Terry's Sports, and Friends of the Custer Museum in Challis; The Story Teller and Salmon Rexall in Salmon; the North Fork Store in North Fork; Gravity Sports, Hometown Sports, McCall Air Taxi, Blue Grouse Books, and the Ponderosa Natural History Association in McCall; Wheeler Drug in Cascade; Hatch's Books in Ontario, Oregon; Food For Thought in Caldwell, Hazzy's in Nampa, Stark's Office Supply in Weiser; The Book Gallery, Parnassus Books, Idaho Mountain Touring, the Boise Airport Gift Shop, The Book Shop, and the Benchmark in Boise.

Margaret Fuller

Sawtooth Wilderness and National Recreation Area

White Cloud – Boulder Mountain Area

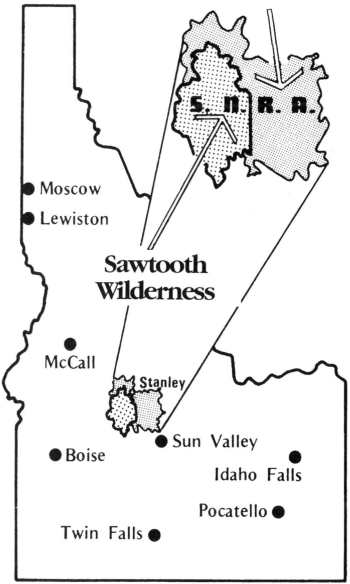

CONTENTS

trails in the SAWTOOTH MOUNTAINS

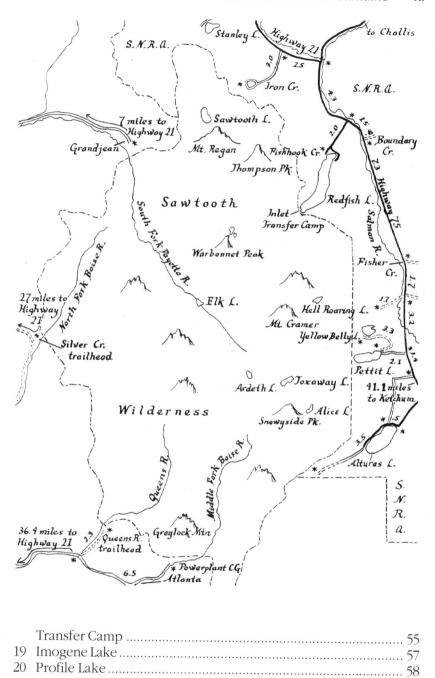

trails in the WHITE CLOUD MOUNTAINS

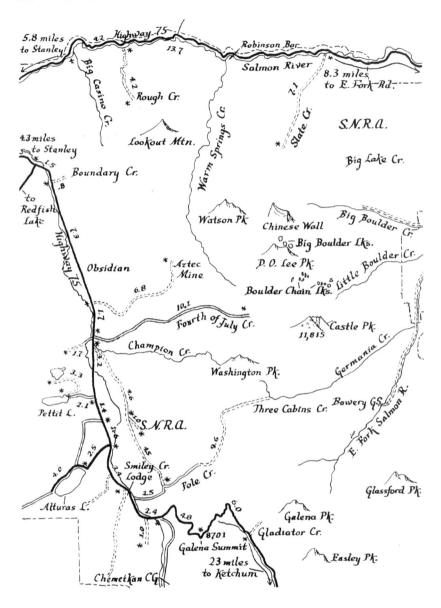

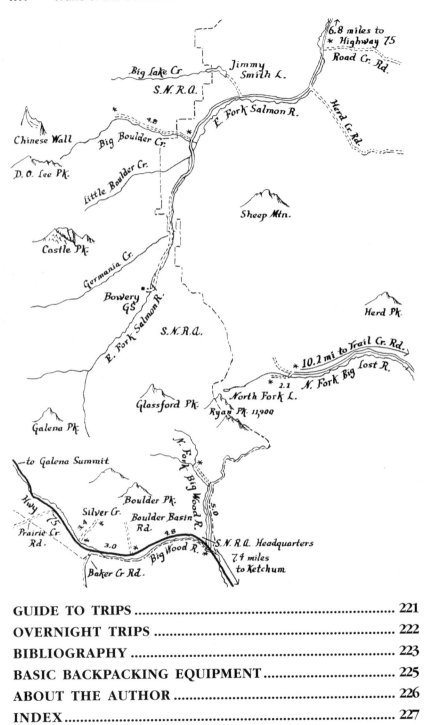

Hikers and the Grand Mogul

Photographs

All photos are by Margaret Fuller, unless noted otherwise

INTRODUCTION

About the area

A few miles north of Sun Valley, Idaho, the Sawtooth Mountains rise thousands of feet above the headwaters of the Salmon River, like rows of saws set on edge. To the east of the Sawtooths above wooded and wrinkled foothills the White Cloud Mountains soar in summits of vanilla ice cream. Closer to Sun Valley, along the Big Wood River, swirl the pink and gray stripes of the Boulder Mountains. The lack of crowds adds to the unique beauty of these three ranges of the Sawtooth National Recreation Area. In this area, the highest summit is Castle Peak (11,815 feet) in the White Clouds.

The Salmon River, which separates the Sawtooths on the west from the White Clouds on the east, runs north down the Sawtooth Valley from its headwaters to the town of Stanley, where it turns east. Here a tributary, Valley Creek, flows into the river from a series of meadows called Stanley Basin. This basin separates the northern Sawtooths on the west from the Salmon River Mountains of the Frank Church — River of No Return Wilderness on the east. In June, camas flowers turn the meadows to lakes of blue.

Big sagebrush cloaks the dry parts of these valleys with soft gray green. In the center of the valleys, meadows and a strip of willows follow the coils of Valley Creek and the Salmon River. An occasional sheepherder's wagon with curved white top shows visitors traditional ranching is still being conducted. Place names such as Hell Roaring Lake remind us frontier days here lasted into the twentieth century.

At the west edge of the valleys, forested moraines embrace large glacial lakes: Alturas, Pettit, Yellow Belly, Redfish and Stanley. Five-mile long Redfish is the best known and most popular. From the head of this lake, buff and gray needles march up a U-shaped canyon. The entrance to the canyon is guarded on the south by the points and pinnacles of the Grand Mogul and on the north by the pleated crown of Mt. Heyburn. Farther north when there is no wind, Stanley Lake reflects the two offset granite triangles of McGown Peak.

Purposes of this guide

This guidebook was written to help spread visitors out, first by giving them information on little-used trails as well as standard ones, and second by encouraging experienced hikers to explore trailless areas. Another purpose of the book is to make known the beauty of the Sawtooth National Recreation Area, so that there will be advocates for preserving the White Cloud and Boulder Mountains, which are not yet designated wilderness.

Changes in this edition

Because many more people are now using some of the trailless areas covered in the book, mention of non-system trails and paths in all trailless areas has been removed. For off-trail hikes only the terrain and landmarks are described. My maps show the routes, but in many cases there is no path, or there are several paths. Be aware that paths in trailless areas may be animal paths and mislead you. Or they may lead to dangerous slopes. Instead of following paths, use a compass and topographic map to find the way. To prevent erosion, avoid walking on non-system trails or paths, especially those that run straight up slopes. In trailless areas, walk on rocks whenever possible, and when it isn't, spread out your party to avoid damaging the plants and soil.

New regulations

In 1997, under a three-year test plan, the SNRA started a recreation user fee system that requires the purchase of low-cost day or annual passes. The money will be used to maintain and improve recreation in the SNRA. Passes may be obtained at all SNRA offices and from local vendors. Failure to buy one may result in a citation and fine. In addition, a new Sawtooth Wilderness plan will probably require separate but free permits for all those entering the Sawtooth Wilderness. The plan includes new restrictions on campfires, group, sizes, and stock use. Be sure to call the SNRA for the latest information on passes and regulations.

Information in this guidebook

The author is a hiker, so the guide gives information and times for foot travel, but horses can use most of these trails and mountain bikers can manage some of them. However, mountain bikes are not allowed in the Sawtooth Wilderness. The scenery, the trails, and the need to protect the wilderness quality remain the same for all trail travelers.

This guidebook is the one that hikers here often carry in their backpacks. The first edition was published in 1979 and a complete revision, containing 24 new hikes, was published in 1988. For it the author hiked again all but seven of the original hikes. She also consulted with Mose Shrum, supervisory forest technician for the Sawtooth National Recreation Area. The second edition was named an Idaho Centennial book by the Idaho Centennial Commission in 1990.

This third edition contains five new hikes, but one hike in the second edition, Ocalkens Lakes, has been removed to protect wildlife. For the three new hikes where the author had help with the hike descriptions the names of the helpers are listed at the bottom of the hike. Since the last edition, the author has hiked several trails for a third time and has checked changes in the trail system with SNRA trail supervisor Jay Dorr.

Town of Stanley

Visitor services

The main business district of Stanley, the largest settlement, is log buildings and dirt streets, overlooked by the sharp towers and snow-filled chimneys of the Sawtooths. Only three blocks long by two blocks wide at its heart, in the last few years the town has extended from this section along its two highways, Idaho 21 and Idaho 75. Food, gasoline, lodging, gift shops and guide services are available here as well as to the south at Redfish Lake, Obsidian, Smiley Creek, and Galena Lodge, to the east at Clayton, and Sunbeam, and on the west side of the Sawtooths at Grandjean and Atlanta.

Services include large developed campgrounds at Alturas, Redfish and Stanley Lakes and on the Wood River north of Ketchum. Smaller ones are at Iron Creek, Pettit Lake, Atlanta, Grandjean and along Highway 21 and the Salmon River Canyon. You can also camp at undeveloped sites along the backcountry dirt roads.

HISTORY

Fur trapping

Mountain Shoshoni Indians, also called Sheepeaters, lived along the Salmon River and its tributaries for centuries before Alexander Ross visited the area with his fur trappers in 1824. As he crossed the divide between the Big Wood River and the headwaters of the Salmon, he discovered and named a small pond, Governors Punchbowl. Other trappers soon arrived: Warren Ferris of the American Fur Company in 1831, John Work of the Hudson Bay Company in 1832 and Captain Benjamin Bonneville's men in 1833.

Mining

When gold was discovered 30 years later, people began to settle here. In 1863, as Boise Basin miners began to spread out from Idaho City they soon found gold and silver quartz lodes. One discovery to the southwest on the South Fork of the Boise River started the settlement of Rocky Bar. Prospectors from Rocky Bar and elsewhere soon found gold in the Sawtooths. In 1864, placer gold was discovered in the Stanley Basin and placer and lode gold at Atlanta. The basin was named for John Stanley, one of those prospectors.

In 1865, a wagon road was built from Rocky Bar to Yuba City near Atlanta on the west side of the Sawtooths. It acquired the name, Boiler Grade, when a boiler being packed along it fell off the road. Because the area was remote, the first stamp mill didn't reach Atlanta until 1867, and the first three mills made little profit. By the mid-1870's, the Monarch and Buffalo mines were smelting ore at Atlanta. This first boom had declined by 1884, but Atlanta has had several more: from 1902-11, in 1916, from 1932-36 and from 1980 to the present. The peak from 1932-36 was the most profitable. In those years Atlanta produced more gold than any other Idaho area, reaching $6 million by 1938.

Near Atlanta on the North Fork of the Boise River, silver was found on Silver Mountain in the 1860s. Little mining occurred until Matthew Graham, a miner at Atlanta and Rocky Bar, had some ore from Silver Mountain assayed in 1885. The ore was so high grade, he built a mine and a road to it from Trappers Flat in 1887. A 20-stamp mill and mile-long tram were installed in 1888. By then the population had reached 350, most of it in the largest settlement, Graham. When the venture failed in 1889, the mine, tram and buildings were sold at sheriffs' sales for $500 and the mill for $9,500. On nearby Black Warrior Creek, mining occurred from 1900 to 1910 at the Double Standard, Rice Mammoth and Overlook Mines.

In 1864, a road was built from Idaho City to Banner, near Lowman, and a pack trail ran from there to Cape Horn in the Stanley Basin. By 1869, miners were placer mining in Stanley Basin and hydraulic mining at Robinson Bar down the Salmon River from Stanley. By this time, Stanley had a store, run by Arthur McGown. When mining on the Yankee Fork of the Salmon began in 1876, miners from that area also spread into the Stanley Basin and Sawtooth Valley.

They soon made rich discoveries. Levi Smiley found a quartz lode at the head of Smiley Creek in 1878, and in 1879 E.M. Wilson discovered the lode of the Vienna Mine on nearby Beaver Creek. By 1880, the Pilgrim, Columbia and Beaver prospects had been developed at Sawtooth City, which was served by a toll road from Ketchum. Eastern developers provided a 20-stamp mill for the Vienna Mine at Vienna, which at its height had 800 residents.

There were also mines along Alturas Creek and in Eureka Gulch. By the winter of 1883-84, the boom was so great that the road to Ketchum was kept open all winter. Beginning in 1886, mail was also carried between Sawtooth City and Atlanta on a sketchy road over Mattingly Creek Divide. By 1892 when the last mine operating, the Silver King, burned, the boom at Sawtooth City and Vienna was over. However, a 75-ton flotation plant was constructed and the Vienna Mine operated again for a few years in the 1930s.

Mining also occurred in the White Cloud and Boulder Mountains, but was much later and less extensive. The lead-silver deposits of the Livingston Mine, the most successful, at $2.3 million, were located by A.S. and W.S. Livingston in 1882. Its first ore was shipped by pack train. In 1922 a road, 200 ton mill and three-mile tramway were built and the mine operated until 1930. Some activity still persists on the patented claims.

Jess Baker located claims at Baker Lake near the head of Little Boulder Creek in 1922, and in 1939 molybdenum was discovered here. In 1967, the American Mining, Smelting and Refining Company (ASARCO) obtained these claims and located another 50. Their application to build a road in 1970 was opposed by environmental groups. The controversy over the proposed mine led to the formation of the Sawtooth National Recreation Area in 1972.

The first claims in Washington Basin at the head of Washington Creek were located in 1882. There were two mills, but only $50,000 in lead and silver was produced.

The settlement of Galena, near today's Galena Lodge, was founded in 1879 around lead and silver mining claims. The mines grew to have a 20-ton smelter, 800 people, four general stores and a stage line to Hailey.

Ranching

In Sawtooth Valley, David Clark started the first year-round ranch in 1899 at a hot spring. He was named postmaster of the first post office, called Pierson, in 1902. The name of it was later changed to Obsidian and moved to near where Sessions Lodge now stands.

Nearby on Fisher Creek in 1901, Frank Shaw was the second settler in the valley, and his cabin now stands in the Stanley City Park. A few sheep grazed Stanley Basin by 1879. Large bands were brought in by Frank Gooding (later governor) in 1887. By 1907 the area was being overgrazed: there were 364,000 sheep in the Sawtooth Forest Reserve.

The Forest Service

The first supervisor of the Sawtooth Forest Reserve was F. A. Fenn. The second was Emil Grandjean, a professional forester from Denmark. In 1908 when the Forest Reserves were changed to National Forests, the Sawtooth Forest was split, with the western part becoming the Boise National Forest. Grandjean became its first Supervisor and kept the position until 1923. The Sawtooth Forest was divided into three ranger districts: Wood River, Salmon River and Boise River. Each of these was subdivided into several guard districts.

One of these districts was the Pole Creek District in Sawtooth Valley. William Horton served as its ranger for 20 years. His log ranger station, built in 1909, is the site of an interpretive trail. The fenced area around it shows the difference in vegetation the lack of grazing within it has caused since then. Within the fence grazing was limited to the few horses kept at the station. In 1913 the station installed the first telephone in the area.

Many Forest Service buildings, roads, trails, and campgrounds were constructed by the Civilian Conservation Corps from 1933 to 1941. CCC camps were located at Redfish, Ketchum and on Big Smoky Creek south of the Sawtooths. During those years, a drought caused many fires in Idaho. The 1,424-acre Germania Creek fire, was one of the first to be fought. Putting it out cost $1,054.

Exploration

The first to explore the Sawtooths extensively was photographer and guide Robert Limbert, the man who in the 1920s successfully advocated a national monument for Craters of the Moon. He also built Redfish Lake Lodge and with John Ewald climbed several Sawtooth peaks.

Climbing

The next to climb in the Sawtooths were the famous American mountaineers, Robert and Miriam Underhill. In 1934 and 1935 they climbed at least 20 of the major Sawtooth Peaks, including Mt. Heyburn. They were guided and packed in by a local rancher, Dave Williams. Articles written by the Underhills attracted more climbers, including members of the Iowa Mountaineers. Paul Petzoldt, founder of the National Outdoor Leadership School, and five others from the Iowa Mountaineers made the first ascent of Warbonnet in 1947 and the group made several other first ascents. Beginning in the late 1940s, the northwest mountaineer, Fred Beckey, also made first ascents, such as Big Baron Spire and North Raker. Louis Stur made the first ascent of the Finger of Fate with Jerry Fuller in 1958. Stur is best known for the route he pioneered on Mt. Heyburn, called the Stur Chimney.

Rock layers near Ocalkens

Formation of the National Recreation Area

The beauty of the rugged peaks led people to campaign to set the area aside for public enjoyment. As early as 1911, women's organizations in Idaho proposed a national park in the Sawtooths, but a series of bills to establish a park have failed in Congress. In 1937 the Forest Service established the 200,042-acre Sawtooth Primitive Area to keep the Sawtooths pristine. In 1972, after studies and public hearings, Congress created the Sawtooth National Recreation Area, to be administered by the U.S. Forest Service. The bill also designated the Sawtooth Primitive Area as a 216,383-acre wilderness in the National Wilderness System. The act stated that the purpose of the Sawtooth National Recreation Area was to protect the plants, trees, wildlife, and fish, especially the salmon, and to conserve and develop the area for public recreation and enjoyment.

The act directed the Secretary of the Interior to study the area and the adjacent Pioneer Mountains for a national park. The study, completed in 1976, recommended that 686,080 acres become a pair of national parks and some of the land around them a national recreation area. The recommended parks have never been established because most Idahoans feel park status would bring too many problems.

GEOLOGY

Sawtooths

The Sawtooth Range is an uplifted fault block bounded by faults, and the Stanley Basin is a depressed fault block called a graben. It is filled with glacial outwash. Joints, that is cracks in the granite rock of the Sawtooths are close together. This jointing has made the ridges sawtoothed because the glaciers on both sides easily carried off the broken rock, leaving only narrow ridges between them. Water from snow and rain then froze in the cracks, breaking off more pieces until only splintered, knife-edged ridges were left. The rock of the western, northern, and southern Sawtooths is the 88-million-year-old Idaho batholith, which is pale gray and beige. The rock in the east-central section is the 44-million-year-old Sawtooth batholith, which is pink or peach. A batholith is molten rock that pushed up and cooled underground, rather than erupting from a volcano or rift.

White Clouds and Boulders

The 20-mile-long band of white rock giving the White Clouds their name is limestone and related rock from the Paleozoic Era more than 250 million years ago. Much of the white rock has been changed by contact with molten granite to a type of rock called calc-silicate, similar to marble, but containing silicate minerals as well as calcite. Other types and colors of Paleozoic metamorphic and sedimentary rocks, such as argillite, quartzite, limestone and conglomerate, surround the band of white in a highly mineralized belt, which is 8 miles wide by 38 miles long and runs north-south through the center of the area. There are major deposits of zinc, fluorite, low grade gold and even lower grade molybdenum. At the lower elevations in the eastern and southern part of the White Clouds, the vast volcanism of the Challis volcanics has left rhyolite and basalt lava and volcanic ash tuffs. The Challis volcanics are about the same age, 44 million years old, as the Sawtooth batholith. When first deposited they covered half of Idaho. In places, mudflows in these volcanics formed lakes. Sullivan and Jimmy Smith Lakes in the White Clouds are examples of lakes formed this way. The Boulder Mountains have geology similar to that of the White Clouds except that the rock is more colorful. There are outcrops of Challis volcanics and Paleozoic sedimentary and metamorphic rock.

PLANTS AND ANIMALS

Plants and trees

Vegetation in the Sawtooth National Recreation Area changes with elevation, rock, soil and exposure to the sun. The lower slopes and valleys contain big sagebrush, the grasses Idaho fescue and bluebunch wheatgrass, and patches of lodgepole pine, Douglas fir and subalpine fir. Huckleberries, which have red leaves in the autumn, often grow under the Douglas fir. The foothills of the White Clouds show the vegetation differences between north-facing and south-facing slopes with open areas on the south slopes and woods on the north slopes up to 8,500 feet or higher.

Along the streams, aspens and willows grow, with snowberry and elk sedge under the aspen. Sedges are similar to grasses but their stems are triangular and their flower parts more tufted. The large wet meadows fill with the sapphire blossoms of camas in late June and early July. Other common wildflowers in wet areas are elephant's head and white wyethia. Where it is drier, sulphur plant, scarlet gilia, paintbrush, sego lily and littleflower penstemon grow. On the western side of the Sawtooths near Atlanta and Grandjean, it is low enough for ponderosa pine. Shrubs associated with the pine are snowberry, ninebark, serviceberry and chokecherry.

Most glacial moraines in the Sawtooths, such as those around Redfish Lake, are covered with lodgepole pine. Higher up, especially where it has been glaciated, subalpine fir, Douglas fir, snowberry, mountain alder, elk sedge and grouse whortleberry grow, and groves of aspens and lodgepole mark old burns. Grouse whortleberry, common here, is a low-growing relative of the huckleberry with tiny pale green leaves and miniature red berries. The most varied vegetation occurs around lakes in the cirque basins. Subalpine fir, Englemann spruce, elk sedge, alpine bentgrass, alpine willow, grouse whortleberry, western ledum (Labrador or trapper's tea), and red mountain heath (mountain heather) all grow here. So do *Kalmia* (a tiny bog laurel), shooting star, mountain or explorer's gentian, and mountain bluebell.

Near timberline, at around 10,000 feet, whitebark pine and an occasional limber pine replace the other trees. Whitebark pine has 5 needles and the dark purple pitchy cones never fall of their own accord. Here also are found subalpine sagebrush, elk sedge, and Idaho and sheep fescue. Wildflowers include mountain sorrel, white mountain heath, and alpine buttercup.

Places with unique vegetation occur, such as high ridges and lakes in the White Clouds with alpine vegetation. Rare plants here include the endemic White Clouds milkvetch, found only in the White Clouds. This ground-hugging plant has gray hairy compound leaves and pale yellow irregular flowers.

Other places with unusual vegetation are the fens, areas of peat similar to bogs, that have recently been discovered in Sawtooth Valley. These fens are watered by streams and precipitation rather than groundwater like bogs. One of their rare plants, a sundew, has tiny reddish leaves with hairs bearing sticky secretions around the edges. With the sticky secretions, it traps insects and digests them.

Wildlife

Most of the wildlife and birds are seen in several different vegetation types. A few like the mountain goat, occasionally seen at high elevations, have a narrower range. A few bighorn sheep, which live in rocky areas at various elevations, are found in one high basin in the White Clouds. More common wildlife includes antelope, elk, black bear, cougar, lynx, bobcat, mule deer, coyote, beaver and muskrat. There are a few wolverine, and some of them are being studied by scientists. Smaller animals include squirrels, mice, shrews, pikas, chipmunks, gophers, badgers, porcupines, rabbits, raccoons, otters, foxes, martens, weasels and skunks. Rainbow, eastern brook, cutthroat, bull and California golden trout and steelhead swim in the lakes and streams. There were two runs of chinook salmon and one of sockeye, in the Salmon River and Redfish and Alturas creeks, but few chinook are left, and the last, lone wild sockeye arrived in 1994. Kokanee, small landlocked salmon, occur in the larger lakes, especially Redfish. The nearby fish hatchery is raising sockeye and chinook to try to re-establish the runs, but the genetic stock will not be the same.

Birds

Birds include ducks, Canadian geese, owls, and three forest grouse: ruffed, blue and Franklin. Other birds are robins, woodpeckers, sparrows, chickadees, warblers, juncos, bluebirds, magpies, hawks, thrushes, ospreys, snipe, killdeer, siskins, golden eagle, dipper, and water pipit. The dipper is unusual because this small dark gray bird runs underwater all year to look for insects. One of the most beautiful is Idaho's state bird, the mountain bluebird, with its brilliant turquoise color.

Endangered species

Two species listed as endangered by the federal government live here: the peregrine falcon and the sockeye salmon, although the wild form of the sockeye may be extinct. The gray wolf vanished many years ago, but has been reintroduced to the Frank Church Wilderness north of the SNRA, so a few may travel south to the Sawtooth National Recreation Area. Here they are considered a threatened species, but north of Interstate 90 in northern Idaho they are listed as endangered. Other threatened species in the S.N.R.A. are the bald eagle and chinook salmon. The grizzly bear vanished many years ago; the last grizzly was seen in the 1940s. Grizzly reintroduction is planned for the Selway–Bitterroot Wilderness well to the north of here.

The only federally endangered plants in Idaho, Macfarlane's Four O'clock and Water Howellia, are not found in the Sawtooth National Recreation Area. The plants referred to as rare are listed in other categories, as candidates for listing by the federal government, as sensitive species by the Forest Service and Bureau of Land Management, and as sensitive species by the Idaho Native

Mountain goat and kid

Plant Society. An example of these plants is the White Clouds milkvetch, which is found only in the White Clouds.

ACTIVITIES

Commercial activities are few, and most today are based on recreation, such as lodges, guest ranches, and outfitters. Some cattle and sheep are driven and trucked to summer ranges here, but their numbers are strictly limited. Logging is mostly restricted to firewood cutting.

Hunting and fishing

Recreation activities predominate. Hunting is permitted in accordance with Idaho fish and game laws. Streams and lakes are stocked by the Idaho Fish and Game Department, but it is difficult to keep them stocked in the Sawtooths because many lakes are infertile and streams are steep. Fishing is usually better in the White Clouds because the types of rock found there dissolve more easily, releasing nutrients to nourish the invertebrates the fish eat.

Trail travel

Trail travel is another main recreation use, with hiking, backpacking, and horseback riding and horse packing the most popular. Some of the trails are used by mountain bikers and motorcyclists. Most non-wilderness trails in the area are open to mountain bicycles, but several are too steep and rocky to be safe or fun to ride. Travel plan maps that show which trails are open to motorcycles and which roads are open to motor vehicles are available from Forest Service offices.

This guidebook describes trails suitable for hikers, mountain bikers, backpackers and horseback riders, as well as some cross-country routes only for hiking.

Water sports

Sailing, jet skiing, motorboating, canoeing are popular on the lakes, and whitewater rafting and kayaking on the Salmon River below Stanley. People water ski and even scuba dive although the lakes are so cold wet suits are usually worn. Most sunbathers enjoying the beaches at the lakes swim only a little because of the cold water.

Winter

In winter, snowmobiling and cross-country skiing are the main activities. The SNRA headquarters has information on the locations and conditions of groomed snowmobile and cross-country ski trails. Backcountry outfitters lead cross-country ski treks where the guests stay in yurts.

BACKCOUNTRY TRAVEL

Preparing for a backcountry trip

The new regulations mean it is essential to check with a Sawtooth National Recreation Area office before your trip. Information can be obtained at the **Sawtooth National Recreation Area Headquarters**, Star Route, Ketchum, Idaho, 83340, (208) 726-7672, on Highway 75 ten miles north of Ketchum; at the **Stanley Ranger Station**, Star Route, HC 64, Box 9900, Stanley, Idaho, 83278, (208) 774-3681, just off Highway 75 between Redfish Lake and Stanley; at the **Lowman Ranger Station**, Lowman, Idaho, 83637, on Highway 21 east of Lowman; or at the **Boise Front Office**, 3493 Warm Springs Ave., Boise, Idaho, 83712. These offices have maps and information on trails and access roads as well as passes, permits, and the current regulations.

The Boulder and White Cloud Mountains have fewer restrictions than the Sawtooth Wilderness. While campfires are allowed at most lakes in the Boulders and White Clouds, they are not allowed in many places in the Sawtooths. In the Sawtooth Wilderness, campfires should be built in fire pans or on fire blankets and the **cold** ashes scattered after use. At present, mountain bikes and trail bikes are permitted on certain trails in the Boulders and White Clouds, but not on trails in the Sawtooth Wilderness. In the Sawtooths, grazing is regulated, and party sizes and the number of stock are more limited, with fewer stock allowed in the more pristine areas. In the wilderness, dogs must be on leash.

Trails and their conditions

Most trails have register boxes at or near the beginning. All hikers and riders should register so that their presence and destination will be known for sure if problems arise. However the sheets from the register are collected only occasionally, so always let someone know where you are going and when you'll be back.

Because conditions change with weather and season it is wise to check with one of these offices before a trip. Travelers should be aware that snow or high water can block some trails before July 15, and that it is likely to snow any time after September 15. Occasionally it snows sooner, or even in the middle of the summer. September and October weather can be beautiful even though cold (15 to 25 degrees) at night. Most of these trails can be traveled from about July 10 through October 15, but the times they open and close vary greatly from year to year. Trails that open earlier or later than most are listed in the Guide to Trips in the Appendix.

Horse travel

When traveling by horse, use gentle horses trained to hobble or picket and stand quietly. The training should be done before they are taken into the mountains. The horses should also be conditioned by regular exercise before the trip, and should be accustomed to being with each other.

In an average season the high passes are not safe for horse travel until after the first week of August. Trying to cross with stock before the trails are bare of snow is hazardous and causes erosion of the fragile soils. When trail conditions are unsafe, lead horses across the problem spot, or turn back. Use caution in passing hikers. Stock users should check with a SNRA office about the number of stock permitted per party.

Horses at campsites

The horse traveler should tie stock near campsites only when loading. Otherwise use the designated tie area if there is one. Tying pack and saddle stock within 100 feet of streams, springs or lakes is prohibited. Tying stock to live trees for more than one hour also is prohibited.

Or the horses can be picketed. Picketing a horse to a log is safer and better for the grass than using a picket pin. Usually it is best not to picket more than one or two horses. The rest should be hobbled. Whether tied, picketed, or hobbled, for safety, avoid leaving stock alone for more than a few hours.

Grazing within 200 yards of lakes is not allowed because grazing damages fragile alpine meadows. It takes many years for this damage to be erased because plants at high altitudes have a very short growing season. Your stock will have much less impact on soils and vegetation if you camp with them at lower elevations, short of the lakes, and take day trips to the high lakes. The impact of a horse party can be reduced by using backpacking foods and lightweight gear so that fewer horses are needed.

Feed

It is a good practice to carry as much feed as will be needed, but bringing hay into the wilderness is not allowed. Some outfitters have found alfalfa cubes are the most satisfactory feed to carry for their horses. The cubes are cheaper than pellets and keep the horses from chewing poles and trees as they tend to do when fed pellets.

Llamas

Some outfitters offer llama trips, and a few rent llamas, but llama use hasn't yet become widespread in Idaho. Most llama outfitters will not rent animals without a wrangler. Information on sources of llamas is available from the Idaho Outfitters and Guides Association. Learning to use llamas requires some orientation and practice, and the llamas used for packing should have already been trained by their owner to halter, lead and walk on trails carrying packs. Llamas are so smart, success with them is easier if you can convince them you are smarter than they are. They don't like going uphill very well, but will go readily if you keep insisting. They are fun animals to use for packing and are easier for the inexperienced to manage than are mules or horses. It is still necessary to keep checking the animals and their equipment during travel to prevent problems. When using llamas it is important to remember horses are afraid of them. Someone should walk ahead of the llama handlers so if a horse party appears the llamas can be led off the trail before the horses see them and spook.

Obtaining packers

When planning and preparing for a backpacking trip, you may find it impossible for your family to carry everything needed to be safe, comfortable and well fed. To help carry enough, families, especially those with young children, may want to arrange with an outfitter for horses, mules, or llamas to carry their gear. The wrangler and animals can accompany you the entire trip, or the packer can carry your gear in and come back and get it in a few days. You can arrange either to ride or walk in to your base camp. This arrangement is called spot-packing and is much less expensive than the first method. To obtain a list of packers and outfitters contact the Idaho Outfitters and Guides Association, P.O. Box 95, Boise, Idaho 83701.

Mountain bicycling

When using a mountain bike certain precautions are needed for your safety and that of other trail users. For the safety of yourself and others, be a good citizen when riding your mountain bike. Always ride in control. Sound the bell or horn or call out at corners to warn of your presence. Yield to hikers and horseback riders. Be sure horses, mules or llamas hear you coming and

The Temple

hear you talk so they know you are a person. Move your bike off trail on the downhill side if possible to let horses pass. Stay on designated roads and trails and avoid riding during and after rain and on naturally boggy sections. When riding on the highway to complete a loop trip, ride single file. Stay as close to the edge of the road as possible and watch constantly for traffic.

Most bicycle injuries are from failure to control your bicycle, not from collisions. To prevent injuries, wear a bicycle helmet with a hard outside shell and foam-padded interior. Gloves, long pants and a long-sleeved shirt are also important. To prevent catching your pant legs in the chain or gears, tuck them into your socks or wear gaiters.

Ride carefully, looking ahead to anticipate hazards. Practice riding on gentle, smooth surfaces, to develop the skill needed on steep, uneven slopes. It is especially important to practice skidding on gentle, even slopes so you can control a skid on loose rocks or rough ground. It is also important to brake before a curve, not within it.

To prevent problems in an emergency, carry the same 12 essentials as for hiking, plus bicycle tools, pump and a tire patch kit. To be sure your gear stays dry, put it in plastic bags inside the bicycle bags. Use rear mounted bags; handlebar bags make control of the bicycle difficult.

Mountain bikes are prohibited in the Sawtooth Wilderness Area. They are allowed on trails and roads, but not off-trail, in all other sections of the Sawtooth National Recreation Area. However, some trails and trail sections are too steep or rocky to be safe for mountain bikes. When in doubt, walk your bike.

SAFE HIKING

Conditioning

The strenuous exercise of hiking will be difficult unless you are in good physical condition. It can also be dangerous for those who are out of condition. They can get so fatigued they will have an accident. In addition, fatigue makes a trip less enjoyable. To get into condition for hiking, have a physical exam and then exercise vigorously for several weeks before any long hike or backpacking trip. The exercise should be something which strengthens the heart and lungs, such as bicycling, running, swimming, or hiking short distances.

Adjusting to high altitude

Hiking will also be difficult if you forget to allow time to adjust to the higher altitude. The lower the elevation of your home the more time you will need. Lack of adjustment to the altitude can cause the severe headache and nausea of altitude sickness. Occasionally life-threatening conditions such as pulmonary or cerebral edema can result from too rapid an ascent to high altitude. Spending one to three days at the elevation of the trailhead before starting to hike will help prevent symptoms, but full adjustment by the body can take as much as three weeks. Because the altitudes in the SNRA are only moderate, altitude sickness is less often a problem here than it is in higher mountains.

Heart rate

To avoid causing problems with your heart, on the trail, take your pulse occasionally. Taking the pulse for five seconds and multiplying by 12 is accurate enough for this purpose. Slow down now and then, so the rate doesn't stay above your target heart rate for more than 20 to 30 minutes at a time. Your target heart rate is figured by subtracting your age from 200 and then taking 80% of that. To help keep the rate at a safe level, stop and rest for 10 minutes every half hour. If the rate climbs above your maximum rate, which is 200 less your age, stop and rest immediately. Wait until it drops to your resting heart rate before continuing, and then hike more slowly.

Avoid hiking alone

Another safety precaution is to hike with others, because if an accident happens someone will be there to take care of you and go for help. In case of injury a lone hiker is likely to find no one around to go for help or treat him or her for shock or bleeding. On a cross-country hike, hiking alone could be fatal because an injured hiker might never be found. Those who insist on going alone anyway should take a survival kit and signal flare and stick to well-traveled routes. They should also consider carrying a sleeping bag even on a day hike, to help prevent hypothermia at night in case of injury.

Creek crossings

One of the main hazards hikers face is creek crossings. In this book unless a bridge is mentioned, hikers cross creeks at fords by wading or cross on stones or temporary fallen logs. Bridges and logs may have washed away in spring runoff by the time of your trip. Early in the season, some of the crossings without bridges are dangerous or impassable. Only experienced hikers or riders should attempt them before July 15. In wet years, creek crossings will be hazardous even longer, and weaker hikers may have problems even in late summer.

To cross a creek safely, unfasten the waist belt of your pack so it won't hold you underwater if you fall. A couple of years ago a woman drowned in the Sawtooths when she forgot to unfasten her pack when crossing a creek on a log. Keep your boots on to protect your feet. The safest place to wade is wide and gravelly. Wading is safer than attempting to cross on slippery wet logs or rocks. When wading, face upstream, and move diagonally, using a stick for balance. Move only one of your three "legs" at a time. Change to dry socks on the other side to prevent blisters.

Mine shafts

Another danger, especially in the White Clouds, is old mines with dangerous shafts and tunnels. Plan your trip to avoid them. If you must pass any, keep away and watch children carefully.

SAFETY FOR ALL
WILDERNESS TRAVELERS

Hypothermia

Because it can snow here any day of the year, when planning trips be aware of the danger of hypothermia. Hypothermia, or the dangerous loss of body heat in cold and wet conditions, is probably the greatest danger in these mountains. It can occur in temperatures as high as 50 degrees F in rain or wind. Wind chill can make the effective temperature much lower than what the thermometer shows. Death can occur in only minutes.

To prevent hypothermia, keep dry and warm. Put on raingear when it first starts to rain and under it wear clothes which stay warm when wet, such as fleece, pile or wool. To prevent a large heat loss from your head, wear a warm hat that covers the ears. Use several light layers of clothing so you can remove layers to prevent sweating, because damp clothing adds to your heat loss. To protect against wind, the outside layer should be tightly-woven fabric. You should also eat often to maintain body heat.

If it is impossible to stay dry and warm, it is best to make camp and build a fire. To be able to make camp on a day hike, carry a tarp, tube tent or aluminized plastic space blanket. When backpacking, a nylon tent with waterproof floor and separate rain fly gives the best protection against rain, wind, or snow.

To recognize hypothermia in yourself or others, notice any persistent shivering. A shivering person should get out of the wind and rain, change into dry clothes, drink hot liquids, and climb into a warm sleeping bag. If you have waited too long to do this and the person is only semi-conscious, very gently remove clothing and place him or her into a sleeping bag with another person. That person should also be nude because skin to skin contact transfers body heat most effectively. In severe hypothermia like this, any exertion, rough handling, or attempts at rapid rewarming can cause death because the condition affects the heart. Horse parties should be aware that horses can also get hypothermia, and need to be sheltered from wind and protected from cold to prevent it.

Giardia

Another hazard is the clear mountain water. In recent years a protozoa, *Giardia lamblia*, has been brought into the area. This bug can cause severe diarrhea and painful stomach cramps from six days to three weeks after exposure. The only way to be sure the water is safe to drink is to boil it for five minutes or filter it with a water filter. Therefore, a water filter or kettle is essential.

Ticks

There are few animal hazards. The main one is ticks. Only a few carry Rocky Mountain Spotted Fever and tularemia. The minute tick that carries Lyme disease may also be found here.

The common larger ticks inhabit the brush all over the SNRA from May until mid-July. During those weeks all backcountry travelers should inspect themselves for ticks at least twice a day. To get a tick to back out, put insect repellant or white gas on it, or cover it with oil or grease. Or you can try to pull the tick out with tweezers VERY slowly so it will relax its grip. If part of it remains under the skin it can cause serious infection. Therefore, if bitten by a tick, see a doctor after your hike.

Sawtooth Lake

Use caution around wild animals

Some of the larger animals can be a hazard. It is unwise to feed, disturb, or even approach wild animals. Deer can kick with their razor-sharp hooves. Chipmunks and ground squirrels sometimes carry bubonic plague. Any animal may bite if fed by hand, and handouts make animals dependent on humans and unable to survive winter. Black bears are seldom a problem here but the SNRA has 150 to 200 of them. They are commonest in the brushy canyons on the west side of the Sawtooths. In these areas it is wise to avoid smelly food like bacon, and to hang food at night on a tree limb ten feet from the ground and six feet out from the tree trunk. Even if you don't hang your food, protect it at all times from chipmunks and ground squirrels because they can crawl into your pack and tear into the food in seconds.

The Twelve Essentials

For safety even on a day trip every backcountry traveler needs to carry the following essentials:

1. Extra clothes – wear or carry all of these: long pants, a sweater, an insulated parka, a rain poncho or jacket, rain pants or chaps, a wool hat, and wool gloves or mittens.

2. Extra food beyond the needs of the trip.

3. Pocket knife.

4. Waterproof matches or a full butane lighter (take both, or two packets of matches stored in different places in case you lose one). Waterproof matches won't light unless struck on the abrasive strip on their box, so be sure to take the box.

5. Firestarter -- the purchased stick, jelly or paraffin type or make some at home from paraffin and corrugated cardboard, or gather pitch in the forest before the trip.

6. First aid kit, including prescription pain medication for use in case of accident.

7. Flashlight -- be sure it works and has extra bulbs and batteries.

8. Topographic map -- know how to interpret it.

9. Sunglasses -- if it snows, traveling over snow without eye protection will cause severe headache and even snow blindness.

10. Compass -- know how to use it to find where you are.

11. Full water bottles and water filter, or pan for boiling water.

12. Emergency shelter -- a space blanket, tube tent or tarp.

Topographic maps

A topographic map or maps of your trip, showing the landmarks and elevation changes, are essential. The sketch maps in this book are intended only for planning and are inadequate for trail travel. The U.S. Geological Survey maps are the only topographic maps with adequate detail. They may be ordered from the Distribution Branch, U.S. Geological Survey, Box 25286, Federal Center, Building 41, Denver, Colorado 80225, or bought in some outdoor and office supply stores. For travelling access roads, the less-detailed Forest Service maps of the Sawtooth and Challis national forests give enough information.

Topographic maps will last longer if they are covered with adhesive plastic film. To cover them, place a piece of clear adhesive-backed vinyl shelf paper the same size as the map on a table, backing side up. Peel off the paper backing, and place the map on top of the sticky vinyl surface, printed side down. Then trim off any unwanted edges, and fold the map so the plastic side is out.

First aid

Before setting out, be sure someone in your party has had a course in first aid or else take a copy of an up-to-date first aid book with you that you have already read. In administering first aid, first make sure the person is breathing and apply CPR (cardio-pulmonary resuscitation) if he or she is not. Then stop any bleeding, and treat for shock. It is important to treat for shock because it can kill even when the injury itself is not fatal.

Emergency evacuation

If the injured is unable to walk but not seriously hurt, and the party is large, the least expensive alternative is to carry him or her out. However, a person with a suspected neck or back injury should not be moved by amateurs. A helicopter is available for emergencies, but is extremely expensive, and its use must be approved by the Forest Supervisor in Twin Falls. Because of recent budget cutting, there are few trail crew members and wilderness rangers, so it is uncommon to meet a Forest Service employee with a radio in the backcountry.

When going for help, leave one person with the victim and send two people out if possible. Write down the information on the injury and your requests for action for the authorities to avoid mix-ups. Those who go out for help should contact the appropriate county sheriff, who is responsible for all search and rescue. Different parts of the SNRA are in different counties, so have different sheriffs. The northern section of the western part of the Sawtooth Wilderness is in Boise County with Idaho City as the county seat. The southern section of the western part of the Sawtooth Wilderness is in Elmore County (Mountain Home). The northern section of the rest of the SNRA is in Custer County (Challis), and the southern section of the rest of the SNRA is in Blaine County (Hailey). An emergency clinic is located at Stanley; this clinic has its own ambulance. The nearest hospital is at Sun Valley.

A makeshift litter for carrying someone out can be made from two poles and a sleeping bag. Rip the stitching out at the foot of the bag, insert the poles, and tie the person on top of the bag securely. For warmth, jackets or another sleeping bag can be wrapped and tied around the victim.

What to do if lost

Getting lost seldom happens if you know how to use a topographic map and compass. Because these mountains are only lightly wooded they have many recognizable landmarks that show up plainly on the topographic map. These landmarks usually make it possible to find the way back to the trail or a road.

If confused, sit down and orient the topographic map to the landscape using your compass. To do this, set the compass on the map and adjust it and the map so the needle points north, parallels the side edges of the map, and points to the top of the map. Now turn the map with the compass on it so the needle points to 19 degrees east of north. (This 19 degrees, called the angle of magnetic declination, is the difference between the direction of the north magnetic pole and the true north pole here. The magnetic declination varies with the location.) When you have turned the needle to 19 degrees east of north, the north mark on the compass points to what is north in your surroundings and on the map.

On topographic maps in this area, the dark brown lines, called contour lines, show 200-foot differences in elevation, and the light brown contour lines 40-foot differences. Some of the topographic maps of other areas have different scales and contour intervals. Close-together lines designate cliffs and far-apart lines show flat areas. Once you have oriented the map, try to match the flat areas, cliffs, and peaks you see in the terrain around you with those on the map.

If you are unable to match them, make camp and build a fire. The fire can signal others where you are, but keep it small to avoid starting a forest fire. Setting up camp and keeping the fire going will help you avoid panic. Panic can cause those who are lost to rush about madly to the point of exhaustion, and this can cause death.

BACKCOUNTRY MANNERS

People using wild areas like the Sawtooth National Recreation Area have no excuse for poor backcountry or wilderness manners. An informal code of wilderness behavior has been developed over the years by land management agencies and wilderness groups.

Meeting other parties

The code directs respect for other travelers. When meeting a horse party, stand quietly on the downhill side of the trail while they pass. If you are downhill from the trail and a horse stumbles, it can recover its footing by stepping uphill without stepping on you. If you have llamas with you and meet horses, get the llamas off the trail and out of sight before the horses spook from seeing them.

Trash

Federal law requires you to BURN or CARRY OUT all trash. Trash includes aluminum foil envelopes, which won't burn and when placed in a fire release toxins into the soil. SNRA forestry technician, Mose Shrum says: "Put them in your litter bag and make the rangers smile." Rangers like Mose have to carry out hundreds of pounds of trash every year; every hour of trash collecting is one hour less they can work on trail maintenance and improvement. With the new funding cutbacks, you may have to carry out other people's trash as well as your own to make your campsite enjoyable. The overall idea of the code is to try to leave the land the way you found it, or, if possible, in better condition.

Stoves lessen the impact of wilderness campers

Backcountry laws

Some items in the code have the force of law. Burying trash or garbage is illegal. It is also illegal to remove or collect any natural objects except berries and mushrooms and, with an Idaho license, fish and game in season. So is removing items other than trash that have been left by humans.

That means prehistoric artifacts and historical remnants. These objects are part of the heritage of our country, and heavy fines and jail sentences await those who remove them.

Taking shortcuts between trail switchbacks is also illegal. It causes erosion and washouts. No one wants to have their taxes used to repair this kind of erosion. To extend this code to traveling in trailless areas, avoid paths and game trails, walk on rocks whenever possible, and spread out your party to minimize trampling of the plants and soil.

Camping

Good wilderness manners require backcountry travelers to use backpacking or other portable stoves for cooking. Wood fires scar the earth and rocks and require chopping up dead trees that house animals and birds. For this reason, in some backcountry areas in the SNRA, fires are prohibited. In an area not closed to fires when a warming fire is needed, use an existing fire ring if there is one. Otherwise, dig a hole for the fire and cover it after you have put out the fire. Cutting green trees or branches is prohibited throughout the SNRA and within the Sawtooth Wilderness, cutting dead trees and branches is illegal.

In some places, campsites have been posted with signs closing them to camping. Please obey these signs, so the trampled vegetation will grow back and the trees will recover from root damage. Camping within 100 feet of main trails is prohibited in the Sawtooth Wilderness.

Campfires prohibited in some areas

In the Sawtooth Wilderness, campfires are prohibited within 200 yards of any lake in the following drainages: Pettit Lake Creek, Alpine Creek Lakes near Alturas Lake, Scenic Creek, and the Goat Creek that is a tributary of the South Fork of the Payette. Campfires also are prohibited within 200 yards of Sawtooth, Alpine (near Sawtooth L.) Alpine (above Redfish L.) Saddleback and Goat lakes. In the White Clouds, campfires are prohibited within 200 yards of the following lakes: Cirque, Cove, Sapphire, Sheep, Slide, Tin Cup, Gunsight, Four Lakes Basin, Scree, Shallow, Castle, and the highest Chamberlain lake.

Dogs

The code requires you to keep your dog out of lakes and streams and bury its waste. Collapsible nylon bowls are available for water and your trowel makes a handy pooper-scooper. You should also avoid letting your dog annoy wildlife or other campers, especially since the wildlife can be a porcupine. In the Sawtooth Wilderness, dogs must be leashed during the summer.

Avoid damaging vegetation

Respect for the land means choosing and setting up your campsite to avoid damaging the vegetation. Camping in meadows harms the grass and trenching tents kills it. Since the growing season in mountains is very short, the grass won't grow back for many years. The higher the elevation the more fragile the vegetation is. To avoid causing damage to high lake basins, camp in the canyons below them, and take day hikes to the lakes. Camping lower down has benefits: an easier trip, fewer other campers, and fewer mosquitoes.

In setting up camp, do not trench your tent. Instead, if rain threatens, use rocks to divert water from the tent and a tarp or poncho laid on top of the tent floor to keep gear dry. A tarp under the floor will work only if it is the exact dimensions of the tent; if it is larger it will collect water and send it under the floor. Before leaving, be sure to replace any rocks used.

Keeping water clean

Another provision in the wilderness code of ethics is keeping the water clear and beautiful. No one wants detergent foam in drinking water or old noodles at the edge of the lake. To keep the water clean, wash dishes, bathe, and do laundry away from lakes and streams. Use biodegradable soap. Your wash pan can be a cook pot, a folding plastic pan or even a large ziploc bag.

Strain the used water, and dump it at least 50 feet away from lakes, streams and campsites. Burn or carry out the food particles strained from the water. Use a pan for cleaning and rinsing fish, and be sure to burn or carry out the fish entrails.

Sanitation

In addition, keeping the water clean requires proper sanitation. For a toilet dig a hole about six to eight inches deep at least 150 feet from lakes, streams, springs, or campsites. The 150-foot distance is required by law in the Sawtooth Wilderness. Cover the hole completely with earth after use. Latrines can be dug for large groups, but should be long, shallow trenches at least 300 feet from water and should be partly covered after each use. Cover a latrine completely before leaving camp and restore the ground to its original appearance. Burn or carry out toilet paper, because animals will dig it up and scatter it.

PLANNING THE TRIP

Hike data in hike descriptions

To help you plan your trip, the beginning of each hike description in this book lists data on the hike. It includes the round trip mileage from the nearest trailhead, highest point reached, elevation gained, elevation lost (return climb) if any, time to allow on foot, topographic maps and the location and quality of the access road. For the descriptions which begin at a trail junction some distance from a trailhead an additional line says: "This section one way: x miles, y feet gain." All other mileages given are round trip. In each trip description and in the Guide to Trips in the Appendix, the routes are rated according to hiking difficulty.

Glossary

To understand the hike descriptions, you may need a few definitions. The word **talus** means loose boulders and rocks with no dirt between. A **rock bench** is a large rounded or flat place of solid rock. **Switchback** means the trail doubles back on itself. The term **cairn** refers to a small pile of rocks marking the route. **Transfer camp** means a trailhead with a campground located beside it. **Blazes** are cutouts in the bark of trees. They are shaped like upside-down exclamation points and are used to mark the official trails.

Mileages

Mileages in this book may not agree with Forest Service signs, but all mileages have been checked against Forest Service trail logs and the author's experience in hiking the trail. Mileages for trails never logged have been calculated with a map measuring instrument, taking into account switchbacks not shown on the topographic maps. The landmarks described here may change or disappear due to natural causes or trail rerouting.

Access roads

In planning, consider the access road as well as the trail. As trails and roads are rerouted and upgraded, mileages may change from those given here. The access roads are described as paved, dirt and primitive. Dirt and primitive roads may become impassable after rain or snow. Most primitive roads require a vehicle with a high clearance and may be open only part of the summer due to mud, snow, or washouts. Expect to drive less than ten miles an hour on primitive roads. In planning, remember that mountain bikes, trail bikes and carts are not allowed in the Sawtooth Wilderness.

Avoiding crowds

To plan your trip to avoid crowds consider going into the Sawtooths from the west or exploring the White Clouds or Boulder Mountains. The west side of the Sawtooths has one third as many visitors as the east. Trails to lakes are longer, but the canyons more beautiful than those on the east side. A list of little-used trails is in the Guide to Trips and most trails in the Appendix also get little use. Another way to avoid crowds is to take trips on weekdays or in September.

How to reach the S.N.R.A.

Idaho Highway 75 bisects the area. This highway goes north from Ketchum and Sun Valley over Galena Summit to the Sawtooth Valley and then east to Challis down the Salmon River. By road, Stanley is 60 miles northwest of Sun Valley, 135 miles north of Twin Falls, and 55 miles west of Challis. You can also drive northeast from Boise on State Highway 21 and turn off on gravel roads to Atlanta or Grandjean or continue on Highway 21 to Stanley. It is 130 miles from Boise to Stanley, 100 miles from Boise to Grandjean (7 miles unpaved) and 100 miles from Boise to Atlanta (40 miles unpaved).

trails in the SAWTOOTH MOUNTAINS

Mt. Regan and Sawtooth Lake from trail to McGown Lakes

ALTURAS LAKE AREA

1   Frenchman Creek

Map 1

round trip: 4.6 to 12 miles
elevation gain: 160 to 1,260 feet
highest point: 8,700 feet
maps: Alturas Lake, Frenchman Creek
time: 3½ to 6 hours
difficulty: easy to moderate
access: At a sign for Frenchman Creek 34 miles north of Ketchum, turn south off Highway 75 onto the Frenchman Creek Road. There are two roads that join in 200 yards. (Avoid a road leading southeast from the east road.) Continue along the road to a ford at 1 mile which requires a high wheelbase, four-wheel drive vehicle. Don't attempt it before midsummer. The Forest Service plans to reroute the road here and build a new crossing. Currently, it is best to go left 200 yards, turn right to the creek, and walk across it on small logs.

This dirt road makes a pleasant hike or mountain bike ride in June and July. At that time, cinquefoil, avens, elephant's head, and forget-me-not color the meadows. The track passes under the grayish-orange rock towers of an unnamed mountain that resembles a stegosaurus. From beaver ponds and a large meadow at 2.5 miles, hikers can look up the canyon to four peaks, one with a 400-foot black face. Back down the canyon, the face of Castle Peak peers through a gap in the wooded ridges. In early summer, snow stripes the gray, making the peak resemble a pile of sticks.

From the creek crossing at the campsite, a 100-yard walk across a small meadow brings you to the road. Hike along the road as it winds through lodgepoles above the creek, climbing 120 feet in the first mile. Although traffic is light, always watch for vehicles. Where a couple of logging roads branch off, keep to the most well-worn track. At 1 mile, the track parallels a narrow meadow fenced with logs to enclose a trout study area. From here, you can look ahead on the right at the towers of the stegosaurus mountain. The next section at the edge of the meadow has several mudholes.

At 1.3 miles, sagebrush appears on both sides of the creek, and at 1.5 miles an avalanche trough scores the opposite canyon wall. The track fords a side stream at 1.8 miles that has carved a foot-wide, foot-deep slot in the road. Just above are the plates and towers of the stegosaurus mountain. At 2 miles, the meadows widen to 200 yards across the canyon from a big talus slope. In this section, there are more mudholes, and the peaks at the head of the canyon

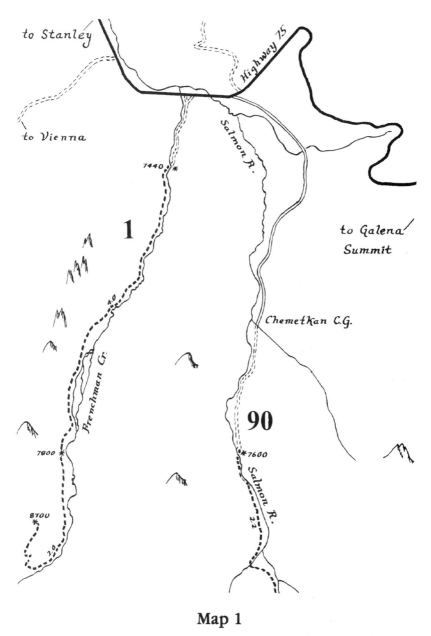

Map 1

begin to appear. At 2.3 miles, three small ponds on the creek hide in the willows. From here you can look down the canyon through a gap in the hills and see Castle Peak's serrated top and slanted sides.

Next, the track returns to the edge of the trees, with views of the meadows. At 2.5 miles, the peak with the black cliff rises above the ridges at the head of the canyon. From 3 to 3.5 miles the road is in the forest. At 4.5 miles the track begins to switchback up the west canyon wall, where it ends at 6 miles.

2   Alturas Lake Shore
Map 2

one-way distance: 2.5 miles
elevation gain: 200 feet
elevation loss: 200 feet
highest point: 7,080 feet
maps: Alturas Lake, Snowyside Peak
time: 2½ hours
difficulty: easy except for a ford of Alturas Inlet
access: From Highway 75, 39.5 miles north of Ketchum, turn left (west) on the Alturas Lake Road and drive 2.2 miles to an unsigned road on the left. This road splits immediately; take the left branch and go .1 mile to a parking spot just before a gate bars motor vehicles. Or park in the first day use area beyond the lake's outlet, walk across the road bridge, and take a path down the outlet to the lakeshore trail.

This shaded walk through lodgepole and Douglas fir forest lets hikers view the glowing cobalt of Alturas Lake, and listen to the sound of its water lapping on the rocky shore. Across the lake, rows of outcrops emerge from sandy slopes like vertebrae. From near the finish, the white peaks of the White Clouds float in the distance like meringues. The trail passes two beaches of apricot sand drifted with pine branches, twigs, and needles. To walk the whole trail, you must bushwhack to reach the inlet and then wade it.

To reach the trail, follow the access directions above. From the small parking area, a path leads over a lodgepole-covered hill and down to the first beach, where it disappears. At the left (south) end of the beach, the trail begins. It stays within 10 to 75 feet of the shore for .5 mile, occasionally passing the fragrant shrub, western Labrador tea.

At .5 mile, the trail turns left (south) up away from the lake, meets an old road, and follows it for 200 yards. After the path crosses a knoll, it reaches a bench 50 feet from the lake at 1 mile. In the next section, the trail continues close to shore, and at 1.5 miles goes over boggy areas in standing water. Then it passes through a clearing, and turns away from the lake about 250 feet. At 1.8 miles, the trail fords two four-foot creeks, then zigzags onto a bench about 75 feet from the shore. At 2 miles, the trail comes out on the beach and ends.

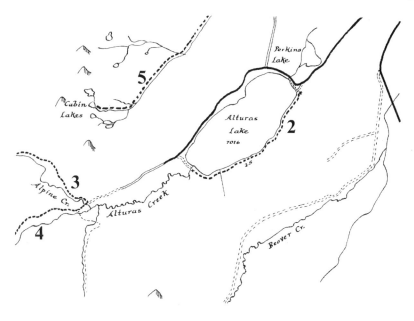

Map 2

For the next half mile, hikers must walk on the beach, stepping over logs and around a deep water hole. Just before the inlet, the beach ends. Here, it is necessary to bushwhack through the willows and around trees that have fallen into the lake. At 2.5 miles is the inlet. Go 75 feet upstream to a wide sandy place to ford it. In a wet year, it is still knee deep at the end of July. In early summer, the ford is treacherous. Across the inlet is parking for a day use area.

This trail was built and is maintained by volunteers. Please respect their hard work. *(Researched with the help of Wayne Fuller)*

3   Alpine Creek Lakes
Map 3

round trip: 6.2 miles to the end of the trail, 7.6 miles to the west lake, 10.4 miles to the north lakes

elevation gain: 500 feet to the end of the trail, 1,442 feet to the west lake, 2,087 feet to the north lakes

highest point: 9,167 feet at the north lakes

map: Snowyside Peak

time: 3½ hours to the end of the trail and back, 7 hours for the west lake, 8 hours for the north lakes

ability: expert

access: From Ketchum, drive north 39.5 miles on Highway 75 to the Alturas Lake Road. Turn left (west) on the paved road and drive along the north side of the lake. Continue past the end of the pavement to a ford of Alpine Creek at 6.5 miles.

warning: The Alpine Creek drainage is closed to stock. No campfires are allowed.

Several wild and lonely lakes in rugged country are scattered beyond the end of the maintained trail in Alpine Creek Canyon above Alturas Lake. The largest lake is the closest, but reaching it requires a careful climb beside a rushing waterfall. At the lower end of the lake, a cracked gray monolith stands guard over this waterfall and two tree-masted islands. At the head of the lake, a jumble of granite peaks forms a wrinkled backdrop for the cliffs and ledges surrounding the clear blue water. Satellite lakes hide among the jumble. From the waterfall, the zigzag wall dividing the north branch of Alpine Creek from Alice Lake is visible. Under this wall, four more lakes are strung on a separate creek, one of them right under the dragon's back of Snowyside Peak.

To reach the trailhead, follow the access directions above. Park in the parking area (7,080 feet) on the near (east) side of the ford. Walk north 50 yards into the woods to find the level trail, which begins to climb at .5 mile. At 1 mile, it passes a rock knoll and drops into a sagebrush basin. From here, there is a fine view of the jagged north wall of the canyon and the peaks at the head of it. This mile makes a fine walk.

The trail continues through sagebrush and strips of trees. At 1.7 miles, it comes beside the aqua-green creek. Just beyond is a large campsite in the woods. From here, the trail ascends the canyon through forest and over granite benches. It stays out of the canyon bottom at first, then drops to edge a flat meadow. At 2.5 miles, the way crosses above another meadow on a sagebrush hillside, then re-enters woods and fords a side creek. The trail reaches the main creek (7,580 feet) 3.1 miles and 500 feet above the trailhead. Here the official trail ends. The routes up both the west and north canyons to the lakes are challenging and can be hard to find.

To reach the large lake in the west canyon, go up the main creek 20 yards, then cross it on logs. On the other side, zigzag up a wooded ridge, cutting northwest towards the outlet of the lake and the waterfall on it. At 3.2 miles, 200 feet above the crossing, is a rolling grassy area with a view of the waterfall.

Keep left (south) of the creek and climb over ledges and through willows beside the falls. A handhold may be needed now and then. The 8,522-foot lake is at 3.8 miles. There are several good campsites on three peninsulas on the south shore.

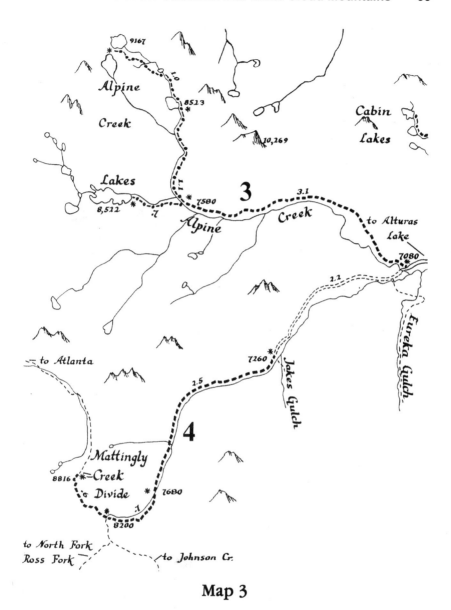

Map 3

To reach the lakes in the north canyon, from the end of the official trail at 3.1 miles, go up the creek on the right (east) for 100 yards. Then follow a line of oval blazes that turn up away from the creek. At 3.5 miles, return to the creek, and go along it, continuing through a rolling meadow dotted with subalpine firs to the 8,523-foot lake at 4.2 miles.

Circle this lake, and go along a stream to a narrow pond at 4.4 miles, staying east of the lake, stream, and pond. At the upper end of the pond, cross the creek to the west. Well west of the creek, climb between rounded ledges past two more ponds to a 9,167-foot lake at 5.2 miles. From here, Lake 9,050 is an easy walk to the southwest. Snowyside Peak may be climbed with caution from the saddle above Lake 9,167 by hiking and scrambling.

4   Mattingly Creek Divide
Map 3

round trip: 12 miles
elevation gain: 1,736 feet
highest point: 8,816 feet
time: 6½ to 8½ hours
maps: Snowyside Peak, Marshall Peak
difficulty: strenuous
access: Turn west from Highway 75 at Alturas Lake, 39.5 miles north of
   Ketchum. Drive 4.5 miles on the paved road, then 2 miles on a dirt road to
   a ford. The old sheep bridge that used to provide a dry crossing for hikers is
   gone.

At Mattingly Creek Divide, across the creek from the red and white mountain heather, jagged peaks crowd the canyon wall. Four rock towers, one brick red and the others gray, peer over a gap like giant chessmen. Hikers seldom climb to the divide, although trail bikers often ride to the Johnson Creek Junction, .6 mile below it.

To reach the trailhead, follow the access directions above. This hike begins at the ford of Alpine Creek (7,080 feet) on the Alturas Lake Road except for those with four-wheel drive, high wheelbase vehicles. This road is not recommended even for 4-wheel drive vehicles. Beyond the ford, the road is level through the forest, but is washed out in places between the ford and a junction with the Eureka Gulch jeep trail at .3 mile. This side road goes 3 miles with a 1,580-foot elevation gain to the old mines of Eureka. From the Eureka junction, the main road winds along over rocks and through forest to a register box at Jakes Gulch (7,260 feet) at 2.2 miles. Here the road is closed to motor vehicles.

The first part of the trail continues as a road through the forest. It was a rough wagon road to Atlanta in the days of Sawtooth City. The track reaches an open sagebrush area at 2.7 miles below striped outcrops. From 2.7 miles to a ford of Alturas Lake Creek at 4.7 miles (7,680 feet), the trail runs through large sagebrush-grass meadows, crossing six intermittent streams on the way.

At 4.7 miles, ford the creek to the left (south) side or cross on an upstream foot log. Beyond the ford is a campsite. In the next 1.2 miles, the route climbs

1,200 feet through thick forest. At 5 miles, it crosses a side stream. Note that the first intersecting trail shown on the map does not exist. The creek now runs below the trail in a 40-foot ravine.

At 5.4 miles (8,200 feet), a .5 mile side trail leads to a junction of the Johnson Creek and North Fork of the Ross Fork trails 240 feet above. This Johnson Creek Trail (another is near Graham) goes 7.6 miles with a 2,055-foot descent to the Ross Fork of the Boise River jeep trail. From its junction with the Johnson Creek Trail, the North Fork of Ross Fork Trail, descends 1,835 feet in 5 miles to the confluence of the North and South forks of the Ross Fork. This point is 3.5 miles up the Ross Fork from the junction of the Johnson Creek and Ross Fork trails.

From the side trail, the Mattingly Divide Trail continues to the head of the canyon where it returns to the right side of the creek at 5.7 miles. Then it climbs a hill to the summit (8,816 feet) at 6 miles.

The divide and the trail from it down Mattingly Creek give cross-country access to a lake at the head of the south fork of Alpine Creek and to two small lakes on the side of Mattingly Peak. The trail down Mattingly Creek drops 2,866 feet in 6.4 miles from the divide to the Middle Fork of the Boise River Trail, 4.5 miles above the Powerplant Campground at Atlanta.

5   Cabin Lakes
Map 4

round trip: 7.5 miles for the four main lakes
elevation gain: 1,998 feet
highest point: 9,078 feet
maps: Alturas Lake, Snowyside Peak
time: 7 to 8 hours
difficulty: strenuous
access: On Highway 75, 39.5 miles north of Ketchum, turn left (west) on the Alturas Lake Road. Drive 3 miles to a junction with the Cabin Creek Road and turn right (north). Drive .7 mile to a sign for the Cabin Creek Trail. Then turn left (west) onto a dirt road and drive .4 mile to a parking area.

The sandy crest of McDonald Peak, sprinkled with pines, bars the canyon above the five small Cabin Lakes. At the first and deepest lake, cracked gray cliffs and a rippling waterfall plunge into the aquamarine water. Above this lake on granite shelves, the highest lake sprawls among rocky peninsulas, flowered turf, and golden sand. The lower two lakes are surrounded by marsh grass. They are really only one lake with two lobes divided by a ten-foot wide channel.

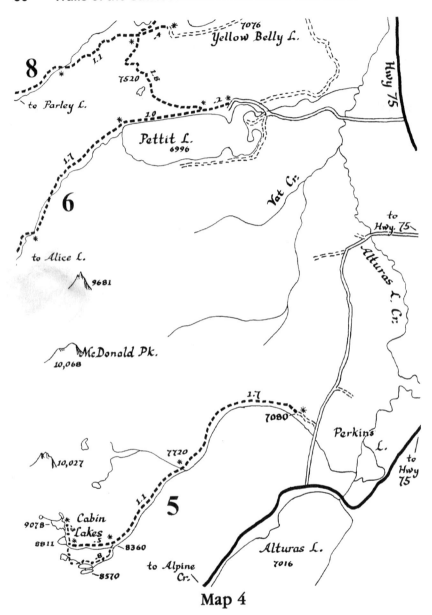

Map 4

To reach the trailhead, follow the access directions above. The parking area (at 7,080 feet) is at the end of a side road signed Cabin Creek trail. From the trailhead, walk northwest through trees and up a sagebrush hillside for .1 mile to the register box. The route then goes west along Cabin Creek below a sagebrush ridge.

At .8 mile, the trail begins alternating between woods and open grassy areas. At 1.7 miles, it ascends a side creek for 200 yards before fording it. The way continues to climb, occasionally crossing streams. At 2.8 miles, beyond a grassy basin and a ford of another side creek, the trail approaches the main creek and disappears in a dry streambed. (Here a route to the twin lakes turns off. Returning by this trail allows a loop trip.) Where the tread reappears beyond granite ledges, continue on the right (north) side of the main creek. The trail climbs between rock ledges and through trees above the creek to the first lake (8,811 feet) at 3.3 miles where it ends.

To reach the 9,078-foot upper lake, go .2 mile around the east side of the first lake and turn northeast up a gully that is to the right of the creek between the lakes. Climb this gully to the lake at 3.6 miles. To reach the twin lakes from the first lake, go south over a ridge to a small lake that dries up in midsummer and follow a creek down to the north one of the two lakes. Return from these lakes to the main trail on the .4 mile trail you passed on the way up that turned off .5 mile below the first lake. From the junction of the two trails, it is a 1.3 mile loop to see the first lake and the twin lakes. Seeing the highest lake too will add another .6 mile.

PETTIT LAKE AREA

6   Alice Lake
Maps 4 and 5

round trip: 10.6 miles
elevation gain: 1,600 feet
highest point: 8,596 feet
maps: Alturas Lake, Snowyside Peak
time: 8½ hours
difficulty: strenuous
access: On Highway 75, 42.5 miles north of Ketchum, turn left (west) on the Pettit Lake Road. Go 1.6 miles on a gravel road to a four-way junction. Turn right (north) and go .5 mile to the Tin Cup hikers' transfer camp.
warning: This trail is heavily used. For a true wilderness experience, choose another. No campfires are allowed.

The gnarled lodgepoles and subalpine firs on the granite peninsulas at Alice Lake seem arranged by a supernatural landscape gardener. Two ponds just below the lake huddle close to the peach-colored skyscraper wall of El Capitan. Across the upper end of the blue green lake parades a row of dragon peaks, one of them with two heads looking in opposite directions.

Pond below Alice Lake

To reach the trailhead, follow the access directions above. The trail starts out through trees and sagebrush to a view of 6,996-foot Pettit Lake, then goes along 20 feet above the shore. At .2 mile, a side trail leads 1.8 miles and 524 feet over a ridge to the Toxaway Lake Trail. This cutoff trail allows loop trips from Pettit Lake.

The Alice Lake Trail leaves Pettit Lake at 1.2 miles and continues level through Douglas and subalpine firs, blueberry and grouse whortleberry for .6 mile before beginning to climb. At 2.1 miles, it edges the base of cliffs. The trail crosses the creek to the east side on a narrow footlog at 2.9 miles. Then at 3.5 miles, it fords back to the right (west) of the creek. Here the canyon opens out and divides.

The path switchbacks through talus and brush above a log-strewn pond. Then it goes along the base of a 600-foot cliff into the right branch of the canyon at 4 miles. At 4.1 miles, the trail crosses to the left (east) of the creek on a logjam, then returns to the west on logs at 4.3 miles. Ahead the route climbs a knoll in the center of the canyon in switchbacks not on the map. Above a waterfall at 4.8 miles, the trail returns to the east on a bridge, then levels out.

At 5 miles, the way returns to the west (right) on logs, just before the first of two shallow blue-green ponds. Alice Lake appears at 5.3 miles. The path runs along its shore to a peninsula at 6 miles, where it turns up to go on to Twin

Lakes. Avoid the overused campsites on this peninsula. Three ponds above the upper end of the lake can be reached by cross-country hiking.

7   From Alice Lake Over Snowyside Pass to Toxaway Lake

Map 5

loop trip from Pettit Lake: 18 miles
elevation gain: 2,404 feet
this section one way: 5.1 miles, 804-foot gain, 1,000-foot loss
highest point: 9,400 feet
map: Snowyside Peak
difficulty: strenuous
access: use directions in Hike 6 (Alice Lake) and hike to Alice Lake.
caution: Snowyside Pass is usually blocked by snow until early to mid-August. To avoid danger and to avoid damaging the soils, wait until the snow melts from the trail before traveling it. The trail is subject to landslides, so be sure to check with the SNRA before traveling over the pass, especially if traveling with stock.
warning: No campfires are allowed.

The trail up Snowyside Pass from Alice Lake first passes Twin Lakes, which are divided by a strip of granite outcrops. In season, reflected snowbanks whiten their dark blue water. The two-headed dragon peak is closer now and two peninsulas in the lower lake reach out toward it. From the upper lake, talus and flower-filled grass sweep to the slabs and cliffs of Snowyside Peak. From the trail up Snowyside Pass, Twin Lakes appear as sapphires inlaid in a gray granite brooch. Above them, a whole row of dragon peaks marches toward the pass from Alice Lake. On the other side of the pass, the trail zigzags down beside wildflower gardens to two turquoise ponds.

This hike description begins at 8,596-foot Alice Lake where the trail leaves the lake for Twin Lakes. For directions for hiking to this point, see Hike 6 (Alice Lake). At times, the trail cribbing on the south side of the top of the pass falls away, and the trail becomes too narrow for safe horse use. Repairs sometimes are delayed because of funding.

From Alice Lake, 6 miles and a 1,600-foot climb from the trailhead, the trail ascends west up the creek between Alice and Twin Lakes. At a marshy meadow and pond, it turns right into woods, then left across boulders to a sign (at .8 mile) for a .2 mile path to Twin Lakes.

From this sign to the ponds above Toxaway, the trail has been rerouted since the topographic map was printed. Half way around Upper Twin Lake and well above it, the route heads north into a meadow with a pond. Then it switchbacks

Twin Lakes from Snowyside Pass

left, right, and then .6 mile to the left (west). It jogs again before the 9,400-foot pass at 1.9 miles. The trail crosses the pass at a notch northeast of the one on the map. This pass may not be open to stock until after the first week in August. Hikers can travel it sooner, but crossing the snow on the north side is hazardous.

On the far side, the path follows a stream as it descends 14 zigzags over rocks, turf and mountain heather to the first pond at 3.2 miles. At the second pond, the trail descends to the shore, across from an inlet that in season gurgles through the white flowers of parrot's beak.

Below this pond, the trail runs beside the thin sheet of the stream as it slides over granite to a third tiny pond. Then the route angles down through boulders and subalpine firs, making more switchbacks than shown. At 3.8 miles, the trail crosses the creek on logs below a waterslide. At 4 miles, the trail passes a campsite just above Toxaway Lake.

The route goes along above the north side of the lake on granite benches and in forest, crossing two or three side streams. From the trail, the White Clouds and the scalloped gray wall of Parks Peak are visible in the distance. A junction with the trail to Sand Mountain Pass and Edna and Imogene lakes is at 5.1 miles (8,400 feet) above a peninsula of rock benches and tiny trees.

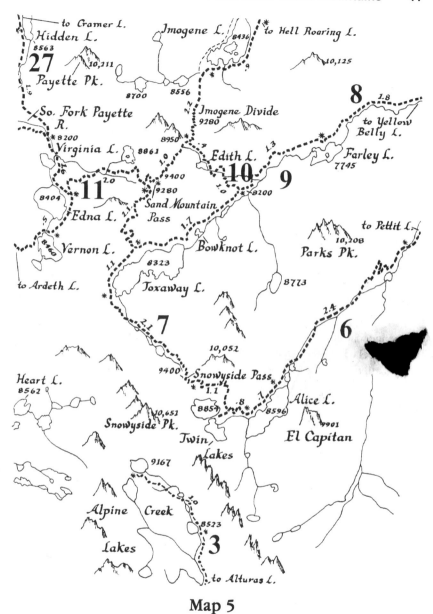

Map 5

8   Farley Lake
Maps 4, 5 and 6

round trip: 6 miles
elevation gain: 724 feet
highest point: 7,800 feet

map: Snowyside Peak
time: 5 hours
difficulty: easy except for ford
access: On Highway 75, 42.5 miles north of Ketchum, turn left (west) on the gravel Pettit Lake Road. Go 1.6 miles to a four-way intersection. Turn right (north) and cross a bridge over the outlet. On the other side of the bridge, turn right (north) again on a road to the Tin Cup horse transfer camp. At .5 mile, keep straight ahead (east) where a road turns off to the horse camp. Continue on the primitive, rocky road to a signed trailhead at the west end of Yellow Belly Lake, 3.3 miles from the bridge.
warning: No campfires are allowed.

Three granite islands, one with a crew of trees, sail the teal blue water of Farley Lake below the furrowed cliffs of Parks Peak. From these cliffs, white ribbons of water plunge into the clear depths. Across the lake from the cliffs and falls, avalanche chutes clogged with tiny firs gouge the sides of an unnamed orange mountain. Just below the lake, the creek thunders into a meadow between jaws of rock.

To reach the trailhead, follow the access directions above, but don't take a enger car up the Yellow Belly Lake Road. In early season and when it rains, el drive is needed. An alternate route is to begin hiking on the Alice L Trail from Pettit Lake and at .2 mile, turn off on a cutoff trail over a 524-foot forested ridge. This 1.8 mile trail meets the Yellow Belly Lake Trail .4 mile above Yellow Belly Lake.

From the west end of Yellow Belly Lake (7,076 feet), the trail runs through sagebrush flats and forest to the Mays Creek junction. Here the cutoff trail comes in from Pettit Lake. A .2 mile path to the north leads to 7,097-foot McDonald Lake, a shallow green lake in marsh grass and partially burned woods.

From this junction, the trail continues through woods to a log crossing of Farley Lake Creek at 1.5 miles. This crossing can be difficult in early summer, especially in wet years. Then the trail begins to climb in forest, passing a waterfall on the creek at 2.4 miles. A rocky meadow with small trees is at 2.5 miles. From the switchbacks above it, the White Clouds and Castle Peak appear to the east and a large waterfall plunges below.

At 3 miles (7,800 feet) is an overlook of the lower end of 7,745-foot Farley Lake. Here a path turns down to some campsites. There are also sites on a peninsula at 3.3 miles, and more sites off-trail at the upper end of the lake.

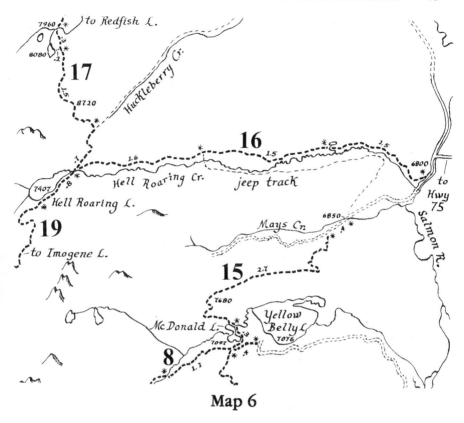

Map 6

9 Farley Lake to Toxaway Lake
Map 5

round trip: 11.4 miles
elevation gain: 1,247 feet
this section one way: 2.4 miles, 600-foot gain
highest point: 8,400 feet
map: Snowyside Peak
time: 8 hours
difficulty: strenuous
access: Hike to Farley Lake by following directions in Hike 8.
warning: No campfires are allowed.

Granite peninsulas scallop the flower-embroidered shores of mile-long Toxaway Lake, the longest backcountry lake in the Sawtooths. Drowned peninsulas, decked with lodgepoles and subalpine firs, create islands. Above the west end of the lake, the shoulder of Snowyside Peak resembles a dinosaur with a triangular, jagged back and a massive head which looks right down at the blue-green water. To the left of the dinosaur, the fissured gray and orange face of Parks Peak borders the lake.

To reach 7,745-foot Farley Lake where this hike description begins, start at Yellow Belly or Pettit Lakes. To reach either lake, follow the directions in Hike 8 (Farley Lake). It is 3.3 miles and a 724-foot climb to the peninsula midway along Farley Lake where this hike description begins.

From here, the trail runs above Farley Lake across rocks and among aspens, sagebrush and subalpine firs. Beyond the lake, the trail climbs above a horseshoe-shaped lagoon on the creek, then re-enters forest. At .6 mile, there are talus, meadows, and ponds. The path goes over a lodgepole ridge with a view of the White Clouds. The trail bridges the outlet of Edith Lake at 1 mile and continues through forest to a junction with the Edith Lake Trail at 1.3 miles.

Just beyond the junction, the main trail comes to a narrow pond with a good view of Snowyside Peak. Above the pond, the creek slides over glacier-polished granite. The path edges another marshy pond before arriving at green Bowknot Lake at 2 miles. Two peninsulas almost cut this marshy lake in two below a miter-shaped shoulder of Parks Peak. The trail winds on through lodgepoles, subalpine firs and granite benches to Toxaway Lake at 2.4 miles. Staying 50 vertical feet above the north shore, the route goes half way along the lake to a junction at 3 miles with the Sand Mountain Pass Trail. There are many campsites on the peninsulas on both sides of the lake.

10 Edith Lake

Map 5 or 7

round trip: 11.2 miles to the lake, 12 miles to the junction with the Imogene Divide Trail
elevation gain: 1,874 feet
this section one way: 1.4 miles to the junction, 750-foot gain
highest point: 8,950 feet at the junction with the Imogene Divide Trail
map: Snowyside Peak
difficulty: strenuous
access: Following directions in Hike 8 (Farley Lake) and Hike 9 (Farley to Toxaway Lake), hike to the Edith Lake junction.
warning: No stock is allowed in the Edith Lake Basin from the junction with the Toxaway Lake Trail to the summits of Sand Mountain Pass and the Imogene Divide.

Little Edith Lake huddles under corrugated peaks below Imogene Divide and Sand Mountain Pass. It is a pleasant spot to rest or camp before tackling one of these passes. Northwest of the lake, the fluted cliffs of a sharp-pointed

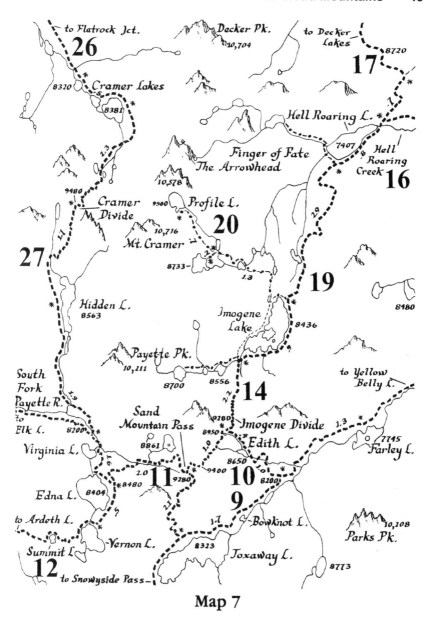

Map 7

orange peak stairstep down to the notch of Imogene Divide. On the south side of the lake, high white granite peninsulas slide into blue-green water.

To reach the Edith Lake junction (8,200 feet) where this hike description begins, follow the directions listed above. This junction is 4.6 miles and an 1,124-foot climb from the trailhead at Yellow Belly Lake. From the junction, the trail switchbacks up through granite outcrops on the south side of Edith Lake's outlet. A ford to the north side where the creek slides over granite slabs is at .5 mile. The trail returns to the south side of the creek at .8 mile, then hops back to the north again just below the 8,650-foot lake at 1 mile. After edging the east and north sides of the lake, the path passes a miniature pond at 1.2 miles. It wanders up a slope of grass and rocks to a tinier pond and a junction (8,950 feet) at 1.4 miles with the trail from Sand Mountain Pass to the Imogene Divide.

11 Toxaway Lake to Edna Lake
Map 5 or 7

round trip: 20.8 miles
elevation gain: 2,204 feet
elevation loss (return climb): 876 feet
this section one way: 4.1 miles, 880-foot gain, 876-foot loss
highest point: 9,280 feet
map: Snowyside Peak
time: 2 to 3 days
difficulty: strenuous
access: Using the directions in Hike 8 (Farley Lake) and Hike 9 (Farley to Toxaway Lake), hike to Toxaway Lake.
caution: Sand Mountain Pass is usually snow-covered until mid-July or early August. To avoid danger and to avoid damaging fragile soils, wait until the snow melts from the trail before traveling it.

Mountains with delicate points and smooth sides ring Edna Lake. Between them to the north, the canyon of the South Fork of the Payette drops away, giving an end-of-the-world effect. The wide expanse of blue water and groves of firs and pines are relaxing. From the trail, the prongs of the Rakers stand out in the distance. On the way to the lake from the pass, a pond, sometimes called Rendezvous Lake, gleams in a meadow of tiny firs below a gabled orange mountain.

This hike description begins at the junction (8,400 feet), on the north side of Toxaway Lake, which is 6.3 miles and a 1,324-foot climb from Yellow Belly Lake. To get there, follow directions in the hikes listed above. The route begins by climbing a ridge in switchbacks as long as .2 mile. Only a few of these are on the map. From this section, sandy slopes drop hundreds of feet to the lake. The trail gradually circles left of a rocky hill. At 2.1 miles it drops to a notch called Sand Mountain Pass (9,280 feet). Here the trail to the Imogene Divide turns off to the north and climbs to 9,400 feet in .3 mile.

The trail on to Edna Lake zigzags west down through whitebark pines to the edge of the meadow surrounding Rendezvous Lake (8,861 feet) at 2.8 miles. From here the trail descends grassy slopes on the north side of a creek and crosses the outlet of Rendezvous Lake at 3.3 miles. A junction with the trails to Ardeth Lake and Grandjean is at 4.1 miles in tiny firs above Edna Lake. Campsites may be reached from either trail.

12 Edna Lake to Ardeth and Spangle Lakes
Maps 7 and 16

round trip: 29 miles via Edith Lake
elevation gain: 3,390 feet
elevation loss (return climb): 1,881 feet
this section one way: 5.1 miles, 1,186-foot gain, 1,005-foot loss
maps: Snowyside Peak, Mt. Everly
time: 3 to 4 days
difficulty: strenuous
access: The shortest way to reach Edna Lake, where this hike description begins, is to hike in 9.3 miles from Yellow Belly Lake by way of Edith Lake. See Hikes 8, 9, 10, and 11.

Spangle Lake is round, deep, and dark blue, but Little Spangle is the opposite: sprawling, shallow, and olive green. At dawn here, below a ridge of short gray cliffs, white granite slabs and islands spangle the water with reflections. From the grass and granite shore of tiny Summit Lake near the divide between Edna and Ardeth Lakes, gray granite boulders and benches climb to the summit of Glens Peak.

The shortest route to Edna Lake is from Yellow Belly Lake by way of Edith Lake. It is 9.3 miles and a 2,324-foot climb by that route. For directions, see the hikes listed above. From the junction (8,480 feet) with trails from Grandjean and Ardeth Lake above the east shore of Edna Lake, take the trail towards Ardeth Lake. It goes south above the shore, then climbs to Vernon Lake at .5 mile. Here carved granite slopes rise to the crumbled cliffs of a triangular peak. There are campsites on the east shore of the lake and near the inlet. A side trail goes south around the lake to a pond above it.

Take the main trail around the north side of Vernon Lake. The trail crosses the outlet on logs and then, at .8 mile, the creek from Summit Lake. The path zigzags through woods, returns to the north side of the creek, and arrives at Summit Lake at 1.5 miles. At the west end of the lake, the ground rises to the 8,866-foot summit of the divide between Edna and Ardeth, which is a 464-foot climb from Edna Lake.

Now the trail drops 638 feet in switchbacks over loose rocks and through trees to 8,228-foot Ardeth Lake at 2.4 miles. At 2.7 miles, the trail fords the outlet of Ardeth Lake to a junction at 2.8 miles with the Tenlake Creek Trail. A good campsite is west of this junction and others are off trail to the southwest.

The trail on to Spangle Lakes climbs the side of a ridge to a meadow and pond at 3.1 miles. Then it switchbacks in rocks to the 8,952-foot divide at 4.3 miles, 724 feet above Ardeth Lake. From the divide, you can climb Glens Peak cross-country over large boulders. The view from this peak is worth the effort.

From the Ardeth-Spangle Divide, the trail drops only 367 feet to a meadow on the east side of 8,585-foot Spangle Lake. Then it goes along the shore to a junction with the Middle Fork of the Boise River and Benedict Creek trails at 5.2 miles. There are plenty of campsites around both Spangle Lakes, but mosquitoes can be bad in wet years, especially at Little Spangle.

13   Ingeborg, Rock Slide and Benedict Lakes
Map 16 or 22

round trip: 36 miles
elevation gain: 3,700 feet
elevation loss (return climb): 2,536 feet
this section one way: 3.5 miles, 310-foot gain, 655-foot loss
highest point: 8,920 feet
map: Mt. Everly
difficulty: strenuous
access: Hike to Spangle Lakes from Yellow Belly Lake (14.5 miles, 3,390-foot gain) or from Atlanta (14.5 miles, 3,145-foot gain). See Hikes 8, 9, 10, and 11 or 53 and 56.

A scalloped ridge of crumbling granite lines the west side of Lake Ingeborg and continues down the canyon of Benedict Creek, where a single scallop drops talus into Rock Slide Lake. Farther down, Benedict Lake and its meadows are trapped between invisible summits hidden behind granite benches. From the trail between Ingeborg and Rock Slide Lakes, the orange and black fangs of the Raker Peaks stand out ahead. One of these resembles the end of a deformed foot, with a big toe, but only three little toes.

This hike description begins at Spangle Lakes at the junction of the Middle Fork of the Boise River Trail with the trail from Ardeth Lake. This spot can be reached in 14.5 miles (3,390-foot climb), from Yellow Belly Lake or in 14.5 miles (3,145-foot climb) from Atlanta.

The trail to Lake Ingeborg first fords the stream between the lakes, then edges the south shore of Spangle Lake. Next it switchbacks up the side of the canyon to a pond under a row of cliffs at .6 mile. Here the trail turns north and

Lake Ingeborg

climbs to 8,890-foot Lake Ingeborg at 1.1 miles. It edges the right shore of the lake near campsites, then goes up a few feet to a 8,895-foot divide.

From the divide, the way drops past a marsh to Rock Slide Lake (8,668 feet) at 2.1 miles. This lake is so small it has few campsites. The trail descends to a pond and junction with a trail to Three Island Lake at 3 miles. This side trail climbs 200 feet in .6 mile to that lake.

Below this junction, the trail keeps dropping, crosses the creek and zigzags down to the shore of 8,240-foot Benedict Lake at 3.5 miles, where there are several campsites. The trail continues down Benedict Creek 4.6 miles to the South Fork of the Payette River in a 1,060-foot descent.

14 Sand Mountain Pass to Imogene Lake
Map 7

round trip: 25 miles from Yellow Belly Lake
elevation gain: 2,654 feet
elevation loss (return climb): 1,294 feet
this section one way: 4.1 miles, 450-foot gain, 1,294-foot loss starting at Sand Mountain Pass
highest point: 9,400 feet
map: Snowyside Peak
difficulty: strenuous

access: Use directions from Hikes 8, 9, and 10 to hike to Toxaway Lake and then to the junction of the Edna Lake and Imogene Divide trails on Sand Mountain Pass.

caution: Sand Mountain Pass and the Imogene Divide are usually blocked by snow until mid-July or early August. To avoid danger and to avoid damaging fragile soils, wait until the snow melts from the trails before traveling them.

Next to a pleated orange ridge, the Imogene Divide overlooks a dozen 100-yard switchbacks, set in gray talus. In the distance below them, white granite peninsulas notch the edges of sapphire blue Imogene Lake. The high point on the trail is .3 mile towards the Imogene Divide from the junction with the trail down to Edna Lake. From this point, the curved gap of Imogene Divide is visible to the north, and the dinosaur back of Snowyside Peak and dark crags of Parks Peak to the south.

To reach the junction on Sand Mountain Pass where this hike description begins, follow directions in the hikes listed above. It is 8.4 miles and a 2,204-foot climb to this junction from Yellow Belly Lake. From the junction (9,280 feet), the trail towards Imogene Lake zigzags to 9,400 feet at .2 mile. Then it switchbacks down through talus, scree, and whitebark pines. Above a tiny pond in the grass at 1 mile is a junction (8,950 feet) with the Edith Lake Trail.

Next the way climbs 330 feet up a sandy slope, dotted with whitebark pines, to 9,280-foot Imogene Divide at 1.9 miles. Then the trail switchbacks down the north side of the pass into timber, reaching a stream at 2.8 miles. At 3.2 miles, beside a marsh along the inlet of the 8,336-foot lake, the trail meets a path that goes around the west side of the lake. There are several campsites on both sides of the lake.

Take the main trail along the east side of the lake past three peninsulas with campsites. From this trail, ribbed, jagged mountains near Mt. Cramer are seen down the canyon below the lake. The trail joins the path from the other side of the lake just below the lower end of the lake 4.1 miles from Sand Mountain Pass.

HELL ROARING AREA

15 Mays Creek Trail to McDonald Lake

Map 6

round trip: 6.2 miles
elevation gain: 830 feet
elevation loss (return climb): 583 feet
highest point: 7,680 feet
maps: Mt. Cramer, Obsidian, Snowyside Peak
time: 5½ hours
difficulty: moderate
access: On Highway 75, turn left (west) 45.7 miles north of Ketchum onto the Hell Roaring–Decker Flat Road. After crossing a bridge over the Salmon River, turn left (south) to a junction at 1.6 miles. Take the left branch and park before a ford of Mays Creek at 1.7 miles unless it is late in the season and there is little water. The trail begins .4 mile beyond the ford.

The Mays Creek Trail is a pleasant, shady walk with veiled glimpses of peaks to the west and south. Missing from the topographic map, this trail leads over a ridge from Mays Creek to McDonald Lake. Shaped like a melting hourglass, the lake is surrounded by marsh grass, willows, huckleberries, lodgepole pines, and shrubby cinquefoil. Up the canyon loom unnamed peaks and across the canyon a sphinx-like shoulder of Mt. McDonald peers over a ridge. The trail links the Yellow Belly and Hell Roaring Creek Trails, making loop trips possible.

To reach the trailhead, follow the access directions above. To avoid mud and rocks, park before the ford of Mays Creek at 6,850 feet. When the Mays Creek Road beyond the ford climbs a hill, turn left (south) at blazes onto an old logging road. Walk 200 yards to a "no motorized vehicles" sign, where the trail begins .4 mile from the ford. The hike mileage is measured from the ford.

The path winds up the side of a wooded ridge to its crest at 1.2 miles. Here it turns west along the top of the ridge. At 2.3 miles (7,680 feet) the route drops south off the ridge, at first straight down, then in long switchbacks on grassy shelves. The trail then follows the shore of the 7,097-foot lake, fording the outlet at 3.1 miles into an area of burned trees. The path then goes south to a junction with the Yellow Belly Trail at 3.4 miles, .4 mile west of Yellow Belly Lake.

16 Hell Roaring Lake
Map 6

round trip: 9.2 miles
elevation gain: 607 feet
highest point: 7,407 feet
map: Mt. Cramer
time: 6 hours
difficulty: moderate
access: From Highway 75, turn left (west) 45.7 miles north of Ketchum and in .3 mile cross the Salmon River on a bridge. Park on the west side of the bridge and walk left (south) on the road for .3 mile to a sign for the trail. Parking is limited at the sign. It will also be possible until a new trailhead is constructed to drive 1.5 miles farther to a junction with the Mays Creek Road and then turn right and drive 3.4 miles up a jeep road that leads to the 3-mile point on the trail. From the end of the jeep road, access to the main trail requires crossing Hell Roaring Creek on shaky logs. This crossing is hazardous in early summer. The rough road has deteriorated over the last few years and now requires four-wheel drive plus a high wheelbase. When the new trailhead is completed, the road will be closed to motor vehicles at the Mays Creek junction.

This shady trail climbs along the white water of Hell Roaring Creek and then ambles through woods carpeted with red-berried grouse whortleberry. Silvered logs and lime green marsh grass enclose the lower end of the blue-green lake. Behind the upper end, the slanting 800-foot Finger of Fate points at the sky. To the left of it, an accordion-pleated headwall leads to the slabs and talus of Mt. Cramer. To the right of the finger, granite gnomes bear the fanciful names of The Arrowhead and The Birthday Cake.

To reach the trailhead, follow the access directions given above. The trail is often dusty and has little water except in the first 1.5 miles where it is close to the creek.

From the trailhead near the Salmon River .3 mile east of Hell Roaring Creek, the trail angles over to the creek, climbing as it goes. Then it runs parallel to the creek in lodgepoles and pale orange boulders capped with black and gray lichen., Next, the path turns away from the creek and winds along parallel to it. At .5 mile, it returns 150 yards to the creek.

At .7 mile, the ground flattens, and the creek meanders in hairpin curves. The trail winds along between a flat forest and little hills covered with boulders and lodgepoles. At 1.2 miles, an old trail from the Salmon River bridge joins. Off to the right at 1.5 miles is the lower end of a pond set in apricot boulders. For a view of peaks reflected in the pond, go around to the upper end of it. The

Hell Roaring Lake

trail continues through flat lodgepole woods, intersecting with the spur trail from the end of the four-wheel drive road at 3 miles.

From the junction with the spur trail, the main trail leads through lodge-pole forest, past a couple of meadows. It crosses an intermittent stream at 3.8 miles. At 4.6 miles is a junction with a trail to Redfish Lake just above 7,407-foot Hell Roaring Lake.

Here, turn left (southwest) and cross the creek on a bridge for the best view of the Finger of Fate and surrounding mountains. There are several campsites on both sides of the lake.

From the upper end, a side trip reaches an unnamed lake right under the Finger of Fate. To do this, leave the main trail at 5.4 miles and work your way around the west end of the lake to the inlet at the west corner of the lake. Go up the right (north) side of this inlet 1 mile to the 8,200-foot lake, which is 6.4 miles from the trailhead and 800 feet above Hell Roaring Lake.

17 Hell Roaring to Decker Creek and Lakes
Map 6

round trip: 14 miles
elevation gain: 1,920 feet
elevation loss (return climb): 760 feet
this section one way: 2.4 miles, 1,360-foot gain, 760-foot loss
highest point: 8,720 feet
time: 8 hours
map: Mt. Cramer
difficulty: moderate, with .1 mile cross-country
access: Follow directions in Hike 16 to hike to Hell Roaring Lake.

Sheets of white granite embrace a flock of blue tarns and then soar to the crinkled walls and sloping snowfields of Decker Peak. The true summit is the 10,704-foot peak 1.3 miles southwest of the Decker Peak marked on the topographic map. The lowest of these tarns, the two Decker Lakes, shimmer on branches of Decker Creek just west of the trail from Hell Roaring to Redfish.

This hike description begins at the junction at the lower end of Hell Roaring Lake (7,407 feet). To reach it, follow the directions for Hike 16 (Hell Roaring Lake). Hell Roaring is a 1.8-mile walk and 200-foot climb from the end of the four-wheel drive road, and a 4.6-mile hike and 400-foot climb up the new trail from the Salmon River. From the junction at the lower end of the lake, the trail toward Decker Creek and Redfish Lake switchbacks northeast in woods to meet the Huckleberry Creek Trail at .7 mile. This trail has come 3.8 miles with a 1,430-foot elevation gain from Decker Flat.

The main trail continues to the 8,720-foot crest of the ridge at 1 mile, 1,360 feet above Hell Roaring Lake. From the north side of the ridge, the snowy face of Decker Peak appears through the trees. At 1.5 miles the trail turns north and drops down a ravine along a stream which is often dry.

To reach Decker Lakes, turn west off the trail where the ground flattens at 2.2 miles and climb 100 feet cross-country to the largest lake (8,080 feet) at 2.4 miles. Do not try to go up Decker Creek to the lake because the slope is steep and has downed timber. To reach the smaller, upper lake, circle the larger lake on either side and cut northwest .1 mile. Decker Creek is .3 mile north of the turnoff to the lakes.

Do this hike in early summer, as the lakes have little water later. The best campsites are along the trail, not at the lakes. There is no water between Hell Roaring and Decker Lakes.

18   Decker Creek to Redfish Inlet Transfer Camp

Map 8

through trip from Hell Roaring Creek Road: 11.2 miles; 14 miles from the new trailhead
elevation gain: 2,714 feet
elevation loss: 2,767 feet
this section one way: 6.7 miles, 794-foot gain, 2,207-foot loss
highest point: 8,554 feet
map: Mt. Cramer
time: 9 hours plus time to set up a car shuttle and to take the boat ride from Redfish Inlet back to the lodge by prearrangement with the lodge
difficulty: strenuous
access: Follow directions in Hikes 16 and 17, and hike to the unmarked turnoff to Decker Lakes 4 miles from Hell Roaring Lake.

From this trail, lodgepole pines screen views of the pale shapes of the White Clouds and the immense turquoise of Redfish Lake. From the descent to the lake, the fractured beige wall of Mt. Heyburn begins the string of peaks that make up the walls of Redfish Canyon. These walls are accented with avalanche chutes like great claw marks.

To reach the beginning of this hike description – at the turnoff for Decker Lakes, .3 mile above Decker Creek (7,960 feet) – follow directions in the Hell Roaring and Decker lakes hikes. After descending to the creek, the trail climbs north, drops northeast and then begins to climb seriously. At a 90-degree bend at 1.1 miles, an old trail to Decker Flat goes off to the right. At 1.4 miles, the main trail turns left (west) up the center of a ridge with a view of the White Clouds near the top.

At 2.2 miles, the path switches north with glimpses of Redfish and Little Redfish. Then the trail drops 200 feet to the head of an all-year stream. It climbs along the side of another ridge at 2.6 miles. The route runs north along the center of this ridge to its 8,554-foot high point at 3 miles. From here, Mt. Heyburn can be seen ahead and the Grand Mogul to the left. From the brow of the ridge at 4 miles, Redfish Lake appears below and Cabin Creek Peak in the Salmon River Mountains in the distance.

At 4.8 miles, the Bull Moose Trail goes off 4.5 miles to Decker Flat with a 1,020-foot elevation loss. Then at 5.1 miles in a low point in the ridge, a trail heads northeast to Sockeye Campground, which is near the lower end of Redfish. It is 4.2 miles with a 1,060-foot elevation loss to that campground. At this junction, if you have arranged for a boat ride or are prepared for the 5-mile

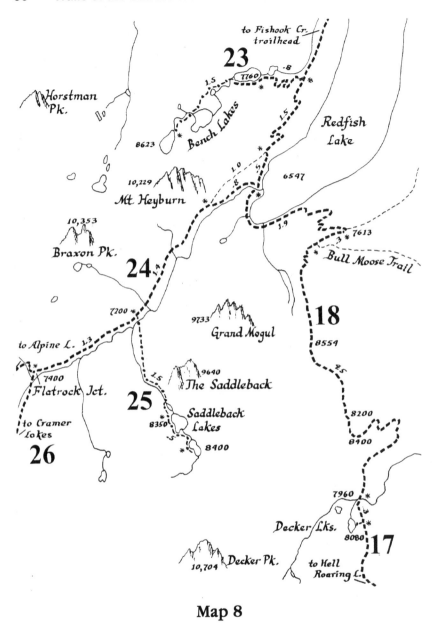

Map 8

walk around the lake, take the trail to the left (northwest) toward Redfish Inlet. This trail zigzags down the side of the ridge within 30 feet of the lake at 6 miles.

At 6.4 miles the trail drops to the beach and disappears in the sand for 50 yards before it returns to forest. At high water, you must wade or take a rough path through the brush here. Next the trail bridges a creek, then climbs 160 feet to meet a side trail to the Lily Pond at 6.7 miles, (labeled Lily Lake on the topographic map). The pond is .2 mile up this path and has a beautiful view of Mt. Heyburn. Go around the lower side of the pond to see a waterfall that descends in four steps on Redfish Lake Creek. To see a much larger falls, continue above the upper side of the pond southwest along a hillside above the creek.

From the Lily Pond junction, the main trail descends to the shore and crosses a bridge over Redfish Creek. Beyond the bridge, the path goes through a pole fence into the transfer camp at 7 miles. It is 5 miles and a 973-foot climb around the lake to the road from here.

19 Imogene Lake
Maps 6 and 7

round trip: 16.6 miles from new trailhead
elevation gain: 1,636 feet
this section one way: 3.7 miles, 1,029-foot gain
highest point: 8,436 feet
maps: Mt. Cramer, Snowyside Peak
time: 8 hours
difficulty: strenuous
access: Follow the directions in Hike 16 (Hell Roaring Lake) to hike to the
lower end of Hell Roaring Lake where this hike description begins.

The arms of Imogene Lake turn one of its high granite peninsulas to an island in early summer. Above the upper end of the lake, a wide shoulder of Payette Peak holds fluted cliffs. Below the peak, a chain of little lakes set in grass and wildflowers skips up a hanging valley. Above the east side of the lake, orange needles climb a wall of unnamed mountains. The chain of little lakes, Imogene Divide, the unnamed lake sometimes called Lucille, and Profile Lake all make beautiful side trips from Imogene.

To reach the junction at the lower end of Hell Roaring Lake (7,407 feet) where this hike description begins, follow the directions in Hike 16. From the junction, hike along the lake on the trail along its left (southeast) shore. At the head of the lake at .8 mile, the trail switchbacks up ledges and through forest across the canyon from crinkled cliffs. From here to Imogene, it has been re-routed from what is shown on the topographic map. Between 1.6 and 2 miles, the path goes along an open hillside amid tiny trees.

At 2.1 miles, the trail circles the left side of a small snow pond that is not shown on the topographic map. The path edges a tiny pond full of water lilies at 2.6 miles. At 2.7 miles, it runs along the east side of a larger, sprawling pond where the dark pleated cliffs of the canyon of Profile Lake are visible. At 3.5

miles, the trail crosses logs to the west side of Imogene's outlet, then goes along the right side of another water lily pond. At 3.6 miles, the trail crosses the outlet again to the east before arriving at the 8,436-foot lake at 3.7 miles.

To make a side trip to the chain of tiny lakes at the head of Imogene, follow the trail along the east side of the lake to a meadow at 4.6 miles where the trail joins one around the west side. Turn right (north) onto this trail and ford the inlet on its north side. Just before a corduroy bridge over a stream, turn left (southwest). Go up granite ledges along the inlet, passing a waterfall, to the first lake, sometimes called "Esther."

The bays and coves of this shallow lake sprawl between grassy swales and granite benches. Here you look up the canyon to the roof-like side of Payette Peak. To reach the higher lakes, go around the right (north) side of the first lake to a small, grassy lakelet. Continue up the inlet, through ledges and between benches to the third lake, which features boulders, scree, tiny trees, turquoise water, and huge sawteeth on the ridge above. Follow the stream between the lakes to the highest lake at 8,950 feet, 1.3 miles and a 520-foot climb from Imogene. For directions for reaching the large unnamed lake (8,733 feet), (sometimes called Lucille), northwest of the lower end of Imogene, see the following hike description.

20 Profile Lake
Map 7

round trip: 20.6 miles
elevation gain: 2,700 feet
elevation loss (return climb): 240 feet
this section one way: 2 miles, 1,224-foot gain, 160-foot loss
side trip to Lucille Lake: additional .2 mile one way
highest point: 9,500 feet
maps: Mt. Cramer, Snowyside Peak
time: 12 hours or 2 days
ability: expert
access: For access directions see Hike 16 (Hell Roaring Lake) and Hike 19 (Imogene Lake).
caution: This cross-country hike is challenging, and it is easy to get lost among the ponds and granite hogbacks below Lucille Lake. Avoid camping at either lake to protect the fragile lake basins.

Northwest of Imogene Lake, great granite triangles overshadow an unnamed 8,733-foot lake, sometimes called Lucille. Lichens color the giant sawteeth above it dark green. To the right (west) of this wall, orange ledges stairstep to the summit talus of Mt. Cramer. Near the lower end of Lucille, a white granite peninsula thrusts into the turquoise water. Seven hundred feet above Lucille, in a bowl of rocks, blue Profile Lake takes the shape of a bust of George Washington. Between the lakes, the creek connecting them tumbles in waterfalls. Northeast of Mt. Cramer, rock soldiers lead along a ridge to the summit of Sevy Peak.

To reach the lower end of Imogene Lake (8,436 feet) 5.5 miles from the trailhead, where this hike description begins, see Hikes 16 and 19. Take the fishing trail west around the lower end of the lake to the narrow bay at the northwest corner of the lake.

Here, turn off the trail and climb west to the pond shown on the map 50 feet above the lake. From the pond, go north to a slot between rock benches at 8,560 feet and descend it to another pond (8,400 feet) at .5 mile. From this pond, walk directly west along the base of ledges (not following the creek) to a third pond (8,300 feet) at .8 mile. Detour to ford the outlet to the north side 100 to 150 yards below this pond where it spreads out over flat granite. Go around the pond on the north, then climb rock benches along the right (north) side of the inlet. When the inlet splits, continue up the right side of the stream draining Profile Lake, not up the outlet of Lucille, which runs in a gorge. At 1.3 miles, cross the creek on logs below a narrow pond (8,680 feet). From here, Lucille is .2 mile to the southwest (8,733 feet), 1.5 miles from Imogene.

To continue to Profile Lake, return to the lower end of the narrow pond and go up a series of grass-filled gaps in the granite ledges on the left (west) side of the outlet. At 1.8 miles (.5 mile from the narrow pond) is a tiny rocky pond. Above is steep talus above the gorge of the outlet, so turn left (west) away from the creek and climb gentler ledges to the top of a rounded granite ridge. From the ridge, descend carefully to the 9,500-foot lake at 2 miles.

To climb Mt. Cramer, return to the granite ridge and follow it west over slabs and boulders. When it steepens, go up the right side of a rectangular snowbank which is prominent much of the summer. Then follow the southeast ridge of the peak to the summit. It is .8 mile and a 1,216-foot hike from Profile Lake to the summit of Mt. Cramer.

REDFISH LAKE AREA

21 Fishhook Creek Meadow
Map 9

round trip to the meadow: 4.4 miles
elevation gain: 242 feet
highest point: 6,800 feet
map: Stanley
time: 3 hours
difficulty: easy
access: On Highway 75, turn left (south) 56.2 miles north of Ketchum on the paved Redfish Lake Road and drive 2 miles to the backpackers' parking lot.

Pale aqua and crystal Fishhook Creek meanders through this meadow, alternately hiding under high grassy banks and pooling in beaver ponds. At the head of the meadow, a 200-yard beaver dam holds in the largest pond. The pointed towers of Mt. Heyburn jut above the left side of the meadow. To the right of Mt. Heyburn, the double black hump of Horstmann Peak crouches like a black cat. North of the meadow, a ridge of square teeth leads toward the shoulders of Thompson Peak. Between these mountains at the head of the canyon, the umbrella-tent of Mt. Ebert is pitched.

To reach the backpackers' parking lot (6,558 feet) where the hike begins, follow the directions above. On the Redfish Lake Road, keep straight ahead at a junction 2 miles from the highway. The parking lot is on the right, just beyond the junction. From it, walk northwest across the lodge road and find a hiker sign and old road leading west up the right side of Fishhook Creek. Most of the hike is along this old road, which is closed to motor vehicles. During the first .3 mile, the track climbs 120 vertical feet up the creek. Near the top of this climb, a trail to the Redfish Corrals turns right. At the top at .3 mile, a trail to the left goes 3.6 miles with a 1,522-foot climb to Bench lakes and a branch of this trail goes on up Redfish Canyon.

Continue on the old road, avoiding side tracks, through Douglas fir and lodgepole forest. At .8 mile is a junction with a trail climbing north 480 feet in .5 mile to join the Alpine Way Trail. By this shortcut, Marshall Lake is only 5 miles instead of 6 miles from the southern end of the Alpine Way Trail. From where the old road ends at a washout of the creek bank at 1.5 miles, take a blazed trail to the right (northwest) through the trees. The path curves left along the base of a steep ridge. At 2.2 miles (6,800 feet), the meadow begins. The largest beaver pond is .1 mile farther.

The trail continues past the pond through forest as far as a creek crossing at 3.1 miles. Experts can continue cross-country an additional 4 miles to the

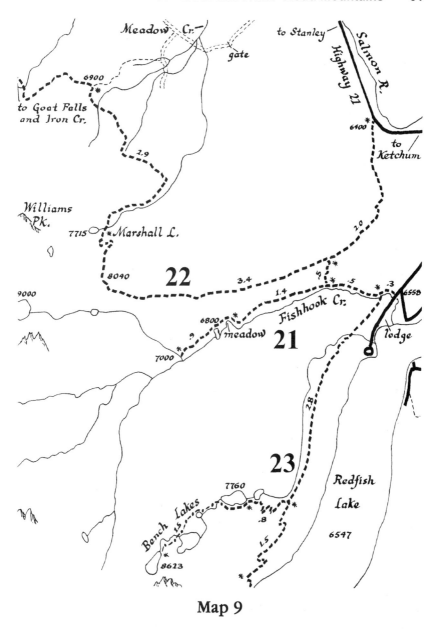

Map 9

Stephens Lakes. This is a difficult route due to a long stretch of talus blocks in the bottom of the canyon.

22 Alpine Way and Marshall Lake
Map 9

round trip: 11.4 miles to lake, through trip 11.3 miles to Iron Creek trailhead
elevation gain: 2,382 feet
elevation loss (return climb): 1,180 feet
highest point: 8,040 feet
maps: Stanley, Stanley Lake
time: 2 days
difficulty: strenuous
access: On Highway 75, 57.4 miles north of Ketchum between the Redfish
    Lake Road and the Stanley Ranger Station, turn left (west) on a paved spur
    road and drive 100 yards to two dirt roads leading left which begin at the
    same point.

Near the beginning of the Alpine Way Trail, across Fishhook Creek soar
the towers of Mt. Heyburn and the black face and nose of Horstmann Peak.
Just off the trail, at 5 miles, tiny Marshall Lake nestles under cliffs laced with
waterfalls. The lodgepoles and subalpine firs edging the shallow green lake blur
the stripes of Williams Peak. Farther along the trail, Goat Falls tumbles in
steps–each short waterfall split into white ribbons by granite boulders.

To reach the trailhead (6,400 feet), follow the access directions above. The
topographic map is confusing because it shows only the spur road to the ranger
station. Drive 100 yards along the right (west) road and park in the trees. Then
walk south along the road for .6 mile. Here it becomes a trail and climbs the
end of a wooded ridge. At 1 and 1.3 miles, the route passes trails to the left (east)
to Redfish Corrals.

Just before the register box at 2 miles is a junction with the cutoff Marshall
Lake Trail which has climbed 480 feet in .5 mile from Fishhook Creek. A few
feet south off trail from the register box is a fine view of Mt. Heyburn and
Horstmann Peak. This viewpoint is a good destination for an evening walk on
the Alpine Way Trail or on the cutoff. At 2.1 miles, a path turns left to another
viewpoint of these mountains.

For more than the next mile, the trail is in the open within a few steps of
this view. At 3.2 miles, the route returns to forest. The way steepens at 4 miles
and at 4.5 miles turns a corner to the north toward the immense fin of Thompson Peak.

Here, expert hikers may turn south to begin a side trip to the round lake
under Thompson Peak. To reach this lake, use caution and avoid steep slopes in
descending to a pond southwest of the trail. The route is easier if you turn off to
the pond before the trail corner at 4.3 miles because the slope is gentler. From
the pond, the climb is steep to the round lake, but not as abrupt as it is going

directly to the lake from the trail. A gully northwest of the pond is the best route to the lake.

Beyond the corner where the route to the round lake begins, continue on the Alpine Way Trail to a high point (8,040 feet) on an open, grassy slope, then descend through woods. At 5 miles, the route drops in switchbacks to a .1 mile spur trail to 7,715-foot Marshall Lake at 5.3 miles. At 5.4 miles, the Alpine Way Trail crosses the outlet of Marshall Lake on logs.

Beyond here, the trail goes northeast down the canyon of Marshall Lake's outlet, then northwest downhill through dense lodgepoles. At 8.3 miles (6,900 feet), a jeep track comes in from Meadow Creek to the west. This track climbs 1.2 miles in 450 feet from a pasture 3 miles southwest of Stanley, but access to it is blocked by posted private property. Skirting the property is so much trouble it is not worth the distance saved.

From the Meadow Creek junction, the main trail turns west along the side of a ridge. At 9.2 miles, the path drops to ford Goat Creek which can be difficult in early summer. Next the route switchbacks a wooded hillside to an unsigned junction (7,400 feet) at 10.0 miles. From here, a well-worn path leads south .4 mile to Goat Falls. From this point, the Alpine Way Trail continues north to the Iron Creek Trail and to Stanley Lake. For a description of this, see Hike 32 (Goat Lake) and 33 (North Alpine Way Trail).

Water on this hike is available only at the two creek crossings and Marshall Lake. The only good campsites are at the lake.

23   Bench Lakes
Map 9

round trip to Lake 2: 7.8 miles, add 1 mile cross-country one way and 863-foot gain to see the higher lakes
elevation gain: 1,202 feet
highest point: 7,760 feet at the second lake, 8,623 feet at the fifth lake
maps: Stanley, Mt. Cramer
time: 6 hours; add 3 hours to see the higher lakes
difficulty: moderate; expert for the upper lakes
access: On Highway 75, turn left (west) 56.2 miles north of Ketchum on the Redfish Lake Road, and drive 2 miles on a paved road to the backpackers' parking lot.
caution: There is no trail to the upper three lakes and reaching them is challenging. Avoid camping at the upper lakes to protect the fragile timberline vegetation.

This hike brings close the pleats and notches of the 1,000-foot face of Mt. Heyburn. In early summer, snow fills the chimneys between the orange and gray towers of the mountain. Each of the blue-green lakes comes nearer to this face, until at the fifth lake the chockstones caught in the chimneys are visible. Below the trail, the clear blue water of Redfish Lake extends to the beginning of Redfish Canyon. The canyon's rows of spiked peaks march toward the lake like a vast rocky parade.

To reach the trailhead, follow the access directions above. From the parking lot (6,558 feet), walk west across the paved lodge road to find the trail at a hiker sign. The trail begins as an old dirt road up Fishhook Creek. At .3 mile, turn left (south) on the trail around the lake to Redfish Canyon. It zigzags through forest up the moraine. Beyond an intermittent stream at 1.2 miles, the trail overlooks the lake as it begins to follow the crest of this moraine, crossing back and forth over the top of it among occasional granite boulders. There is no water. On the north side of the ridge at 3.1 miles, turn right (north) on the side trail to Bench Lakes.

Beyond this turnoff, the Redfish-Baron Lakes Trail continues well above the lake past its upper end and into Redfish Canyon. At 1.5 miles from the Bench Lakes junction, a branch trail drops .5 mile to the Inlet Transfer Camp boat dock at the upper end of the lake. Taking the boat to the end of the lake shortens the distance to Bench Lakes by 1 mile.

To find the branch trail from the boat dock, look for two gaps near the upper ends of two pole fences that run uphill from the dock. The trail begins at the gap in the north fence. Avoid a path that leads from the lower end of the fences along the lake shore.

The branch trail climbs along the ridge, zigzagging above the lake with an excellent view back up Redfish Canyon. It joins the main trail .5 mile from the boat dock. The main trail from here to the Bench Lakes junction has an even better view up the canyon.

From the Bench Lakes junction, the trail to the lakes makes switchbacks not shown on the topographic map. At 3.7 miles is the grassy edge of the first lake, which has few large trees because of an old forest fire. Across it to the north, four sharp-pointed peaks peer over a wooded ridge. The second lake, at 3.9 miles (7,760 feet), nestles below a wooded ridge guarded by Mt. Heyburn. The official trail ends here.

To reach the upper lakes, there are two possible routes. First, you can circle the left (south) shore of the second lake, then cross the inlet and climb along the right (north) side of it to the tiny third lake at 4.5 miles. This lake is just a pond in the woods. To reach the fourth lake from here, circle the third on the right (north) and ascend a steep rocky slope to the lake at 4.8 miles. To save distance, you may wish to avoid the third lake and instead go from the left

(south) side of the second lake directly to the outlet of the fourth lake by compass. To continue to the fifth lake, go around the fourth lake on the north and
cross its inlet. Then climb a wrinkle left (south) of this inlet to the lake (8,623
feet) at 5.3 miles.

24 Redfish Inlet to Flatrock Junction
Map 8

round trip: 7 miles
elevation gain: 853 feet
highest point: 7,400 feet
maps: Mt. Cramer, Warbonnet Peak
time: 5½ hours
difficulty: easy
access: Take the boat from Redfish Lake Lodge to the Inlet Transfer Camp or
   go around the lake on foot. To reach the lodge, turn left (west) on the paved
   Redfish Lake Road 56.2 miles north of Ketchum and drive 2.3 miles, following the signs to the right at a junction at 2 miles.

Jagged peaks fringed with delicate spires line both sides of Redfish Canyon.
Between the peaks, lakes like Saddleback Lakes hide in hanging valleys cut off
by an ancient glacier. Deep blue Redfish Lake, enclosed by glacial moraines,
meets this canyon below the jumbled points of the Grand Mogul and the fluted
cliffs of Mt. Heyburn. The orange Saddleback on the southeast wall of the
canyon at 2 miles is one of the most dramatic peaks lining the canyon. It looks
like an oversized saddle, complete with horn. At Flatrock Junction, the trails to
Alpine and Cramer Lakes diverge. Near it Redfish Creek slides in shining sheets
over white granite. This hike gives you the essence of the Sawtooths with little
effort. Even a boat ride to the trailhead at the upper end of the lake is worthwhile.

To reach the Inlet Transfer Camp where the hike begins, take the lodge boat
or walk 5 miles around the lake. If taking the boat, leave your car in the backpackers' parking lot to avoid congesting the lodge parking area.

The trail to Flatrock starts as paths in the campground that meet 200 yards
to the northwest at a register box. Avoid paths leading uphill northeast of the
boat landing. The trail through the campground joins the trail from the lodge
at .8 mile.

The joined trails continue up the canyon alternating open areas with trees
and giving views of the lake beginning at 1.2 miles. At 1.4 miles, the path
crosses a side creek. Statue-like towers on the canyon wall and enormous boulders along the trail at 1.6 miles create an area called "Garden of the Giants." At

2 miles, the trail crosses another creek, just before the unmarked turnoff for Saddleback Lakes at 2.2 miles.

The route continues in trees and over rock benches beside cascades to Flatrock Junction (7,400 feet) at 3.5 miles. There are campsites and picnic spots a few yards away near the ford of the creek on the Cramer Lakes Trail.

25 Saddleback Lakes
Map 8

round trip: 7.4 miles, from Redfish Inlet, 3 miles cross-country
elevation gain: 1,803 feet
this section: 1.5 miles, 1,150 foot gain; additional .5 mile one-way for the upper lake, 50-foot gain
highest point: 8,400 feet at the upper lake
map: Mt. Cramer
time: 8 hours
ability: expert
access: On Highway 75, turn left (west) 56.2 miles north of Ketchum, and following signs, drive 2.3 miles west to Redfish Lake Lodge. Take the boat from the lodge to the upper end of the lake or hike 5 miles to the Inlet Transfer Camp.
caution: The route is difficult to find and it is easy to get hung up in downed timber or on cliffs. Avoid camping in the fragile lake basin to prevent damaging it. Campfires are not allowed within 200 yards of the lakes.

The top of the Saddleback resembles a saddle for giants complete with saddlehorn. From its summit, an orange granite wall plunges 1,300 feet into the lowest turquoise lake. Climbers call this face "The Elephant's Perch". Across the lakes, the dark gray needles of Goat and Eagle perches face this wall. Above the highest lake, teeth on Decker Peak peer over a striped ridge.

To begin this hike, take the trail up Redfish Canyon from the Inlet Transfer Camp. At 2 miles the trail fords a stream coming from the northwest. Once across it, look for a campsite beside Redfish Creek at 2.2 miles. Here, cross the creek on a complex of logs 100 yards upstream. The crossing is dangerous or impassable in early season and in wet years.

On the other side of the creek, plunge through brush away from the creek for 30 yards and then look for a way to climb south between outcrops. To keep out of downed timber and the gorge of Saddleback Lakes' outlet, avoid going too far up Redfish Creek before climbing away from it.

At .7 mile, in grass and small trees, descend from the outcrops so they are on the left (east). At 1 mile, climb 500 feet beside the cascading outlet. Above the

The Arrowhead from Upper Cramer Lake

cascade at 1.2 miles, cross the creek to the right (west) side. At 1.3 miles, skirt the right (west) side of a narrow sliver of a pond to reach the flat granite benches at the lower end of the first lake (8,350 feet) 1.5 miles from the trail and 3.7 miles from Redfish Inlet Transfer Camp.

To reach the higher lake, go around the right (west) side of the lower lake. This lake (8,400 feet), 2 miles from the trail, is enclosed by sentinels of Decker Peak.

26   Flatrock Junction to Cramer Lakes
Maps 8 and 10

round trip: 13.4 to 14.4 miles
elevation gain: 1,834 feet
this section one way: 3.7 miles, 981-foot gain
highest point: 8,381 feet at Upper Cramer Lake
maps: Mt. Cramer, Warbonnet Peak
time: 10½ hours from Redfish Inlet Transfer Camp
difficulty: strenuous
access: Use directions in Hike 24 (Redfish Inlet to Flatrock Junction) and hike
    to that junction.

At Upper Cramer Lake above a meadow sprinkled with wildflowers, a giant arrowhead emerges from the mountain wall. The outlet of the lake thunders into the water of the middle lake in a short, wide waterfall. Above the lakes, the 800-foot face of Mt. Cramer and the needled ridge of The Temple edge the cirque leading to Cramer Divide. In the distance to the north, a rock feather caps a peak on Baron Divide.

This hike description begins at Flatrock Junction (7,400 feet), which is 3.5 miles and 853 feet above Redfish Inlet Transfer Camp. For directions for reaching this point, see the hikes listed above. From Flatrock Junction, the trail to Cramer Lakes begins with a 25-foot ford of Redfish Creek. A log jam is about 100 yards downstream, but the creek can be impassable in early summer and remains treacherous well into mid-summer in wet years.

The path goes level through woods for .8 mile. It then curves southeast and climbs along the side of the canyon that contains the outlet of Cramer Lakes. From 1.5 to 2 miles the trail switchbacks, then levels in forest that veils Elk and Reward Peaks to the southwest. At 2.5 miles, the path climbs gently along the canyon wall, crossing small side streams, and at 2.7 miles, it runs above an unnamed grassy lake (8,108 feet). The route crosses another side stream at 3 miles and reaches Lower Cramer Lake (8,320 feet) at 3.2 miles. The path continues on the left (northeast) side of the lakes to the middle lake at 3.5 miles and the upper lake (8,381 feet) at 3.7 miles. There are several campsites at all three lakes. From the upper lake, the trail heads through a wildflower meadow towards Cramer Divide.

27 Cramer Lakes to Edna Lake
Map 7

round trip: 29.4 miles
elevation gain: 3,137 feet
elevation loss (return climb): 1,280 feet
this section one way: 7.5 miles, 1,303-foot gain, 1,280-foot loss
highest point: 9,480 feet
maps: Mt. Cramer, Warbonnet Peak, Snowyside Peak
time: 4 days
difficulty: strenuous
access: Using directions in Hike 24 (Redfish Inlet to Flatrock Junction) and Hike 26 (Flatrock Junction to Cramer Lakes), hike to Upper Cramer Lake.
caution: Cramer Divide is usually blocked by snow until early to mid-August. To avoid danger and to prevent damage to the soils, wait until the snow melts from the trail before traveling it.

From Cramer Divide, rows of peaks march in every direction, beginning with the splinters of The Temple which run east from Cramer Divide to the sliced-off summit of Mt. Cramer. This ridge continues east to jumbled Sevy Peak and The Arrowhead, a rock resembling the tip of an arrow sticking out of the mountain. South of the divide, rocks and wildflowers edge the crystal water

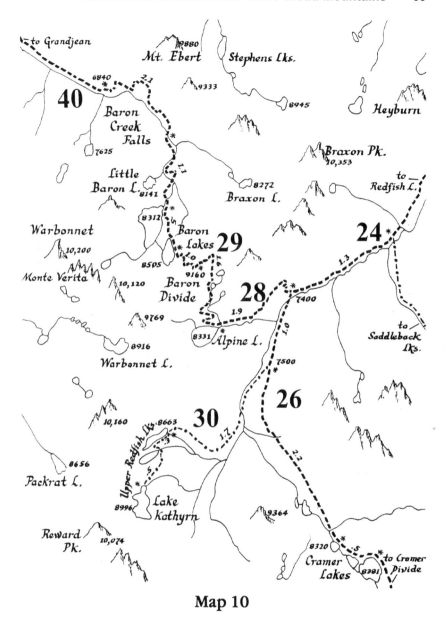

to Grandjean

Mt. Ebert 9880

Stephens Lks.

Heyburn

6840

2.1

40

9333

8945

Baron
Creek
Falls

7625

Braxon Pk.
10,353

Little
Baron L. 8141

1.1

8272

Braxon L.

to
Redfish L.

8312

Warbonnet
10,200

Baron
Lakes 29

24

Monte Verita
10,120

8505

9160

Baron
Divide

28

1.3

Warbonnet L.

9769

8916

8331

1.9

7400

Alpine L.

1.0

to
Saddleback
Lks.

7500

26

30

10,160

.8663

2.2

1.7

Packrat L.

8656

.5

Lake
Kathyrn

8996

9364

Reward
Pk.

10,074

8320

Cramer
Lakes

.5

8391

to Cramer
Divide

Map 10

of Hidden Lake, which filters into a narrow pond in a marsh. From the pond, granite benches and ledges soar east to the wide triangle of Payette Peak.

Above Upper Cramer Lake (8,321 feet) the trail climbs granite benches, crosses a creek at .7 mile and the outlet of a pond at 1.3 miles. Next it switchbacks past a smaller pond in rocks and zigzags up talus below a wall of cliffs to the divide (9,480 feet) at 2.3 miles.

On the other side, the trail drops south in whitebark pines along a ridge, overlooking a narrow blue pond. Then the path zigzags to a crossing of the inlet in a meadow at 3.3 miles. The trail continues down grassy slopes to the shore of Hidden Lake (8,563 feet) at 4 miles. The path edges the west shore of the lake and the narrow pond below it. At 4.9 miles it crosses the outlet of the lake, then descends through forest and angles over to ford the South Fork of the Payette River at 8,200 feet. On the south side of the river is a junction with a trail down the river to Elk Lake and Grandjean and up the river to Virginia and Edna lakes. This junction is 5.9 miles from Upper Cramer Lake.

To reach Edna Lake from here, go up the South Fork trail. The trail fords the river to the east side at 6.4 miles and a creek coming from Sand Mountain Pass at 6.5 miles. It reaches the shore of Virginia Lake, a shallow lake in marsh grass and woods, at 6.6 miles. The route then climbs 200 feet to the lower end of Edna Lake at 6.9 miles. It edges the north side of the lake to a junction at 7.5 miles with trails to Sand Mountain Pass and Ardeth Lake.

28 Flatrock Junction to Alpine Lake
Map 10

round trip: 10.8 miles
elevation gain: 1,784 feet
this section one way: 1.9 miles, 931-foot gain
highest point: 8,331 feet
map: Warbonnet Peak
time: 8½ hours
difficulty: strenuous
access: On Highway 75, turn left (south) 56.2 miles north of Ketchum and go 2.3 miles to Redfish Lake Lodge. Take the boat from the lodge or hike 5 miles around the lake to Redfish Inlet Transfer Camp. Using the directions in Hike 24, hike up Redfish Creek to Flatrock Junction.
warning: No campfires are allowed within 100 feet of Alpine Lake.

From Flatrock Junction the trail to Alpine Lake zigzags 931 feet up cliffs on the side of Redfish Canyon. On the west side of the lake, furrowed cliffs unite into a pointed granite mountain. On the other three sides of the lake, lodgepole pines and subalpine firs decorate granite benches. Above the benches to the northeast, spires peek over a ridge.

Following the access directions above, hike to Flatrock Junction (7,400 feet). The left branch of the trail goes to Cramer Lakes. Take the right (west) branch towards Alpine Lake. This trail switchbacks through grass and brush, crossing back and forth over a side stream. At .7 mile, it comes to cliffs covered with trees. The trail levels out at 1.6 miles and fords an inlet. At 1.9 miles, it reaches the lake (8,331 feet). Campsites on the trail side of the lake are over-used, so try the upper end or across the outlet. Campfires are not allowed within 200 yards of Alpine Lake.

29 Alpine Lake to Baron Lakes
Map 10

round trip: 17 miles
elevation gain: 2,613 feet
elevation loss (return climb): 848 feet
this section one way: 3.1 miles, 829-foot gain, 848-foot loss
highest point: 9,160 feet
map: Warbonnet Peak
time: 2–3 days
difficulty: strenuous
access: Using directions in Hike 24 (Redfish Inlet to Flatrock Junction) and Hike 28 (Flatrock Junction to Alpine Lake), hike to Alpine Lake.
caution: Baron Divide between Alpine and Baron Lakes is usually blocked by snow until mid-July or early August. To avoid danger and to prevent damage to the soils, wait until the snow melts from the trail before traveling it.

From Baron Divide, peaks, crags, and serrated ridges stretch in every direction into blue haze. Below, Baron Lakes perch in a hanging valley at the head of the South Fork of the Payette River. On the south, the cylindrical folds of Monte Verita overhang the lakes. Northwest of that mountain, granite pinnacles create the feathers of a war bonnet, but the peak called Warbonnet is hidden. On the north end of this ridge, Big Baron Spire raises a pinnacle resembling the tip of a bent thumb.

Following the directions in Hike 24 (Redfish Inlet to Flatrock Junction), hike to Alpine Lake (8,331 feet). Above the lake, the trail to the divide makes four 300-yard switchbacks in woods and then climbs along the outlet of a series of ponds, crossing it twice. At .7 mile, the path edges the west side of the first pond.

From the pond, the trail goes towards the head of the side canyon where the ponds are located. At 1.3 miles, it turns from heading north to southwest. The path then zigzags west up rocks to the 9,160-foot divide at 1.6 miles. On the other side, the trail hairpins down through ledges, talus and whitebark pines to the rocky edge of Upper Baron Lake, (8,505 feet) at 2.6 miles. It continues along the edge of the lake, where at 2.8 miles, a path turns off to some campsites. The route descends in woods to the lower lake (8,312 feet) at 3.1 miles. The best campsites are off-trail northeast of Upper Baron Lake and at the lower end of Baron Lake.

30 Upper Redfish Lakes
Map 10

round trip: 14 miles; 5 miles cross-country
elevation gain: 2,449 feet
this section one way: 2.5 miles, 1,496-foot gain
highest point: 8,996 feet
maps: Mt. Cramer, Warbonnet Peak
time: 10½ hours or 2 days
ability: expert
access: Using directions in Hike 24 (Redfish Lake to Flatrock Junction), and
  Hike 26 (Flatrock Junction to Cramer Lakes), hike to Flatrock Junction and
  go 1 mile above it on the Cramer Lakes Trail.
caution: This is a challenging hike and it is easy to get lost or find yourself
  climbing cliffs. Avoid camping in the fragile lake basin to prevent damaging it.

Snowfields splash the 800-foot charcoal gray sawteeth of Elk Peak above the
three Upper Redfish Lakes. Needles guard the ridge between this peak and the
talus cap of Reward Peak. These peaks and needles, plus white granite knolls,
turquoise water, and whitebark pines swollen with burls decorate the upper
lake, Lake Kathryn. The two lower lakes, set between trees, granite outcrops
and flower-splashed meadows, have a different backdrop. On the northeast,
pickets of an orange mountain fence in the aqua water of the twin lakes.

Using the access directions above, hike to a point 1 mile toward Cramer
Lakes from Flatrock Junction. This point is at 7,500 feet and 4.5 miles from the
Inlet Transfer Camp. At the turn off, the trail jogs uphill to the left and begins
to climb. Leave the trail here and descend to Redfish Creek, following it for .5
mile through dense forest, downed timber and boggy areas. Cross the creek at
about .6 mile on logs while the ground is still level.

Go along the right (west) side of the canyon above the creek. Just before
reaching the outlet of Cramer Lakes at .8 mile, the banks of the creek steepen.
Climb away from the creek 100 yards onto a little ridge and follow it. At 1 mile
the creek divides again into three sections. Climb along the right (north) side of
the right branch through shrubs. At 1.2 miles, the canyon gets even steeper and
the branch of the creek you are following splits again, forming outlets for the
two lower lakes. The outlet of the lowest lake, the one to the right (north), is
not shown on the topographic map.

Keep to the right of BOTH streams and work up ramps between granite
ledges, but AVOID the cliffs on the right. This route is easier than the brush
between and to the left of the streams. Each time the creek splits, keep to the
right of all branches of it. The stream runs through a series of cascades and
waterfalls before the granite flattens into pavement at 1.5 miles. At 1.7 miles is

the lower lake (8,663 feet). Go left (south) around the lower lake and cut across a strip of land to the middle lake at 2 miles.

The upper lake, Lake Kathryn, can be reached from the lower end of the middle lake by scrambling .5 mile up a 300-foot ridge to the south. To find this route, cross the outlet of the lake and circle the ridge to the left of it until you can climb between granite benches to the crest. Then follow the flattened summit of the ridge until you can climb down over the benches to the lake (8,996 feet) near its outlet.

IRON CREEK AREA

31 Alpine, Sawtooth and McGown Lakes
Map 11

round trip: 9.6 miles
elevation gain: 1,720 feet
side trip to McGown Lakes: add 1.5 miles one way and 330-foot gain, 255-foot loss
highest point: 8,430 feet
map: Stanley Lake
time: 8 hours
difficulty: strenuous
access: On State Highway 21, 2.5 miles north of Stanley, turn left (west) on the gravel Iron Creek Road and drive 3 miles to the transfer camp.
warning: This trail is heavily used. For a true wilderness experience, choose another. No campfires are allowed within 200 feet of the lakes.

Above the lower end of Sawtooth Lake, the largest lake in the Sawtooth Wilderness, sculptured granite curves from the shore to the cap-like summit of the dominant peak, Mt. Regan. From the trail to McGown Lakes, the twisted rust and silver trunks of dead whitebark pines frame this peak and the immense sapphire platter of the lake. A mile below the lake, the cracked cliffs of Alpine Peak fall to two orange peninsulas which pierce the lime and blue-green water of Alpine Lake. From the trail between the lakes, two hills in the distance to the east resemble potatoes, one with its jacket on and the other opened and topped with sour cream and chives.

To reach the trailhead (6,710 feet), follow the access directions above. The trail begins in a flat lodgepole forest, and comes close to Iron Creek at .5 mile. Then it climbs a rise and winds to a trail junction with the southern branch of the Alpine Way Trail at 1.2 miles. This branch goes south to Marshall Lake and then to a trailhead near the Stanley Ranger Station. From this junction, the Iron Creek Trail edges the right side of a round meadow and climbs gently. At

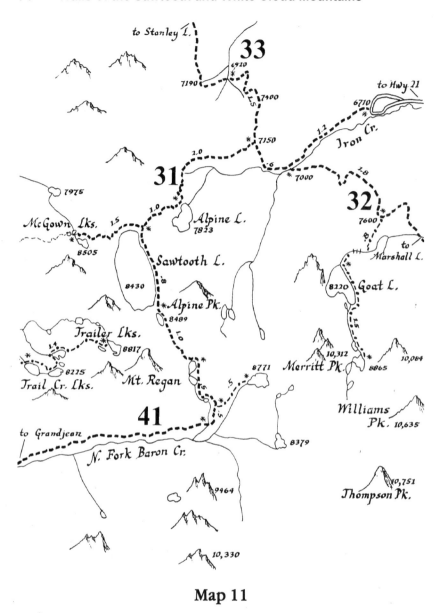

Map 11

1.8 miles, the north branch of the Alpine Way Trail turns off to Stanley Lake. To the south up a side canyon is a sliced-off dome.

The Iron Creek Trail angles up the side of the ridge and makes four switch-backs. At 2.9 miles, it fords cascading Iron Creek on rocks to a wildflower meadow. Then the trail zigzags up a forested ridge to a junction at 3.8 miles with a 200-yard path to Alpine Lake (7,823 feet).

The main trail continues above Alpine Lake zigzagging through granite benches. At 4.5 miles, the path flattens as it bridges a stream, then climbs the headwall to a grassy pond at 4.7 miles. The trail crosses the outlet of Sawtooth Lake and back again on logs to the left (east) side. It reaches a junction a few yards from the edge of the lake at 4.8 miles. The right (west) branch goes 1.5 miles with a 330-foot gain and 255-foot loss to McGown Lakes.

For a good view of the lake (8,430 feet), take the left (south) branch past a snow pond to a grassy area at 5.2 miles. From here it is .8 mile to the south end of the lake, where a pond sits in flowers under the wall of Mount Regan. The only good places to camp near Sawtooth Lake are at two ponds .7 mile below this pond at the head of the North Fork of Baron Creek, and back at the pond toward Alpine Lake.

You may want to retrace your steps to the junction at the head of the lake and take the other trail to McGown Lakes, which are set in gray talus. The main reason for taking this side trip is the excellent view of Sawtooth Lake.

32   Goat Falls and Lake
Map 11

round trip: 6.6 miles; 7.6 miles for the lake
elevation gain: 870 feet; 1,590 feet for the lake
elevation loss (return climb): 80 feet
highest point: 7,400 feet at the falls; 8,220 feet at the lake
map: Stanley Lake
time: 5 to 6 hours
ability: expert
access: On Highway 21, turn left (west) 2.5 miles north of Stanley onto the gravel Iron Creek Road and drive 3 miles to the transfer camp.
caution: Climbing to Goat Lake from the falls is the most dangerous hike in this book. Since the last edition of the book, the steep slope beside the cliffs edging the waterfall has deteriorated. Walking it now is like walking on ball bearings up a steep roof. The only safe route is to climb the cliffs beside the waterfall. Therefore, it is much safer to make the falls your destination.

Goat Falls tumbles in a beautiful series of cascades toward an inky green pond, which is also fed by two other high waterfalls. At Goat Lake, two small permanent snowbanks with aquamarine edges spit large chunks of ice into the water. These snowbanks hang above teal blue water at the base of an 1,800-foot wall. On the wall, rock towers thrust out of the cliffs like gigantic divers ready to plunge. On the other three sides of the lake, shorter cliffs enclose shallower turquoise water. Above the upper end, strands of a braided waterfall weave through lime green grass. Behind the falls, the tip of Thompson Peak holds feathers of rock aloft.

Goat Lake

To begin this hike follow directions above to the Iron Creek trailhead at 6,710 feet (see Sawtooth Lake). Take the Iron Creek Trail to the junction at 1.2 miles (7,000 feet) with the Alpine Way Trail going south.

Turn left on that trail and cross Iron Creek on small, shaky logs. The trail goes east through woods, then turns south in a ravine full of alders and grass at 1.6 miles. It follows a tiny stream up the ravine and crosses it in mud at 2 miles.

The sandy slopes in the ravine have been much eroded, making the way hard to find. Beyond the creek crossing, there are two boggy stretches that must be negotiated with care. Next, the path turns northeast up the side of a ridge and rounds the end of it, still climbing.

At 3 miles, at an unmarked junction, peaks behind Goat Lake are visible. Here the main Alpine Way Trail turns east downhill, but is much less worn than the non-system path to the falls. Go towards the mountain wall and the falls through two open areas. The second open area contains a dry stream bed and a triangular tower of gray cliffs above it. The treacherous ballbearing slope rises above this open area. Keep going to the base of the falls at 3.4 miles.

To continue cross-country to the lake, turn up beside the falls and cautiously scramble up the ledges and cliffs. The first 300 feet are the steepest. At the top of the falls, follow the creek and then edge away from it in boulders. At 3.6 miles, to avoid enormous blocks of talus, cross the creek to the left on a complex of logs or on large rocks. Early in the season, you may need to cross farther up or not at all. Climb along the left side of the creek through forest and over granite outcrops to the 8,220-foot lake at 3.8 miles.

This hike is recommended for expert adults only because of the climb up the ledges and the dropoffs at the lake. Campfires are not allowed within 200 yards of Goat Lake, and camping is discouraged in the fragile lake basin. There is little space for it anyway.

To reach the upper lakes, go around the east side of the lake to the upper end, climbing between the benches and then dropping to the shore. From the left (east) lobe of the lake, aim for a rock ramp leading to the 150-foot high bench on the near (east) side of the two inlets. To get onto the ramp you must scramble up a ten-foot cliff. Climb the ramp to the top of the bench and go along it until you can descend onto the elongated snowfield shown on the map. Walk up the snowfield past the first tiny lake in talus to the largest of the upper lakes (8,865 feet), 645 feet above Goat Lake. A dark knoll separates this lake from a teardrop-shaped lake west of it.

33 North Alpine Way
Maps 11 and 12

through trip: 8.8 miles
elevation gain: 1,530 feet
elevation loss (return climb): 1,720 feet
this section one way: 5.8 miles; 1,090-foot gain, 1,200-foot loss; additional 1.5
miles one way and 849-foot gain to see off-trail lakes
highest point: 7,760 feet at a saddle
map: Stanley Lake
difficulty: strenuous; expert for the lakes
access: On Highway 21, 2.5 miles north of Stanley, turn west on the Iron
Creek Road and drive 3 miles to the Iron Creek trailhead. Then hike 1.8
miles to the Alpine Way Trail.
warning: This trail is closed to stock.

This section of the Alpine Way Trail passes under cliffs and crosses side
canyons lined with spires, crags, and waterfalls. In this northern section, the
towers are those on McGown Peak, the double-pointed mountain of Stanley
Lake. From the high point of the trail, a cross-country side trip reaches two
tiny lakes in a sawtoothed canyon. West of the lower lake, crescent-shaped hol-
lows and wandering veins of white rock etch the gray granite of McGown Peak.
On the east, the lake is guarded by a granite gargoyle. A narrow flower-strewn
moraine holds in the upper lake below triangular sawteeth.

To reach the beginning of this hike description, follow the access directions
above to hike the Iron Creek Trail to the junction with the North Alpine Way
Trail at 1.8 miles. From this junction, the Alpine Way Trail angles up the side
of a grassy ridge to a flat summit at .5 mile. Then it switchbacks down in trees,
crosses a small creek and then Crooked Creek (6,920 feet) on logs at 1.5 miles.
The trail skirts the base of the mountain wall in woods and in sandy areas. At
2.5 miles, it fords a small creek in a gorge, then climbs straight to a saddle (7,760
feet), the high point of the trail, at 3 miles.

To reach the off-trail lakes, turn southwest and go up the end of a ridge. Go
along the east side of the towers of the ridge spine to a notch at .3 mile where
the ridge smooths out so you can follow the top of it. At .5 mile, the ridge ends
in a cirque of grass and rocks. Climb the headwall of the cirque along the creek
mostly on the left side past a waterfall. At the top, continue to a shallow pond
shown as a marsh on the topographic map and turn right (north). Climb through
a gap between two hills to the lower lake (8,575 feet) at 1 mile. To reach the
upper lake (8,609 feet) 1.5 miles from the trail, return to the marsh and walk
past a second pond to the head of the valley.

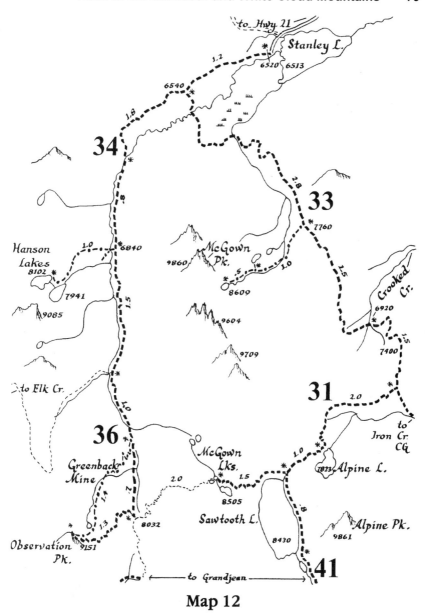

Map 12

From its high point, the trail descends a ridge in trees with a view of towers on McGown Peak. Beginning 3.8 miles from the Iron Creek Trail, it descends in .2 mile switchbacks toward Stanley Lake Creek. At 4.5 miles, the path crosses a side creek on logs or slippery rocks, then descends the left side of the creek in lodgepole and grouse whortleberry. At 5 miles as the ground flattens, the trail turns right (north) toward Stanley Lake Creek, which it fords at 5.5 miles. This ford may be hazardous in early summer.

At 5.7 miles, the trail passes a register box for this trail and at 5.8 miles intersects the Stanley Lake Creek Trail, 1.2 miles from the trailhead at Stanley Lake. Note that the trail from here to the Stanley Lake trailhead is closed in early summer to protect the meadows.

STANLEY LAKE AREA

34 Bridalveil Falls and Hanson Lakes
Map 12

round trip: 8 miles to the falls, 9.6 miles to the lakes
elevation gain: 320 feet to the falls, 1,582 feet to the lakes
highest point: 8,102 feet
map: Stanley Lake
difficulty: moderate to the falls, expert (cross-country) to the lakes
access: Drive northwest of Stanley on Highway 21 for 5 miles. Turn left (west) on the gravel Stanley Lake Road and go 3.8 miles to the Inlet Campground.
warning: The first two miles of this trail is closed in early summer to protect the wildflowers and grasses. Reconstruction is planned soon; check with SNRA headquarters to see whether the trail is open.
caution: The route to Hanson Lakes is difficult and it is easy to get lost or to get onto the hazardous slope beside the waterfall. Avoid camping in the fragile lake basin.

Bridalveil Falls puffs out at the top, then plunges in a veil of lacy water. Beside the falls, clumps of turf hold red paintbrush, magenta mimulus and pale blue bluebells in a bride's bouquet. Higher up, a double-humped monolith, textured by fractures, overlooks the deep turquoise water of the two Hanson Lakes. A natural earth dam stabilized by firs keeps the upper lake from tumbling into the lower.

To reach the trailhead at 6,520 feet, follow the access directions above. At the trail sign, go west through the gate and follow an old road through willows near the creek. At .5 mile, the track turns right (northwest) into a big meadow. After edging the meadow on the north and crossing streams, it enters forest. At 1.2 miles is a junction with the north end of the Alpine Way Trail. Keep straight ahead to the west through trees and more small meadows.

At 2.3 miles, the route begins to climb a step in the canyon. It curves across the hillside, and then turns straight up the canyon again. At this turn, it is possible to walk northeast .2 mile to the edge of the gorge to see Lady Face Falls.

At 3 miles, the trail fords Stanley Lake Creek to the left (east) side. The footlogs here are underwater in early season, and the ford is hazardous then. To see the falls (6,840 feet), at 3.8 miles turn off in a sandy place toward the creek and ford it. Once across, go southwest .2 mile to view the falls at 4 miles. In doing this, avoid the dangerous sandy slope to the right of the falls, and do not try to take it to the lakes.

To reach the lakes safely, return to the ford. At the ford, notice three vertical sandy ridges leading up the canyon wall to the right (north) of the waterfall. To the right of them, a strip of brush parallels the ribs. Zigzag up the right (north) side of this brushy area, skirting the edge of the forest. When the steepness lessens, cut left to a small creek.

Cross this creek and contour across the hillside to a small flat meadow. Traverse a flat, rocky slope and plunge through mossy springs to the outlet of the lakes.

Turn right (southwest) along the right side of the creek to the lower lake (7,941 feet) .7 mile from the ford. Go around the right (north) side of this lake and up the right (northeast) side of the inlet to reach the upper lake (8,102 feet) 1 mile from the ford. For safety on the return, be sure to turn left (north) across the slope .2 mile below the lower lake BEFORE the slope plunges down beside the waterfall.

35 Elk Meadow and Lake
Map 13

round trip: 5.4 miles for the meadow, an additional 1.6 miles one way for the lake
elevation gain: 120 feet; 40 feet additional for the lake
elevation loss (return climb): 40 feet
highest point: 6,805 feet at the lake
map: Elk Meadow
time: 4½ hours for both meadow and lake
difficulty: easy for the meadows (except for the ford); expert for the lake
access: On Highway 21, turn left (west) 10.5 miles northwest of Stanley onto a gravel road and drive 1.4 miles to a junction. Turn left here and drive to a barrrier closing the road at 2.3 miles. Then walk .6 mile along the road to the trailhead. A new trailhead has been completed 2 miles from the highway.

From the vast green bogs of Elk Meadow, views of McGown Peak and the canyon wall of upper Elk Creek entice hikers. Elk Meadow makes a pleasant day hike, especially in late June when the wildflowers are at their best. This route to Elizabeth Lake is easier than the one from Stanley Lake as it avoids a 560-foot return climb, although hikers must still cross Elk Meadow with no

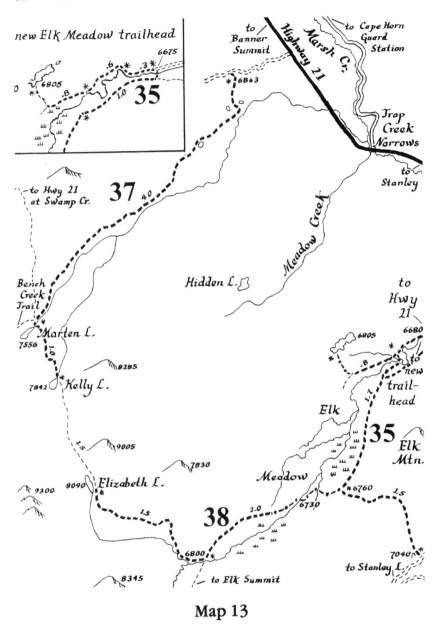

Map 13

trail. In addition, near the beginning you can use a compass to take a short crosscountry side trip through thick woods to a marshy green lake twice as large as Elizabeth Lake, but with a similar view.

The Elk Meadows trailhead has been relocated to the point on the access road where the bicycle and snowmobile trail around Elk Mountain begins at a bridge over the creek. The road is closed here. This point is just before the road goes into a muddy meadow 2 miles from the highway. A new trail segment leads from the bridge 1 mile along the south side of the creek to intersect the old trail about .3 mile beyond where it forded the creek to the south side. The old jeep track and trail on the north side of the creek are blocked off and partly obliterated. Note that the trail shown on the topographic map leading through Elk Meadows on the north side of the creek does not exist, and the actual trail on the south side of the creek is not on the topographic map.

Once across the bridge, go to the right (west). The trail going east leads to a mountain bike route that goes around Elk Mountain on old roads to the Stanley Lake Road. A mile from the beginning of the new Elk Meadows Trail cow paths begin to wander off. To stay on the trail follow the blazes. At 2.2 miles, the trail crosses a tongue of meadow, then returns to forest. At 2.4 miles, the route joins the Elizabeth Lake Trail where it disappears at the edge of the meadow at 6,760 feet at a signed junction. Beyond the junction, the trail shown going across the meadow does not exist.

To reach the unnamed lake from the parking spot near the bridge, find the remnants of the old jeep trail, passing the old trailhead and ford at .9 mile, .6 mile beyond the gate. Continue on the jeep trail until at 1.4 miles it turns up to the right a few yards and ends. Then take out your compass and topographic map and plot a course to the lake. The trail shown on the map to the lake does not exist. Using your compass as a guide, climb over a small hill, down to the upper end of a swampy meadow, and then up to the lake (6,805 feet) 1.7 miles from the new trailhead.

36 Observation Peak
Map 12

round trip: 16.6 miles
elevation gain: 2,631 feet
this section one way: 4.5 miles, 2,311-foot gain
highest point: 9,151 feet
time: 2 days
map: Stanley Lake
difficulty: strenuous
access: On Highway 21, 5 miles north of Stanley, turn west onto the gravel Stanley Lake Road, and drive 3.8 miles to a small parking area beside the Inlet Campground. Using the directions in Hike 34 (Bridalveil Falls and Hanson Lakes), walk up the Stanley Lake Creek Trail to the Bridalveil Falls turnoff where this hike description begins.

View from Observation Peak

From this sandy hill above the Trail Creek–Stanley Lake Creek Divide, the jagged spires of the Sawtooth Range stretch southeast, becoming bluer with distance, to the needles of North and South Raker on the skyline. Across the canyon, dark cliffs sweep to the rounded top of Mt. Regan. One of the blue peaks, Warbonnet, resembles the crest of a dark blue wave rushing east. To the north, the view includes the rounded mountains above Elk Creek and back down the canyon of Stanley Lake Creek, the serrated wall of McGown Peak.

This hike description begins on the Stanley Lake Creek Trail at the ford for Bridalveil Falls at 6,840 feet, 3.8 miles from the trailhead. To reach this point, follow the directions in the hikes listed above. From here, the trail, still an old road, crosses an open area below the cliffs of McGown Peak, then continues in woods. A campsite is at .7 mile beside a side stream flowing through sand. At 1.5 miles, a trail turns off to the right (west) to Elk Creek Summit. It climbs 1,520 feet and descends 1,780 feet in 9.5 miles to the Elizabeth Lake Trail.

Continue on the Stanley Lake Creek Trail. At 2 miles, it threads a narrow meadow below a wall of boulders and cliffs and passes a campsite. Just beyond the meadow, the trail fords the creek to the right (west) side. At 2.5 miles, the old road to the Greenback Mine turns off up the canyon wall. The trail continues along the creek but well above it. At 3.2 miles is the flat of the Trail Creek–Stanley Lake Creek Divide (8,032 feet). You can camp here, but there is no water.

On the divide is a four-way junction. To the left (east), a trail goes to McGown and Sawtooth Lakes. McGown Lakes are 2 miles toward Sawtooth Lake, with a 600-foot gain and 120-foot loss. The trail straight ahead descends 1 mile to the Trail Creek Lakes junction with a 451-foot elevation loss and then goes on down Trail Creek to Grandjean (see Hike 39, Trail Creek Lakes). To the right (west) is a trail up Observation Peak. Take this trail, which climbs 1,119 feet in 1.3 miles, up a sandy hillside sprinkled with whitebark pines to the gentle summit at 4.5 miles.

To see the site of the Greenback Mine on the return, descend north from Observation Peak .7 mile cross-country to a round pond. Follow its outlet .5 mile to a boggy meadow and the mine road. The mine is 200 yards up the road, but the only building remaining is a log crib over the shaft. To return to the trail, descend .7 mile on steep road switchbacks. This 1.4 mile route saves .6 mile over the trail, but the cross-country hiking along the pond's outlet is rough.

37 Marten and Kelly Lakes
Map 13

round trip: 10 miles
elevation gain: 979 feet
elevation loss (return climb): 40 feet
highest point: 7,842 feet
maps: Elk Meadow, Banner Summit
time: 7 hours
difficulty: moderate
access: On Highway 21, turn west 8.5 miles north of Stanley, onto a dirt road
at a sign for Marten Lake. Drive through a creek at .2 mile and continue to
the register box at .7 mile.

Similar tree-dotted cliffs and peaks of rounded triangles back Marten and Kelly Lakes. The lakes differ only because marsh grass edges Marten Lake and red mountain heath and Labrador tea surround Kelly Lake. The trail gives a view to the east across Stanley Basin of the striped ramparts of Cabin Creek Peak. Few take this gentle climb because it is north of the main rocky mass of the Sawtooths. Thus, the stillness may be broken only by the cry of a jay or the sighing of the pines.

To reach the trailhead (6,863 feet), follow the access directions above. The trail starts out in lodgepoles and, at .5 mile, crosses a basin of snow ponds. At 1 mile is a tiny marshy lake with a view of the peaks. At 2.5 miles, the path climbs along the base of an open hillside. In woods at 3.5 miles, the route crosses four sections of a branch of Trap Creek. The largest has a footlog. At 4 miles, the main trail reaches Marten Lake (7,556 feet), which has several campsites.

A hundred yards before the lake is an unsigned junction with a trail to the right (north). This trail splits in a few yards into the Bench Creek and Swamp Creek trails. The Bench Creek Trail goes west 5.4 miles to Highway 21 near the Bull Trout Lake Road, with a 644-foot climb and 1,280-foot descent. The Swamp Creek Trail goes 6 miles north to Highway 21 just south of the Thatcher Creek Campground with a 910-foot elevation loss.

The trail on to Kelly Lake crosses the outlet of Marten Lake on a log, then wanders over a gentle ridge through subalpine firs to a stream crossing at .5 mile. The path rounds the east end of the ridge, and turns south to the lake (7,842 feet) at 5 miles. Camping here is limited. The trail continues beyond Kelly Lake 1.5 miles with a 491-foot gain and 243-foot loss to Elizabeth Lake.

38 Elizabeth Lake
Map 13

round trip: 10 miles
elevation gain: 1,410 feet
elevation loss (return climb): 360 feet
highest point: 8,090 feet
time: 8½ hours
maps: Banner Summit, Elk Meadow
ability: expert
access: From Highway 21, turn west 5 miles northwest of Stanley onto the gravel Stanley Lake Road. Drive 3.4 miles to the second junction, which is marked Elk Mountain. Turn right (west) and drive to a trailhead at 5.2 miles.

This little lake of marshy edges and green water hides behind lodgepole pines and subalpine firs. It is enclosed in ridges of crumbled granite cliffs. Beyond the lower end, two small jagged peaks cling to the wall of Elk Creek Canyon. Just before the lake, McGown Peak and the White Clouds seem to float in the distance to the southeast. On the way to the lake, the creeks and bogs of Elk Meadow make route-finding difficult and wet. Therefore, this route is best for late summer and dry years.

To reach the trailhead (6,960 feet), follow the access directions above. From the register box, take the trail north over a flat ridge and then west down to the edge of Elk Meadow at 1.5 miles where it disappears. Here there is a signed junction with the 2.4-mile Elk Meadow Trail. Although the topographic map shows a trail across Elk Meadow, it does not exist.

From here you must use compass and topographic map to find the trail again going up Elk Creek at the far end of the meadow. Go west over to Elk Creek and ford it to the right (west) side at 2 miles. Do not try to skirt the meadow on the near (east) side because bogs extend from it up into the forest. Early in the summer, pools and streams of water cover much of the meadow, and the ford of Elk Creek is deep and swift.

Beyond the ford, cut over toward the woods at the far side of the meadow, crossing two or three side creeks on the way. Aim for the willows where the far edge of the meadow jogs toward you. The trail should appear along the edge of the forest at 3 miles. This point is on the west side of the meadow near its upper end. The route enters the woods and passes a tiny log cabin. Sixty yards beyond the cabin is a junction before a ford of Elk Creek at 3.5 miles. The Elk Creek Trail continues across the ford 6 miles to Elk Creek Summit with a 1,780-foot climb. Then it goes an additional 3.5 miles and 1,520 feet down to the Stanley Lake Creek Trail.

At this junction, turn right (west) on the Elizabeth Lake Trail. It goes along the right (north) side of Elk Creek and then a side creek. Avoid cow paths before the trail starts to climb. The trail is the least-used path and crosses the other paths at right angles. At 3.8 miles, it climbs straight up the wooded hillside. The way turns away from the creek at 4 miles and then turns back to the left at 4.3 miles.

At 4.8 miles it crosses a branch of the creek to the left (west) side. The route goes west up a steep ridge and then follows the top of it. At 5 miles, an unsigned path drops left (west) 100 yards to the lake (8,090 feet). The trail continues 1.5 miles with a 243-foot climb and 491-foot loss to Kelly Lake.

GRANDJEAN AREA

39 Trail Creek Lakes
Map 14

round trip: 10.2 miles
elevation gain: 2,820 feet to the first Trail Creek Lake
highest point: 8,000 feet at the first Trail Creek Lake, 8,817 feet at the highest Trailer Lake
side trip to Trailer Lakes: 1.4 miles one way and 880 feet additional gain
maps: Grandjean, Stanley Lake
time: 9 hours for the lower Trail Creek Lake, 4 additional hours for Trailer Lakes
difficulty: strenuous; expert for cross country route to the upper lakes and Trailer Lakes

access: On Highway 21, 37.2 miles northwest of Stanley, turn left (east) onto the gravel Grandjean Road. Drive 7.1 miles to the trailhead in the campground.

caution: Avoid camping in the fragile basin of the upper lakes.

The lowest Trail Creek Lake reflects a dark triangular peak with hunched shoulders. At the base of the peak, a tilted slab touches the blue-green water with one corner. Lodgepoles, subalpine firs and granite benches lead along the opposite shore to the inlet, which cascades down a flower-dusted notch. Cliffs of the triangular peak also hang over the second lake, but a grassy peninsula and talus soften its shoreline. In front of granite knolls and whitebark pines, marsh grass and Labrador tea wreathe the dark green water of the third lake. On the skyline above it, jagged teeth march to the summit of a peak roofed with sloping slabs.

From the third lake, it is possible to continue to Regan and Trailer lakes. Above the island dotting round green Regan Lake, peach talus climbs to cliffs scribbled with stripes. The highest of the two Trailer Lakes is only a turquoise pool in the rocks above the fish-shaped largest lake, which looks up with a talus eye. Above it, pale orange cliffs sweep to the lumpy summit of Mt. Regan.

To reach the trailhead (5,180 feet) on the east side of the campground, follow the access directions above. Note that the trail climbs 2,820 feet to the first lake. There is little shade, so the climb can be hot on a warm day. The trail first leads through woods to a bridge over Trail Creek. At a junction on the other side at .2 mile, turn left (north) on the Trail Creek Trail. This trail twice switchbacks up a sagebrush hillside, then follows the creek on a steep, grassy slope across from rock towers.

At 1 mile, the trail hairpins away from the creek, then returns to it in brush at 1.2 miles. The route crosses to the left (north) side of the creek at 1.5 miles on footlogs which will be underwater and dangerous in early season.

From the ford, the route makes a big switchback up a talus slope, and at 1.7 miles returns to forest and brush. At 2.4 miles, the trail zigzags up a brushy slope. It is washed out for a few yards at 2.9 miles just before it fords the creek again to the south.

In the next section, 16 switchbacks up to 200 yards long climb 320 feet up granite ledges in .3 mile. At 3.3 miles the trail runs gently along the ravine of the creek and crosses it back to the left (north) on a log at 3.5 miles. At 3.9 miles, after the creek splits, the way crosses the north branch of the creek in alders to the right (east) side. The next section has another 20 switchbacks, but they are in woods and climb only 300 feet in .5 mile.

The sign for Trail Creek Lakes is at 4.4 miles (7,581 feet). The main trail climbs 451 feet in 1 mile to the Trail Creek–Stanley Lake Creek Divide. Take

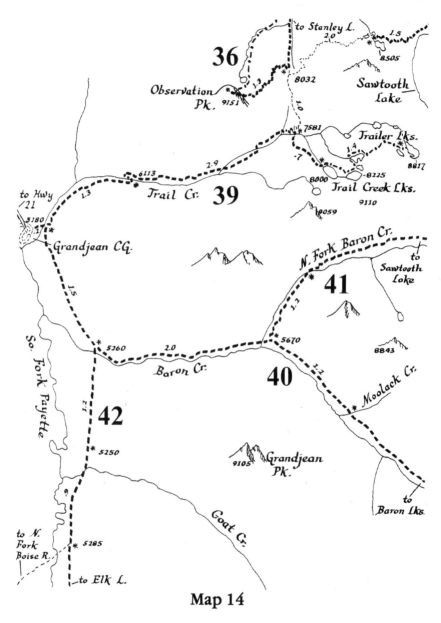

Map 14

the Trail Creek Lakes Trail across Trail Creek in mud and up a hillside, and then up the right (west) side of the outlet of the lower lake. On the way, the route skirts a talus slope occupied by pikas. The lower lake (8,000 feet) is at 5.1 miles. Campsites are at the lower end and half way around the left (north) side of the lake.

The Second Trail Creek Lake

There is no trail to the upper lakes. To reach them, go around the north shore of the lake and climb east up a ravine to the left of granite benches. In a dry creek bed, turn right (south) cross-country to the lower end of the second lake (8,225 feet), which is .5 mile from the outlet of the lower lake.

To reach the third lake (8,245 feet), go half way along the north side of the second lake. Then turn left (north) and walk past a pond to the lake at .7 mile.

To get to Trailer Lakes, go around the third lake on the north to its upper end. From here there are two possible routes, both difficult. The steeper route climbs the inlet shown on the map in a gully of tiny trees. From this gully, continue up a slot in the rocks to the flat sand and granite benches near the smallest, highest lake, which is .1 mile above the large, fish-shaped lake (8,817 feet).

The second route gives a view of Regan Lake on the way. To follow this route, head north from the north side of the third lake near the upper end for 200 yards up a little canyon. Turn east and go between a series of granite knolls to a low saddle (8,600 feet), 1.4 miles from the lowest Trail Creek Lake. Regan Lake is .2 mile below to the north. To reach the Trailer Lakes from here, go east above cliffs along the side of the ridge.

40 Baron Creek Trail to Baron Lakes
Maps 14 and 10

round trip: 22.4 miles to the upper lake
elevation gain: 3,325 feet
highest point: 8,505 feet
maps: Grandjean, Stanley Lake, Warbonnet Peak
time: 2 to 3 days
difficulty: strenuous
access: From Highway 21, 37.2 miles west of Stanley, turn right (east) and drive 7.1 miles on the gravel road to the Grandjean Campground.

The trail from Grandjean to Baron Lakes ascends a canyon shadowed with spires and embroidered with waterfalls. At Baron Lakes, the face of Monte Verita resembles the pipes of an organ. The ridge connecting this peak with a shoulder of hidden Warbonnet Peak holds a row of tilting feathers. To the northwest, the summit of Big Baron Spire resembles one small crooked feather. Below the lakes, the great pleated wall of Baron Peak forms a backdrop of sawteeth.

To reach the trailhead at 5,180 feet, follow the access directions above. Beginning at the end of the campground, the trail bridges Trail Creek to a junction at .2 mile with the trail to Trail Creek Lakes. Stay on the level South Fork of the Payette River Trail, which rambles under lodgepole and ponderosa pines and through grassy areas.

At 1.7 miles, turn left (east) on the Baron Creek Trail, which climbs along the left (north) side of Baron Creek through forest and open brush below granite cliffs. At 3.6 miles, the trail fords the North Fork of Baron Creek, where a footlog is usually present. This ford is hazardous in early summer and wet years, and always requires care. There is a campsite beyond the ford. At 3.7 miles, the North Fork of Baron Creek Trail turns off to Sawtooth Lake.

As the trail continues up the canyon on the left (east) side of Baron Creek, the folded face of Grandjean Peak is above the south wall. At 4.9 miles, it fords Moolack Creek to two small campsites. The route comes close to Baron Creek at 5.5 miles at a campsite marked by a trailside boulder. Above in an open grassy area, the grade steepens. At 6.8 miles, a waterfall tumbles from Tohobit Peak.

Switchbacks begin opposite another falls at 7.3 miles. They climb 1,000 feet in 1 mile, mostly over rocks close to Baron Creek Falls. Above the falls at 9 miles is a campsite.

The trail bridges Baron Creek at 9.4 miles. From here, it is possible to hike up a side creek to the east to the site of an old trail crew camp below Braxon

Lake. The main trail has three more creek crossings (at 9.8, 10.1 and 10.4 miles) but no more bridges. The last ford is just below the lower end of 8,312-foot Baron Lake (10.5 miles). The best campsites are near the outlet.

The trail to the upper lake zigzags through forest and then up the ridge to 8,505-foot Upper Baron Lake at 11.2 miles. The best campsites are off-trail northeast of the lower end of the lake.

Two interesting side trips from the lakes lead to Little Baron Lake and an unnamed lake on the side of Monte Verita. To reach Little Baron Lake, climb through a notch in the ridge from the lower end of Baron Lake and descend 200 feet in forest. For the unnamed lake, go around Baron Lake along the east shore, crossing the outlet of Upper Baron Lake (not shown on the map) and the inlet draining the small lake on the side of Monte Verita. This lake is your destination. Climb the right side of the inlet over grassy slopes and granite benches to the lake (9,020 feet) 1.2 miles from the lower end of Baron Lake and 708 feet above it.

41 North Baron Trail to Sawtooth Lake
Maps 14 and 11

round trip: 19.4 miles
elevation gain: 3,309 feet
elevation loss (return climb): 59 feet
this section one way: 6 miles, 2,819-foot gain, 59-foot loss
highest point: 8,489 feet
maps: Grandjean, Stanley Lake
time: 2 to 3 days
difficulty: strenuous
access: Follow the directions for Hike 40 (Baron Lakes) to hike to the crossing of the North Fork of Baron Creek on the Baron Creek Trail, 3.7 miles from Grandjean.

This trail climbs the canyon of the North Fork of Baron Creek between pleated granite walls trimmed with pinnacles. As it ascends the headwall, orange stripes etch the charcoal pleats of a 1,500-foot face across the canyon. From the top of this climb, it is a short side trip to a round turquoise lake in a bowl of scalloped cliffs. Farther up, the trail passes three aquamarine ponds in talus and wildflowers right under the orange cliffs of Mt. Regan. Around a corner, the high rounded point of Mt. Regan hangs over the pond and the great sapphire sheet of Sawtooth Lake.

This hike description begins at the junction (5,670 feet) of the Baron Creek Trail with the North Fork of Baron Creek Trail, which is 3.7 miles from Grandjean. For directions for hiking to this junction, see Hike 40 (Baron Lakes).

The North Baron Trail switchbacks up a grassy area into brush and Douglas firs. At 1.2 miles, it fords the North Fork to the left (north) side. In late summer, cross on a downstream log and brush pile, but in early summer, pick your way across the treacherous avalanche logs just above the ford. For hikers, the log crossing is hazardous until late summer.

Once across, the trail continues to switchback through brush and rock slabs, then runs through alders, willows and cottonwoods with occasional washed-out sections. At 3 miles, the route crosses open slopes of grass, tiny firs and sagebrush. Then it climbs scree and talus to a ford of the outlet of Sawtooth Lake at 4 miles to the right (east) side. This crossing can be difficult in early summer.

Next, the path hairpins up the wall of the hanging valley containing the lake, crossing back and forth over a white quartz outcrop. When the trail levels (at about 8,240 feet and 4.5 miles) before the first of two tiny ponds in the woods, hikers can take a cross-country side trip northeast to the 8,771-foot round lake under Merritt Peak.

To take this side trip, cut towards the outlet of that lake, keeping just below the edge of the talus, but above the forested gorge. Before the lake, a big snowbank lingers in a hollow. For the last 200 yards, it is necessary to scramble along ledges beside the creek. At the lake, which is .5 mile and 600-feet above the trail, you must climb out of the stream bed to the right to avoid cliffs.

From the turnoff for the side trip, the main trail continues .2 mile to the first pond, which has the first campsites since Baron Creek. The path then threads a wildflower garden and talus to two larger ponds in the talus at 4.7 and 5 miles. There are campsites on the wooded knoll between these ponds. Above the upper pond (8,271 feet), the trail zigzags through talus to its high point opposite still another pond (8,489 feet) in the grass right under Mt. Regan. Then the way drops to the shore of Sawtooth Lake (8,430 feet) at 6 miles. From here, the trail goes .8 mile along the east shore to the Iron Creek Trail (see Hike 31, Alpine, Sawtooth and McGown Lakes).

42 South Fork of Payette River: Grandjean to Elk Lake

Maps 14 and 15

round trip: 23.2 miles
elevation gain: 1,470 feet
highest point: 6,650 feet
maps: Grandjean, Edaho Mountain, Warbonnet Peak
time: 2 to 3 days
difficulty: strenuous

access: On Highway 21, 37.2 miles northwest of Stanley, turn left (east) onto the gravel Grandjean Road and drive 7.1 miles to the Grandjean Campground.

Along the way to Elk Lake from Grandjean, Taylor Spring bubbles from emerald moss at the side of Big Meadows. These vast meadows unfurl five miles of green velvet along the meandering South Fork of the Payette River. Farther up the river at Elk Lake, a fir forest crowds lime green marsh grass. Across the lake, the spired and fractured north wall of the canyon faces rock ridges bristling with trees.

To reach the trailhead, follow the access directions above. The trail crosses Trail Creek on a bridge at .2 mile, then passes a turnoff for Trail Creek Lakes. The route is level for the first 6.5 miles through trees and grassy areas. At 1.7 miles, the Baron Creek Trail turns east. Continue south on the river trail. Right away it fords Baron Creek.

At 2.5 miles the trail has been diverted to an old mining road for .4 mile so that the ford of Goat Creek at 2.9 miles will be easier. Both Baron and Goat Creeks are deep and rushing all summer. The bridges that once were here were removed when they became unsafe. In early summer, and until mid-summer in wet years, these fords are hazardous.

At 3.8 miles, a trail turns off to the right (west) up the North Fork of the Boise River. This trail crosses the South Fork of the Payette in a 120-foot ford, which is hazardous for hikers all summer. The route goes 11.8 miles up a ridge and down the North Fork of the Boise to meet the Bayhouse Trail 1 mile from the four-wheel drive Graham Road. There is a 2,271-foot climb and 1,656-foot elevation loss along the way. Most of the forest along this trail burned in 1994.

The South Fork trail reaches Taylor Spring at 5 miles. The spring is only 140 feet higher than the trailhead at Grandjean. There are several campsites near the spring. The site and grave of Deadman's Cabin is .9 mile south of the spring on an old mining road that is now blocked off and not evident from the trail.

At 6.5 miles, the trail begins to climb. Below Garden Creek at 8 miles are waterfalls on the South Fork and a campsite. Mud slides have caused washouts above here, but the trail has been repaired. There are many switchbacks in brush beyond, but none are shown on the topographic map. A campsite .5 mile below Fern Falls sits off-trail in a grassy area toward the river. Fern Falls at 10.5 miles is actually two short waterfalls. At 11.6 miles, the trail comes close to Elk Lake, (6,650 feet) half way along it. There is one campsite earlier, down a path near the lake at 11 miles, but the more attractive sites lie at the upper end of the lake at 12 miles. In this canyon, water can be obtained from the river when the trail is near it or from stream crossings.

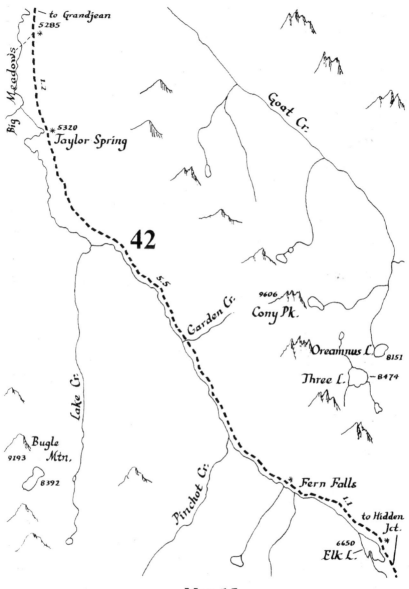

to Grandjean
5285

Big Meadows

1.2

5320
Taylor Spring

Goat Cr.

42

5.5

Garden Cr.

9606
Cony Pk.

Oreamnus L.
8151

Three L.
8474

Lake Cr.

Bugle
Mtn.
9193

8392

Pinchot Cr.

Fern Falls

1.1

to Hidden
Jct.

6650
Elk L.

Map 15

43 South Fork of Payette River: Elk Lake to Hidden Lake Junction

Map 16

round trip: 35.2 miles
elevation gain: 3,020 feet
this section one way: 6 miles, 1,550-foot gain
time: 3 to 4 days
maps: Warbonnet Peak, Mt. Everly, Snowyside Peak
difficulty: strenuous
access: Using the directions in Hike 42 (South Fork Payette River Trail: Grandjean to Elk Lake), hike to Elk Lake.

Along the South Fork of the Payette River above Elk Lake, glacier-polished rocks glide up to spires and turrets on the canyon walls. Similar spires bar the head of each side canyon. Just below Benedict Creek, the river foams in a glistening cascade known as Smith Falls. In this trail section, the route fords Benedict Creek once and the river three times.

To reach Elk Lake (6,650 feet), follow the access directions listed above. Above the lake, the trail climbs through woods to a 120-foot ford of the river to the right (south) side at 1.9 miles. This ford is usually only one to two feet deep, but it may be dangerous or impassable in June and early July. Beyond the ford, the trail climbs to a junction with the Benedict Creek Trail at 2.9 miles. In 3.5 miles this trail gains 960 feet in reaching a junction with the Queens River Trail below Benedict Lake.

The South Fork Trail next crosses Benedict Creek on logs, then fords the river to the left (north) and climbs more steeply. This ford and the Benedict Creek crossing are hazardous in early summer. At Tenlake Creek at 4.7 miles, the trail fords the South Fork again to the south side to a junction (7,640 feet) with the Tenlake Creek Trail.

Between this junction and the Hidden Lake junction, the trail switchbacks up 600 feet through lodgepoles and grouse whortleberry. At the junction at 6 miles (8,200 feet), trails turn off to Hidden Lake and Edna Lake (described in Hike 27, Cramer Lakes to Edna Lake). From Elk Lake to this junction, water can be obtained only at the river crossings and campsites are few.

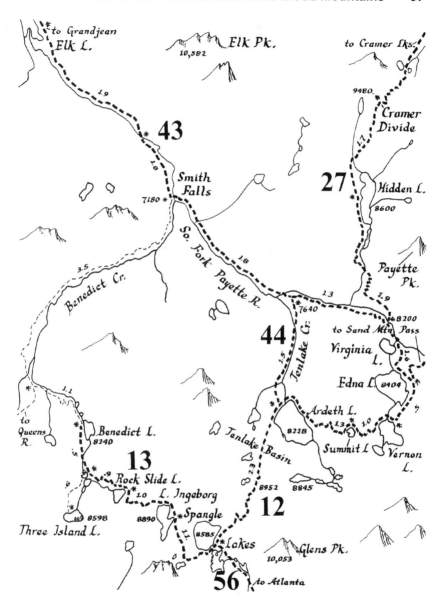

Map 16

44   Tenlake Creek Trail to Ardeth Lake
Map 16

round trip: 35.6 miles
elevation gain: 3,048 feet
this section one way: 1.5 miles, 588-foot gain
highest point: 8,228 feet
map: Mt. Everly
time: 3 to 5 days
difficulty: strenuous
access: Using directions in Hikes 42 and 43, hike 16.3 miles from Grandjean up the South Fork of the Payette River to the Tenlake Creek Trail.

This trail leads to Ardeth Lake, a .5 mile-long blue lake set below the wide triangle of Glens Peak in a basin containing ten lakes. The topmost cliffs of this peak peer at the lake over a 600-foot shelf of solid granite. Two slanting chimneys, usually snow-filled, divide the sides of the shelf into three leaning granite grain elevators. The other nine lakes perch on this shelf, accompanied by dozens of tiny ponds.

This trail begins at 7,640 feet on the South Fork of the Payette River Trail, 16.3 miles and a 2,460-foot climb from Grandjean. The trail ascends Tenlake Creek through thick forest, and at .2 mile fords Tenlake Creek to the right (west). At 1.2 miles just below Ardeth Lake, the route returns to the left (east) side of the creek. These fords have deep, rushing water and are hazardous in early summer. The trail joins the trail from Edna to Spangle Lakes in woods near campsites at the lower end of Ardeth Lake (8,228 feet) at 1.5 miles.

GRAHAM   AREA

45   Bayhouse and Johnson Creek Trails
Map 17

round trip: 15.2 miles
elevation gain: 1,780 feet
elevation loss (return climb): 720 feet
highest point: 7,040 feet
maps: Swanholm Peak, Nahneke Mountain
time: 11 hours or 2 days
difficulty: strenuous
access: From Highway 21 at the Edna Creek Campground 18 miles northeast of Idaho City, drive to the Little Silver Creek trailhead on the rough, primitive Graham Road, which requires four-wheel drive, and often washes out.

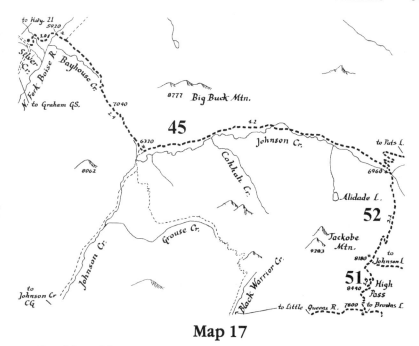

Map 17

caution: Most of the area around Graham, and along the Bayhouse and Johnson Creek trails, including Pats Lake, burned in 1994. It will be a challenge to travel through for several years because the burned snags can fall without warning, especially on windy days. The Forest Service has cut the dead timber back from the road so that it is less likely to fall on passersby, and they are working on cutting snags along the trails. Until they have finished, trail travel will be dangerous. For several years, finding safe campsites will be difficult, and leaving the trail will be dangerous. Before traveling in this area, always call SNRA headquarters for information on the conditions.

From the summit of the Graham Road, the splintered panorama of the entire Sawtooth range outlines the horizon. This road is for the brave, since it is rocky, steep and hangs above deep canyons. It requires four-wheel drive because it is a primitive road that has received little recent maintenance. From the road, the Bayhouse Trail climbs through a burned fir forest over a ridge and down through sparse sagebrush to the Johnson Creek Trail. The trail meanders with the creek in and out of meadows and the remains of lodgepole groves below the granite spurs of Big Buck Mountain. The Graham Road provides the shortest access to Pats Lake (10.1 miles), but Pats Lake will not be a destination hike until enough dead timber has fallen to remove the danger of falling snags. This danger will fall off and then peak again about ten years after the fire. As a day hike on calm days, these trails will provide an opportunity to observe how a forest at mid-elevation regenerates after fire when it is undisturbed.

The road to Graham turns northwest from the Atlanta Road at a point 4.3 miles from the Edna Creek Campground, which is 18 miles northeast of Idaho City. The route follows the Pike's Fork of the Crooked River, gradually becoming steeper and rockier. At a summit 13 miles from the turnoff, the road looks down on the 1,000-foot deep canyon of Jackson Creek. The track skirts the canyon wall to a junction with a side road to Jackson Peak Lookout at 14.6 miles. From this point, the road is suitable only for four-wheel drive vehicles with high clearance. It drops 300 feet into two-mile long Trapper Flat at 15.5 miles. The track next climbs the Crooked River to 8,080 feet with a view of the Sawtooths at 21.7 miles. After ups and downs, the road crests again at 25 miles. In the next five miles, it descends 2,000 feet with some turns so sharp drivers must back up to make them.

At 28.1 miles (32.4 miles from Highway 21), the road reaches the Little Silver Creek trailhead. It continues another four miles, passing the Graham Bridge Campground, to the Johnson Creek Campground.

The level trail from the Silver Creek trailhead (5,904 feet) fords Cow Creek at .2 mile and the North Fork of the Boise River at .8 mile. The crossing may be difficult and hazardous in early summer. A trail turns up the North Fork of the Boise at 1 mile. It climbs 1,656 feet and descends 2,271 feet in 11.8 miles to meet the South Fork of the Payette River Trail 3.8 miles from Grandjean. Most of the area along this trail burned in 1994.

At the junction with the North Fork of the Boise Trail, take the Bayhouse Creek Trail, which climbs southeast 1,140 feet through burned forest and lush meadows. At 1.9 miles, it crosses a branch of Bayhouse Creek. The path reaches a summit, (7,040 feet) at 2.5 miles with a view of the lower end of Johnson Creek Canyon. It drops 720 feet on an open slope to a junction (6,320 feet) at 3.4 miles with the Johnson Creek Trail, which has come 5 miles and 700 feet from the Johnson Creek Campground with four fords of the creek.

Turn left (east) up the Johnson Creek Trail, which winds through burned pines and remnants of brush. At 5.5 miles, the path fords the creek in a sprawling meadow. At the other end of the meadow at 5.9 miles, it fords back again to the north side of the creek. Up the canyon, the horns of two peaks form a headwall behind Azure and Rock Island Lakes. The trail climbs gently in the canyon bottom, and at 6.7 miles begins to climb more steeply. At 7.6 miles, it joins the Pats Lake Trail. There are several campsites along the canyon, but unless you can find a site well away from any burned trees, they will be unsafe. In late summer, there is water only in Johnson Creek and it dries up beyond the first ford in a year with little snow.

QUEENS RIVER AREA

46 Queens River Canyon to Pats Lake Junction

Maps 18 and 19

round trip: 24.8 miles
elevation gain: 3,080 feet
highest point: 8,280 feet
maps: Atlanta West, Atlanta East, Mt. Everly
time: 3 days
difficulty: strenuous
access: On Highway 21, 18 miles north of Idaho City, turn east at the Edna Creek Campground and drive 36.4 miles on a gravel road to the Queens River. Turn left (north) and drive 2.3 miles on a dirt road to the transfer camp.
caution: Because the 1994 Rabbit Creek Fire burned Pats Lake and the Johnson Creek drainage, a loop trip is not recommended. It would be difficult to find campsites safe from falling snags.

Cracked gray cliffs 1,000 feet high line the canyon of the Big Queens River from its mouth to the Pats Lake junction. The first 3 miles of trail run through groves of ponderosa pines draped with yellow-green moss, but higher up, the route traverses open grass, brush or talus with views of fluted peaks ahead. Beyond Nanny Creek, streams pouring down the side of the canyon make bogs on the trail. Near the head of the canyon, a 1-mile side trip leads to an unnamed lake. A dagger-shaped tongue of grass along the inlet cuts into this oval, green lake below a ridge of short cliffs. At the Pats Lake junction, the infant river babbles through moss in a rocky meadow under the gray granite hat of Mt. Everly.

To reach the trailhead, turn right (east) at the Edna Creek Campground 18 miles north of Idaho City onto Forest Road 384. At 13.7 miles, turn left (east) along the North Fork of the Boise River on Road 327. At 26.6 miles, turn left again at a four-way intersection onto the Middle Fork of the Boise River Road 268 and drive to the Queens River Road 206 at 36.4 miles. Here, turn left (north) and drive to the transfer camp at 38.7 miles. There are signs for Atlanta at each turn on the approach, but on the way out, you must find the way by the road numbers. The Queens River Road continues beyond the parking area into an informal campground.

From the parking area, the trail begins as an old road, closed to motor vehicles, which drops left (north) to cross the Queens River on a bridge. At .2

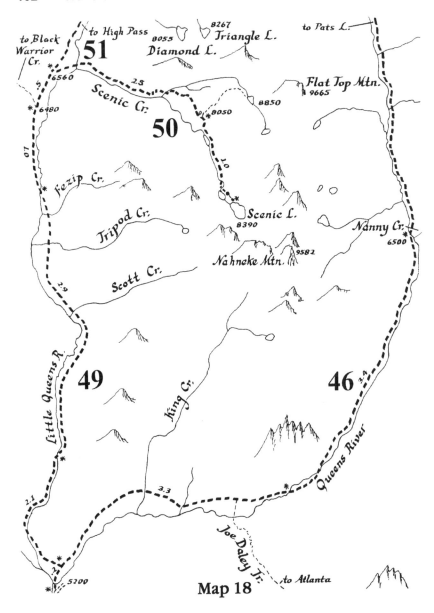

Map 18

mile, the trail splits into the Queens River and Little Queens River trails. A loop trip will take five to eight days.

Of the two, the Queens River Trail climbs more gradually. Take the right (east) trail up the Queens River, which wanders through Douglas firs and ponderosa pines. The trail crosses side creeks at 1.4 and 2 miles under the cliffs of the canyon wall. At 2.3 miles, it approaches the river and appears to cross it on a ponderosa log but doesn't. The Joe Daley Trail joins from the south at 2.6 miles at an unmarked junction. This trail goes 4.5 miles in a 1,320-foot climb over a ridge to primitive roads leading to Atlanta.

At 3.3 miles, the Queens River Trail crosses the river to the right (south) on a log jam 150 yards upstream. This crossing of the Queens River and the next two are hazardous early in the season and until mid-summer in wet years.

Once across the log jam, go back down the creek ten yards, then up a dry side stream to find the trail. From here, it ascends in trees away from the river into brush below the canyon wall.

At 3.8 miles, the path hops a side creek, and at a campsite, returns to the river and crosses it to the left (north) on a log jam 25 feet west of the trail. On the other side, head upstream to find the trail, which soon reaches an open, brushy area extending upstream three miles. On the wall above, waterfalls hide in clefts in the cliffs. Just before Nanny Creek, the route returns to forest, then crosses the river at 6,500 feet in several sections at 6.9 miles to a flat on the right (south) side of the river. Here, beside Nanny Creek, there are campsites.

Beyond here, the trail is in open grass and rocks with ledges above. At 7.9 miles, it is flooded for 60 yards at high water. The grassy and wooded flats at 8 miles have campsites.

Now the way is over grass, with several side streams and only patches of woods. At 9.6 miles, the path jogs 90 degrees to the right (east) for 100 yards at a "trail" sign and cairns, then continues up the canyon. At 10.7 miles, it fords the creek to the left (west) side. Here, you can go off to the right to an unnamed lake (8,200 feet).

To make this side trip, wind west steeply up the side of the ridge. At .5 mile, you are above and to the right of a 100-foot gorge which holds the lake's outlet. Continue along above the gorge until the ground flattens in a grassy area below talus at .7 mile. Here, cut left (northeast) across the small outlet and climb through woods near it. West of a tiny pond, return to the south side of the creek, then climb along the west shore of the lake to a campsite in trees 1 mile from the main trail.

Fifty yards beyond the turnoff for this side trip, the main trail fords the river at 7,360 feet, then climbs through a meadow. The way is marked with cairns, but there is no trail tread. If you are descending the canyon instead, a big blaze shows the location of the ford. Beyond the meadow, the trail is hard to find in woods and bogs. These bogs, and smaller ones in the previous three miles, can be hazardous for stock. Gradually the trail returns to the river, then switchbacks mostly in the open.

At 11.6 miles, it crosses back over the now six-foot wide river to the right (north) and angles along a ridge with black and white striped cliffs across the canyon. At 12.3 miles, among small subalpine firs, the route returns to the left (west) side of the creek, and joins the Pats Lake Trail at 12.4 miles (8,280 feet).

47 Pats Lake Junction to Everly and Plummer Lakes
Map 19

round trip: 29.2 miles
elevation gain: 3,764 feet
elevation loss (return climb): 352 feet
this section one way: 2.2 miles, 684-foot gain, 352-foot loss
highest point: 8,640 feet
map: Mt. Everly
time: 3 days
difficulty: strenuous
access: Hike up the Queens River Trail 12.4 miles to the Pats Lake junction, following directions in Hike 46 (Queens River Canyon).

The trail to Everly and Plummer Lakes climbs under the towering cliffs of the dark gray north face of Mt. Everly. From the white granite benches surrounding the turquoise water of Everly Lake, ledges and cliffs soar to the double-hump of this mountain. The lake is around a corner from the great dark face. Granite benches also enclose Plummer Lake except on the east where cliffs rise 700 feet to two triangular peaks. A scalloped blob of black rock splashes the right hand one, Plummer Peak. Even though the lakes are only .2 mile apart, Everly Lake drains into Benedict Creek, a tributary of the Payette River, and Plummer Lake empties into the Queens River, a tributary of the Boise River.

To reach the beginning of the hike, follow the access directions above. From the junction with the Pats Lake Trail at 8,280 feet, take the Queens River Trail east up through a grassy basin and then woods. The trail passes through two flat meadows to a 8,592-foot divide at .7 mile with a view of the face of Mt. Everly.

Then it crosses a grassy flat and drops through trees to a triangle of trails at 1.2 miles (8,240 feet). This triangle is the only sign of the junction to the lakes. From here, the Queens River Trail drops to the Benedict Creek Trail in .9 mile with a 360-foot descent. Turn right (south) at the triangle and ford a small creek to a meadow. This side trail then winds back and forth through trees and granite outcrops up the right (west) side of the outlet. It crosses the outlet on built-up rocks just below Everly Lake (8,628 feet) at 1.7 miles.

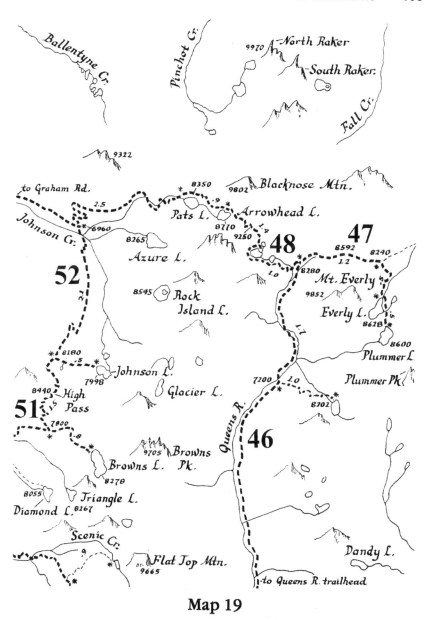

Map 19

The trail goes along the left (east) side of the lake below granite benches to some campsites. From these, a path leads east to a tiny pond, then south up between the benches and down to the north end of Plummer Lake (8,600 feet) at 2.2 miles.

48 Pats Lake Junction to Pats Lake
Map 19

round trip: 31.4 miles
elevation gain: 4,050 feet
this section one way: 3.3 miles, 970-foot gain, 840-foot loss
highest point: 9,250 feet
map: Mt. Everly
time: 3 to 4 days
difficulty: strenuous
access: Hike up the Queens River Trail 12.4 miles to the Pats Lake junction, following directions in Hike 46 (Queens River Canyon).
caution: The divide between the Queens River and Pats Lake is one of the last to open in the summer. To avoid danger and to avoid damaging fragile soils, wait until the snow has melted from the trail before traveling it. The danger of burned trees falling makes camping at Pats Lake hazardous. Instead, camp near Arrowhead Lake. Before traveling the area, call the SNRA headquarters for information on conditions.

The trail to Pats Lake hairpins 400 feet up the canyon wall from the trail junction in less than a mile. Along the way, two ponds hug the grass like blue mirrors on green velvet. At the larger pond, granite hills frame the fissured wall of Mt. Everly across the canyon. Gentians, buttercups and shooting stars carpet the grass in season. From the top of the divide, the view is back into the misty gulf of the Queens River Canyon and ahead into cobalt blue Arrowhead Lake and teal blue Pats Lake below it. Above these lakes, cracks in the wall of cliffs make them resemble a row of buildings.

To reach the beginning of this hike at the Pats Lake junction (8,280 feet) 12.4 miles and a 3,080-foot climb from the Queens River trailhead, follow the access directions given above. From the junction in the rolling meadow, the trail climbs through woods and rock benches to the first pond at .7 mile. A second, larger pond is in turf at 1 mile. At 1.2 miles, the path passes above a third tiny pond in granite benches. Camping at the ponds is poor because of the lumpy turf. Next, the trail passes left of a snow pond in a grassy basin, then switchbacks up granite ledges to 9,250 feet. It drops into a notch (9,200 feet) at 1.7 miles.

On the other side, the trail hairpins down slabs and talus 200 feet in .3 mile to a tiny pond. At 2.4 miles is 8,770-foot Arrowhead Lake, which has only a few, small campsites.

The trail on to Pats Lake (8,350 feet) zigzags down through ledges and burned trees, then circles the north side of the lake well above it. At the lower end at

Mt. Everly

3.3 miles, a path goes 100 yards to campsites along the shore, but at present there is danger from falling trees.

49   Little Queens River to Scenic Lakes Junction
Map 18

round trip: 13.4 miles
elevation gain: 1,360 feet
highest point: 6,560 feet
maps: Atlanta West, Nahneke Mountain
time: 9 hours
difficulty: strenuous
access: Follow the access road directions in Hike 46 (Queens River Canyon) to reach the Queens River trailhead.

The Little Queens River makes a beautiful early summer walk through a rainbow of wildflowers beside the vanilla-scented trunks of ponderosa pines. Above, Douglas firs feather the canyon walls. Along the trail, which is an old wagon road for the first three miles, ruins of silvered wood and remnants of rusted iron from old mines give a feeling of stepping back in time.

To reach the trailhead, follow directions for the hike listed above. At the junction at .2 mile, take the left (west) branch of the trail up the Little Queens

River in an open, brushy forest of Douglas fir and ponderosa pine. It is an old road that bridges the river to the west at 1.1 miles. Once across, it runs at the base of a steep hillside, crossing Browns Creek at 1.7 miles.

At 1.8 miles, the track is in a sagebrush flat beside the ruins of cabins and across the river from an old mine tunnel. At 2.3 miles, it fords the river back to the right (east) in two sections. The ponderosa footlog that used to be upstream here has washed away.

A log cabin is at 3 miles in a grassy flat across from mine diggings. Beyond here, the old road becomes a trail which climbs away from the creek in forest for 2 miles. In this section the trail crosses Scott Creek at 3.9 miles, Tripod Creek at 4.7 miles and Fezip Creek at 5 miles. At 5.2 miles, the path fords back to the left (west) side of the river. In late season, hikers can cross on rocks, but in early summer this crossing will be difficult.

Now the path threads slopes of sagebrush and grass. At 6.2 miles is a junction with the Neinmeyer Creek Trail, which goes 7.6 miles with a 2,080-foot climb and 2,320-foot descent to the Johnson Creek Trail .6 mile south of the Bayhouse Trail junction. The Little Queens River Trail edges a beaver pond, then reaches the Scenic Lakes junction at 6.7 miles.

50 Scenic Lakes
Map 18

round trip: 20.4 miles
elevation gain: 3,190 feet
this section one way: 3.5 miles, 1,840-foot gain
highest point: 8,390 feet
map: Nahneke Mountain
difficulty: strenuous
access: Follow the directions above under Hike 46 (Queens River Canyon) and Hike 49 (Little Queens River) to hike to the Scenic Lakes junction, 6.7 miles from the Queens River Transfer Camp.

On a dark gray face overhanging the turquoise water of the tiny lake below Scenic Lake, two dark gray layers of rock form a V. The thinner of these ends in a melting arrowhead. Above Scenic Lake, a curved line of dark brown splotches the cliffs and two more layers, round and weathered, resemble gigantic brown candles.

To reach the Scenic Lakes Trail, follow the access directions for the hikes listed above. On that trail .2 mile from the junction, there is a ford of the 75-foot wide Little Queens River. This crossing is hazardous in early summer and until August in wet years. Then the way winds above the canyon of Scenic

Creek in alternate forest and open grass. At 1 mile, it begins zigzagging through brush, with a view from one trail corner of a waterfall on the creek. At 1.7 miles, a sign warns that horse travel is not recommended beyond this point because it is difficult for horses, and the area is fragile. Above here, party size is limited to six and the number of stock to eight.

Here the trail becomes a foot path that climbs straight up in grass and brush with a view of towers to the left, then cuts to the right below cliffs. Next it zigzags up to the right of the cliffs, then at 2.1 miles angles along the side of the canyon wall.

The trail descends left of an orange and white outcrop, and circles to the right of a pond to a junction with a line of blazes (no path) to Flat Top Lakes at 2.5 miles. This route climbs 800 feet in .7 mile to the first Flat Top Lake.

The Scenic Lakes Trail winds across a boggy meadow, over a granite outcrop, and along the center of the first of three large meadows. Beyond the first of these, the path runs on the left of the creek between it and granite ledges. In the second, narrower meadow, the trail tread disappears, and then reappears at a cairn on an outcrop half way along the meadow. Now the trail follows the creek next to ledges. After crossing the third, smaller meadow, it fords the creek at 3.2 miles to the right (west). The smaller, unnamed lake, where the official trail ends, is at 3.4 miles. A few small campsites are nearby.

To reach the upper lake, ford both branches of the outlet and go along the edge of the lake below a granite knoll. At the far end, ascend a slope of grass and rocks into woods to the upper lake (8,390 feet) at 3.5 miles. A rocky campsite is on a bench near the outlet, with another site below it.

51 Scenic Lakes Junction to Browns Lake, High Pass and Johnson Lake Junction
Maps 18 and 19

round trip: 21 miles
elevation gain: 3,240 feet
elevation loss (return climb): 260 feet
this section one way: 3.8 miles, 1,880-foot gain, 260-foot loss
side trip to Browns Lake: add .8 mile and 478-foot gain
highest point: 8,440 feet
map: Nahneke Mountain
time: 3 days
difficulty: strenuous
access: Follow directions in Hike 46 (Queens River Canyon) and Hike 49 (Little Queens River) to hike to the Scenic Lakes junction.

Hiker on Scenic Lakes Trail

caution: The Johnson Creek drainage and Johnson Lake area burned in the 1994 Rabbit Creek Fire. Camping in the area is not recommended because of the danger of falling snags. If considering a trip over High Pass to Johnson Lake, call the SNRA headquarters first for information on conditions.

On the east side of Browns Lake, towers top the crinkled wall of Browns Peak. Across from this wall, tiers of cliffs rising to smooth granite mountains echo the shapes of the benches edging the lake. In late summer, the white island cruising near the lower end resembles a sea monster. Farther up at the head of the Little Queens River at High Pass, the orange and black needles of North and South Raker Peaks stick up above a distant ridge to the north like porcupine quills.

To reach the beginning of this hike description, follow the access directions above to hike to the Scenic Lakes junction (6,560 feet), which is 6.7 miles and a 1,360-foot climb up the Little Queens River from the Queens River Transfer Camp. From this junction, the Little Queens River Trail runs in open brush and scattered trees, crosses three side streams and curves east at 1.3 miles. At 1.7 miles, it is in a grassy basin with tiny subalpine firs. Where the route switchbacks left (north) at 1.8 miles in the basin, it is possible to cut off the main trail and go .9 mile trail to Diamond Lake, by fording the river and then climbing

640 feet. At 2.3 miles, the main trail comes to the Browns Lake junction (7,800 feet).

The side trail to Browns Lake climbs east on the north side of Browns Creek over open slopes and through forest. At .4 mile, it crosses the creek to the right (south) in alders. The path runs along the base of granite benches and then up between them to a meadow with campsites in the trees. It reaches the lake (8,278 feet) at .8 mile. Campsites are on the west shore and at the outlet.

From the Browns Lake junction, the main trail switchbacks sandy slopes between lodgepoles to 8,440-foot High Pass at 3.3 miles. From here, the canyon walls of the Little Queens River, and the gray peaks around Browns Lake appear to the south and the Rabbit Creek Fire and the needles of the Rakers to the north.

On the other side, the trail descends left across a sandy slope, switchbacks twice and then continues northwest. Below in a meadow is a small pond which is shown on the map. At 3.6 miles, the trail curves right in woods to an unsigned junction (8,180 feet) at 3.8 miles with a .5 mile side trail to Johnson Lake.

52 Johnson Lake Junction to Johnson Lake and Pats Lake

Map 19

round trip: 30.2 miles
elevation gain: 4,630 feet
elevation loss (return climb): 1,480 feet
this section one way: 4.6 miles, 1,390-foot gain, 1,220-foot loss
side trip to Johnson Lake: add .5 mile one way and 182 feet return climb
highest point: 8,350 feet
maps: Nahneke Mountain, Mt. Everly
time: 4 to 5 days
difficulty: strenuous
access: Following directions in Hike 46 (Queens River Canyon), Hike 49 (Little Queens River) and Hike 51 (Scenic Lakes junction to Browns Lake, High Pass and Johnson Lakes junction) hike to the Johnson Lake junction.
caution: This trail section is not recommended at present because of the danger of snags killed by the 1994 fire falling on tents and passersby. For information on conditions, call the SNRA headquarters.

A gigantic granite breast swells above the upper end of shallow Johnson Lake. To the right of it, a second, smaller peak echoes that silhouette. Huckleberries and Labrador tea surround the misty emerald green lake, which con-

Johnson Lake

tains two granite islands. One is large and plumed with firs and the other is tiny and rocky.

To reach the Johnson Lake junction (8,180 feet) which is 10.5 miles and a 3,240-foot climb up the Little Queens River, follow the access directions above. Watch for this unsigned junction 200 yards into the woods on the north side of High Pass. To take a side trip to Johnson Lake from here, follow the blazed side trail east to a crossing of the outlet of a pond. The path wanders through lodgepoles, then drops to the lower end of the 7,998-foot lake near a campsite, which is .5 mile from the main trail. From a marsh .3 east of the lake, experts can continue .7 mile cross-country to The Hole or Glacier Lake.

From the Johnson Lake junction, descend the main trail through a burned forest to reach Pats Lake. The trail crosses an avalanche area, and at .5 mile makes two switchbacks just above a grassy flat. At .8 mile, the path edges the flat with a glimpse of a small green pond. The route runs down the outlet of the pond, then descends through grass, flowers, and remnants of forest to a ford of Johnson Creek at 2.1 miles (6,960 feet). At 2 miles, the trail joins one down Johnson Creek connecting with the Silver Creek trailhead on the Graham Road. All of the canyon along this trail burned, too.

The trail to Pats Lake above this junction makes switchbacks up to .2 mile long on open slopes of sagebrush and grass with views up Johnson Creek toward High Pass and down the creek toward Graham. At 2.8 miles, the path runs straight along the side of the ridge into a burned forest. It crosses to the south bank of the creek at 3.9 miles. At 4 miles, the way is below talus blocks which pour down from a notch on the skyline to the south. These blocks mark a .5 mile, 400-foot cross-country route for experts to Azure Lake. This point is at the south end of the curve in the trail that is closest to Azure Lake. Just beyond this point, the trail fords the creek back to the north in a meadow.

If going to Azure Lake, use caution and do not attempt it in wet weather. The route goes up along the edge of ledges just to the right (west) of the talus. From the notch on the skyline, descend a narrow ridge to the lower end of the lake where a granite peninsula shelters a campsite. Climbing directly from Pats Lake to Azure Lake is not recommended because of cliffs.

From the Azure Lake turn off, the main trail fords the creek, then climbs between rock ledges, crossing the creek twice more before reaching a path to the lower end of Pats Lake (8,350 feet) at 4.6 miles.

ATLANTA AREA

53 Middle Fork of Boise River: Powerplant Campground to Rock Creek
Maps 20 and 21

round trip: 17 miles from east end of campground
elevation gain: 960 feet
highest point: 6,400 feet
maps: Atlanta East, Mt. Everly
time: 10 hours or 2 days

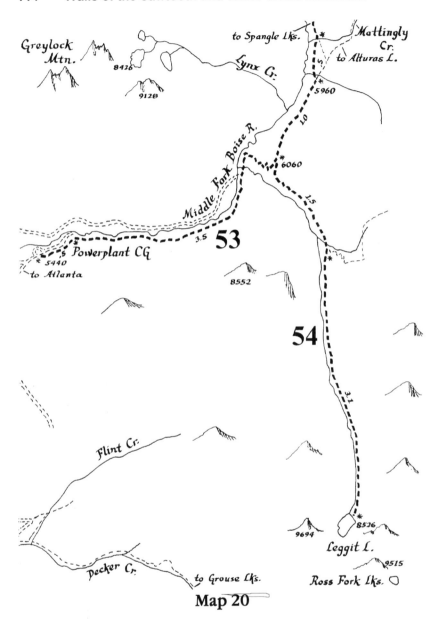

difficulty: strenuous

access: From the Edna Creek Campground 18 miles northeast of Idaho City
   on Highway 21, drive to Atlanta, using the directions found in Hike 46

Middle Fork Boise River Canyon

(Queens River Canyon). Continue 5 more miles on the main road to Atlanta. Go straight ahead where the road forks at the east end of town and drive 1.5 miles to the Powerplant Campground.

The road to the trailhead for this hike wanders through the weathered town of Atlanta. The town nestles in lodgepole pines and aspens in a mountain valley below Greylock Mountain, a crumbling giant with a stubble of pines and rock towers. Some of the old buildings have collapsed, some have been torn down, and others are still used as bars, homes, cabins, and small stores. From the Powerplant Campground near Atlanta, the trail up the Middle Fork of the Boise River plows through thick forest. From the colorful undergrowth of flowers, fluffy grass, and bushes, there is a view of the spires and teeth of the canyon wall.

To reach the trailhead, follow the access directions listed above. Just before the Powerplant Campground (5,440 feet) is a meadow with a trail sign, circular drive and horse loading area. The trail begins to the right (south) of the road here. You can drive .5 mile farther to the end of the campground, but do not park there unless you want to pay for camping. From the campground, the trail is southeast .1 mile. The trail mileage in this hike description is figured from the end of the campground, not from the sign.

The trail parallels the river in forest, across from an old road, passing a meadow and pond at 2 miles. At 2.3 miles, the path comes close to the creek above ten-foot cliffs and at 2.6 miles, it crosses Leggit Creek. The trail turns 90 degrees east, at 2.8 miles, then at 3 miles switchbacks 200 feet up the canyon wall to the Leggit Lake junction (6,060 feet) at 3.5 miles. From this junction, there is a fine view of the canyon.

The main trail continues through forest up the canyon, crossing an intermittent stream at 4.2 miles. At 4.5 miles is the first of two side trails leading to the Mattingly Creek Trail. The main trail crosses Corral Creek in a grassy flat with a view of a dark rock hill, 100 feet high, between the two branches of the Mattingly Creek Trail. At 5 miles, in forest just beyond the second of these junctions, the Middle Fork Trail crosses Mattingly Creek on logs, which can be difficult in early season. Later in the year, Mattingly Creek is the only water source along the trail from here to Rock Creek.

The trail continues 3.5 miles through forest to a ford to the north side of the river at 8.5 miles (6,400 feet) just beyond its confluence with Rock Creek near campsites. In early season, this ford is deep, rushing, and hazardous. Across it is a junction in a wide grassy area with the trail up Rock Creek to Timpa Lake. The main trail continues on up the river 6 miles to Spangle Lakes in a 2,185-foot climb.

54 Leggit Lake
Map 20

round trip: 16.2 miles
elevation gain: 3,086 feet
this section one way: 4.6 miles, 2,466-foot gain
highest point: 8,526 feet
map: Atlanta East
time: 12 hours or 2-3 days
difficulty: strenuous
access: Follow directions in Hike 53 (Powerplant Campground to Rock Creek) to hike to the Leggit Lake junction.

On the way up Leggit Creek, a 1,000-foot dark gray cliff reminds hikers of Yosemite. The 500-foot ridges holding Leggit Lake in a rocky cup make it seem like a lake in the sky. These ridges of talus, grass and ledges end in miniature dark gray peaks, one on each side of the lake. The peaked cap of the western one is split by a chimney.

This hike description starts on the Middle Fork of the Boise River Trail at the Leggit Lake junction (6,060 feet), 3.5 miles and a 620-foot climb from the end of the Powerplant Campground. For directions for reaching this junction, see the hikes listed above. From this junction on a rock knoll 400 feet above the Middle Fork canyon, the trail angles steeply up the canyon of Leggit Creek.

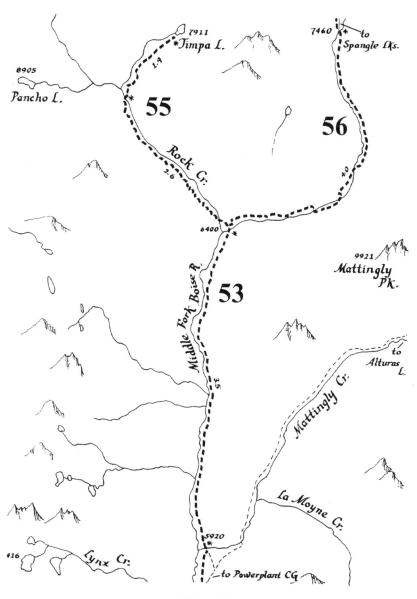

Map 21

Beyond a large campsite at 1.5 miles, the trail goes south towards Leggit Creek. Avoid an old road that leads up the left wall of the canyon to a prospect. The trail tread is indistinct here, but should become obvious in 200 yards. At 1.8 miles, the trail enters a flat, gravelly area opposite the immense black cliff. Beyond the gravel, it crosses a side stream. At 3 miles the forest gives way to rocks, grass, flowers and tiny subalpine firs.

The route becomes steep, rocky and sketchy at 4.1 miles. At 4.4 miles, the trail goes left (east) of the creek to avoid cliffs and disappears. A path will appear that climbs the scree past scattered trees east of the cliffs. Follow it up the ridge ahead to the lake (8,526 feet) at 4.6 miles. A few small campsites are at the lower end. Water is available at two side streams and from the creek now and then in the last 2.5 miles.

55 Timpa Lake
Maps 20 and 21

round trip: 25 miles
elevation gain: 2,471 feet
this section one way: 4 miles, 1,511-foot gain
highest point: 7,911 feet
time: 3 days
maps: Atlanta East, Mt. Everly
difficulty: strenuous
access: Using directions in Hike 53 (Powerplant Campground to Rock Creek), hike 8.5 miles up the Middle Fork of the Boise to Rock Creek.

Turf and marsh grass border the shallow blue-green water of Timpa Lake. On the west side, talus and ledges lead to an elephant-shaped ridge. Across the canyon below the lower end of this small lake, a ridge sweeps up in the center to a wide gable. At the head of the canyon, Chickadee, Surprise, Confusion and Low Pass lakes and several ponds hide off-trail behind wooded knolls and rock ridges.

To reach the junction of the Middle Fork of the Boise River Trail with the Rock Creek Trail, where this hike description begins, follow the directions in Hike 53. From the junction take the Rock Creek Trail, which fords Rock Creek to the left (west) side at .2 mile at a ford that can be dangerous in high water. The crossing is rocky, so it is difficult or dangerous all summer for saddle or pack stock. From it, the path zigzags up the canyon near the creek, which alternates cascades and pools. At 1.3 miles, the trail passes a huge boulder pile, and becomes more shaded and gradual. It crosses the creek back to the east at 2.6 miles on a complex of logs.

Above this crossing, Timpa Creek flows into Rock Creek. The trail zigzags up the canyon of Timpa Creek on the right (southeast) side, then goes straight along the side of the canyon to a sudden ending 50 vertical feet above the 7,911-foot lake at 4 miles. Water is available only at the creek crossings and the lake, where mosquitoes can be a problem.

56   Middle Fork of Boise River: Rock Creek to Spangle Lakes

Map 22

round trip: 29 miles
elevation gain: 3,145 feet
this section one way: 6 miles, 2,185-foot gain
highest point: 8,585 feet
maps: Mt. Everly, Atlanta East
time: 4 days
difficulty: strenuous
access: Hike 8.5 miles from the Powerplant Campground near Atlanta up the
Middle Fork of the Boise River Trail to Rock Creek. For directions see Hike
53 (Middle Fork Boise River Trail–Powerplant Campground to Rock Creek).

In this section of the canyon, Mattingly Peak forms a dark gray bucket edged
by triangular spires. As the trail passes under scalloped cliffs, wildflowers abound,
from delphinium to grass of Parnassus. From Spangle Lakes, Snowyside Peak
resembles a dinosaur with a spine at the neck, a square head with ears, and
gullies outlining its ribs.

To reach the junction with the Rock Creek Trail to Timpa Lake at 6,400
feet, hike up the Middle Fork of the Boise River Trail, following directions for
Hike 53 (Powerplant Campground to Rock Creek). It is 8.5 miles and a 960-
foot climb from the campground to this junction. Just before the junction you
must ford the river in two sections, which is difficult or hazardous for hikers in
early summer, and dangerous for pack stock all summer.

Take the Middle Fork Trail east along the river. The route is in the open in
snowbrush. At 1.1 miles, it crosses to the south bank of the river on a log. The
trail enters the woods and hops a side creek, then returns to the north at 1.5
miles. Next, it climbs 100 feet away from the river under dark gray cliffs.

At 2 miles, the path returns on a log to the right (east) of the river. Then it
enters a grassy field with small trees where a talus-covered mountain is ahead
on the left. The trail jumps two side streams here, passes a pond on the river
and returns to the left (west) bank just before a junction with the Flytrip Creek
Trail (7,460 feet) at 4 miles. This trail gives access to Camp and Heart Lakes (see
Hike 57).

At 4.2 miles, the main trail crosses back to the left (west) side of the river. It
zigzags up granite benches decorated with lodgepole and subalpine firs, then
switchbacks along a ridge. Across the canyon, granite slabs and cliffs hover
above cascades. Parts of an old trail are interlaced with the current trail here.

At the top of the switchbacks, hikers from Spangle Lakes can turn off on a cross-country shortcut to Camp Lake (see Hike 57). At 5.5 miles, the trail crosses the creek and then passes a marsh. It reaches an arm of Little Spangle Lake at 5.9 miles. At 6 miles on the shore of Spangle Lake (8,585 feet), there is a T-shaped junction with trails to Ardeth Lake and Benedict Creek.

57 Camp and Heart Lakes
Map 22

round trip: 28.6 miles
elevation gain: 3,122 feet
this section one way: 1.8 miles, 1,102-foot gain
highest point: 8,562 feet
maps: Mt. Everly, Snowyside Peak
time: 4 days
difficulty: strenuous
access: Using directions in Hikes 53 and 56 (Middle Fork of the Boise River Trail: Powerplant Campground to Rock Creek and Rock Creek to Spangle Lakes), hike 12.5 miles to the junction with the trail up Flytrip Creek.
caution: Avoid camping in the fragile basin of either lake.

At the head of Flytrip Creek, Camp Lake extends from a slim meadow like blue toothpaste from a green tube. Over a wooded ridge from it lurks the orange dinosaur of Snowyside Peak. A fin-like shoulder connects the dinosaur's head to its pointed back. On the other side of the ridge, Heart Lake, edged with Labrador tea and granite, faces this monster. To the south, low ridges divide Heart Lake from P.S. Lake and a matching dinosaur. Between the two dinosaurs, a conical gray peak stands watch.

To reach the Flytrip Creek Trail, hike the Middle Fork of the Boise River from Atlanta 12.5 miles in a 2,020-foot climb or hike 2 miles down the river from Spangle Lakes. For directions, see the hikes listed above. There is a large campsite at the junction (7,460 feet).

The Flytrip Trail fords the river and then ascends the side of the canyon in woods. It crosses an unnamed creek three times before two small ponds appear at 1 mile. The lake (8,520 feet) is at 1.5 miles. Heart Lake at 8,562 feet, .3 mile beyond, is reached by turning right (southeast) over the low, wooded ridge. Both lakes have small campsites.

The Flytrip Creek Trail climbs more than 1,000 feet and begins 1,125 feet lower than Spangle Lakes, so from Spangle Lakes, it is more fun to go cross-country to Camp and Heart Lakes. To do this, turn east over a low ridge 1 mile below Spangle Lakes (just before the steep switchbacks start) and drop to a marsh. From this marsh, go southeast to a larger marsh and cut across at that level, avoiding talus, to the two small ponds .5 mile below Camp Lake on the trail. This route saves 1.5 miles and 600 feet of elevation gain.

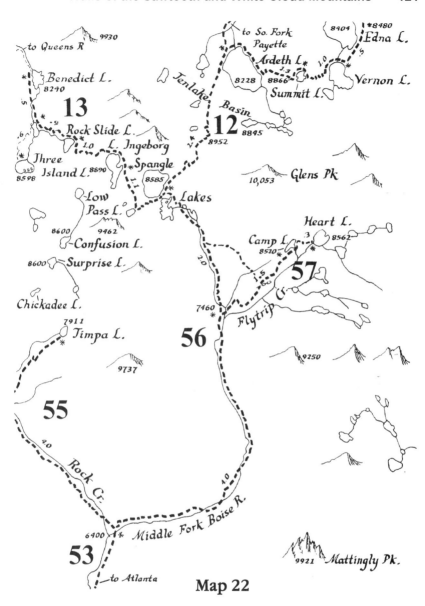

to Queens R
9930

Benedict L.
8240

13

Rock Slide L.
1.0   L. Ingeborg
Three
Island L. 8890   Spangle
8598   8585

Low
Pass L.
8600   9462
Confusion L.

8600   Surprise L.

Chickadee L.

7911
Timpa L.

9737

55

40

Rock Cr.

53

6400   Middle Fork Boise R.

to Atlanta

Jenlake
8228

Basin

12
8952

8845

Lakes

7460

56

Flytrip Cr.

to So. Fork
Payette

Ardeth L.
1.3
8866

Summit L.

8404   *8480
Edna L.

1.0   Vernon L.

10,053   Glens Pk

Heart L.
Camp L.   3   8562
8510   57

9250

9921   Mattingly Pk.

Map 22

trails in the
WHITE CLOUD
MOUNTAINS

Sapphire Lake (Big Boulder Lakes)

GERMANIA CREEK AREA

58 South Fork Champion Creek and Rainbow Lake

Map 23

round trip: 11 miles
elevation gain: 2,155 feet
elevation loss (return climb): 905 feet
highest point: 9,200 feet
map: Horton Peak
time: 11 hours or 2 days
difficulty: expert
access: From Highway 75, turn east 36 miles north of Ketchum on the gravel Pole Creek–Germania Creek Road. At 2.3 miles, turn right, avoiding the Valley Road to the north. At 4.5 miles, turn left (north) at a sign "Trail to Champion Creek" and drive .5 mile to an unmarked trailhead where the road makes a 90 degree left turn.

The trail provides a fine view of the Boulder Mountains and of a 700-foot high fluted wall east of Horton Peak. The Twin Creek–South Fork Champion Creek divide provides a scenic destination for a day hike. On the side of the South Fork of Champion Creek Canyon, Rainbow Lake lies on a bench. Above the lake, a curve of rock, striped rust, white and yellow, forms a rainbow. On the topographic map, a snow pond is labeled Rainbow Lake, but the map is wrong. The lake is east of this pond, in a spot shown as marsh on the map. The lake is marshy around the edges and may appear stagnant in late summer, but is much larger and deeper than the pond.

To reach the trailhead (7,250 feet), follow the access directions above. From the trailhead, the trail starts up the narrow canyon of Twin Creek in dense forest, staying left (west) of the creek for the first .3 mile. The path crosses to the east side, goes 50 feet above the stream, then returns to the west side at .5 mile.

In the next .3 mile, the trail crosses the small creek five more times. Sometimes it runs through narrow jaws of rock, where it has been washed out. Hikers must look at their maps at these places to keep on the correct side of the stream. The canyon opens out into a grassy basin where the trail, now on the right hand side, almost disappears. It goes along a grassy shelf above the creek, then drops to the creek and fords it to the left (south) just beyond where the creek begins a double bend at 1 mile.

There is much downed timber here and it is easier to stay on the right side of the creek in steep sagebrush and pick up the trail again where it crosses back

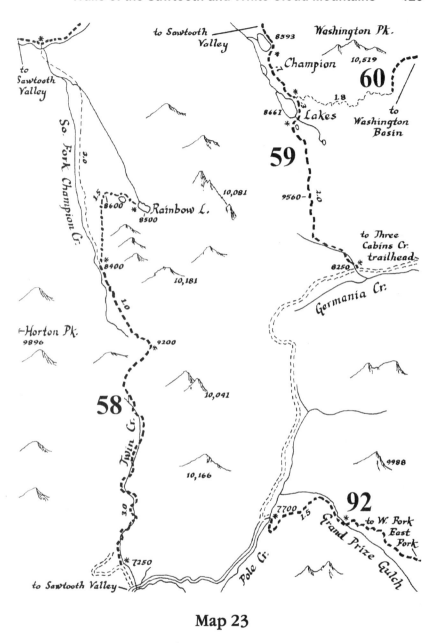

Map 23

to the right at 1.2 miles. There are two more crossings which are not shown on the topographic map. The route returns to the west side in a narrow meadow, where the canyon becomes more open and the trail less distinct. At 1.6 miles, the route crosses to the right side of the creek and becomes clear in the trees ahead.

The path now stays on the right (east) of the creek, but disappears from time to time in the high grass. At the end of the meadows at 2 miles, the trail fords back and forth, then becomes much more obvious as the forest closes in at 2.1 miles. Around 2.4 miles, there are three more fords in a dell of wildflowers. The trail ends up left (west) of the creek.

As the canyon bends, the trail curves right and keeps disappearing under the many small trees. At 2.8 miles, it cuts northeast out of the canyon, climbing 300 feet up a grass and sagebrush slope to a 9,200-foot saddle at 3 miles.

From the top, the wooded summit and sagebrush sides of Horton Peak are seen to the west. When descending the far side of the saddle to the north, the big fluted cliff east of Horton Peak can be seen. To the right (north) of Horton Peak, a wooded mountain has white cliffs at its base. Those who wish to go on to the lake should notice these, because they will turn off the trail opposite them.

At 3.5 miles, the trail passes right of a small wooded knoll, then comes out on open hillsides with a view of a big flat meadow ahead. The trail descends to this meadow, disappearing often. On the return it is difficult to find the spot where the trail leaves the meadow, so notice the landmarks carefully.

The trail stays in trees on the right of the meadow, and crosses a sagebrush area beyond a horse campsite. The meadow has other campsites and makes a good destination for a hike or an overnight trip because it is lush, wild, and remote.

Experts who wish to go on to Rainbow Lake should leave the trail at 4 miles (8,400 feet) just beyond the north end of the meadow. This is opposite the white cliffs on the other side of the canyon, which were mentioned earlier. The trail continues three more miles down the South Fork to Champion Creek with an elevation loss of 800 feet.

To reach Rainbow Lake after leaving the trail, climb north diagonally up the east side of the canyon. Notice a saddle on the opposite wall next to some white cliffs. The notch you are aiming for is across the canyon from this saddle. Keeping below cliffs, walk north to two wooded hills and east through the 8,600-foot notch between them. The notch is .8 mile from the meadow, and a hill marked 8,681 feet on the topographic map is just north of it.

If you are too high on the ridge, find the tea-colored pond below to the east and adjust your route. Descend the other side of the notch through lodgepoles to the pond (8,495 feet) at 1 mile. Partly-wooded granite cliffs on the ridge you have just descended shadow the pond. Go around the pond and then east-southeast through forest to the pale green lake (8,500 feet) at 1.5 miles, 5.5 miles from the Twin Creek trailhead.

59 Champion Lakes
Maps 23, 24, and 28

round trip: 6 miles
elevation gain: 1,310 feet
elevation loss (return climb): 967 feet
highest point: 9,560 feet
maps: Horton Park, Washington Peak
time: 6 1/2 hours
difficulty: strenuous
access: On Highway 75, 36 miles north of Ketchum, just south of Smiley Creek Lodge, turn right (east) on the Pole Creek–Germania Creek Road. Go 2.3 miles on gravel to a junction. Turn right here and go east on the gravel and primitive surface up to Pole Creek Summit at 9.1 miles. Continue down the other side to a grassy hillside at 11.2 miles. Turn left (north) and drive 100 yards uphill to a register box. The last four miles are rough, rocky and muddy and may require four-wheel drive. It is also possible to reach Champion Lakes in 8 miles from Fourth of July Creek by way of a new cutoff to Champion Creek and a trail up that creek.

From a divide on the trail, shadowed canyons lead south to the pink and charcoal gray crags of the Boulders. To the north, the blue-green ovals of Champion Lakes sit in a basin of woods, rocks and meadows below the pearl gray sand of Washington Peak. This peak and a pale gray-striped mountain dominate the upper lake, where mats of pink algae float near shore in late summer. On the west side of the lower lake, a gray and white striped ridge ends in a wall of towers.

To reach the trailhead (8,250 feet), follow the access directions above. From the register box, the trail goes west across a stream, then fords a creek. The path climbs north along the west side of this creek in grass and sagebrush where bluebells grow in season. Around .3 mile, the trail crosses the creek, which is now a tiny stream, several times. At .7 mile, the path turns right (north) uphill and leaves the creek. Without switchbacks, the route steeply ascends a slope of grass, sand and scattered trees. The 9,560-foot divide is at 1.2 miles.

From here, the trail descends loose rock and crumbled ledges for 30 feet, requiring caution. It then angles down steep scree into a gully of tiny firs. The use of horses and mountain bikes on this trail is discouraged because of the steepness and loose rock. Below the gully, the path crosses a dry flat at 1.5 miles, and climbs an 80-foot wooded ridge. On the other side of the ridge, the route drops 300 feet and passes a pond below a meadow leading to the upper end of the first lake (8,661 feet) at 2 miles.

A path goes around the west side of the lake, but the official trail is on the east side where it crosses the inlet in a meadow at the upper end of the lake. Here it disappears, then reappears in the woods beyond, near some campsites. Half way around the lake, at 2.3 miles, a trail turns off to go 1.8 miles with a 1,419-foot climb and 700-foot descent over the white shoulder of Washington Peak to Washington Basin.

The Champion Lakes Trail continues through boggy meadows below the lower end of the lake to the lower lake (8,593 feet) at 3 miles. Here, the best camping is at the upper end. A third small lake is 200 yards west of the trail half way between the two larger lakes. Below the lower lake, the trail continues 6.7 miles with a 1,493-foot elevation loss to a closed trailhead on private land in Sawtooth Valley. A mile above this trailhead, a new trail goes north 3 miles with a 450-foot elevation gain and 250-foot loss to the Fourth of July Creek Road.

60 Washington Basin
Maps 23, 24, 25, 26

round trip: 9.6 miles
elevation gain: 1,900 feet
elevation loss (return climb): 400 feet
highest point: 9,380 feet
maps: Horton Peak, Galena Peak, Washington Peak, Boulder Chain Lakes
time: 8 1/2 hours
difficulty: strenuous
access: On Highway 75, 36 miles north of Ketchum, turn right on the Pole Creek–Germania Creek Road and drive 4.6 miles on gravel and 7.5 miles on a primitive surface over Pole Creek Summit to the trailhead at Three Cabins Creek at 12.1 miles. The trail to Washington Basin is a jeep trail.

The white wall of Croesus Peak, striped with burnt orange, hangs above the old cabins, mines and mill ruins of Washington Basin. On a cloudy day, the stripes on the peak look red, making it peppermint striped. The grooves of chimneys and an "X" in the stripes accent the wall. On the east, this wall merges with the two-toned summit of red, caramel and cream-colored rock called Bible Back Mountain. At the head of the basin, Washington Peak and its shoulders bulge in white pillows. From here the pleated wall of Castle Peak forms a distant backdrop to a narrow green pond in the rocks below.

This hike is on a steep jeep trail. Ordinary passenger cars should be left along the Pole Creek Road at Grand Prize Gulch at 6.5 miles. You may need a high wheelbase and/or 4-wheel drive for three fords at 7.3 miles. If you can get your 4-wheel drive passenger car to the trailhead, it can negotiate the jeep trail

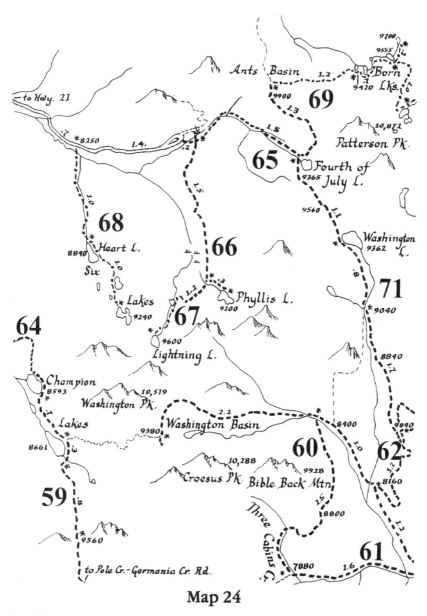

Map 24

for 2.5 miles, but the upper part is suitable only for four-wheel drive vehicles with a high wheelbase. Remember that the mine diggings and buildings are on private property and are historical, so please treat them with respect.

To reach the trailhead, follow the access directions above. From the trailhead (7,880 feet), the jeep road climbs along Three Cabins Creek in forest and sagebrush. After running over talus for 100 yards, at .6 mile it switchbacks to the right onto a steep section. From here, the jeep trail climbs through forest to an 8,800-foot summit at 1.5 miles, 920 feet above the trailhead.

Now the track drops to a ford (8,400 feet) of Washington Creek at 2.5 miles and a trailhead for a mile-long trail down Washington Creek to the Chamberlain Lakes Trail and for a cutoff trail over to upper Washington Creek. Leave passenger cars with four-wheel drive before the ford. From here, the jeep trail climbs through forest, with bridges at 2.6 and 2.7 miles. At 3.6 miles where the slope lessens, the colorful mountain wall is opposite. Several mines, cabins and an excellent view are at 3.9 miles. The road then crosses open grassy slopes as it winds to the head of the basin.

At 4 miles, a branch road leads right to mines just before the crossing of a small creek. Then the track curves down to a usually dry pond. A detour on foot leads to old boilers and mill timbers at the head of this muddy flat. From here the road climbs past ruins and a log cabin to join a track at 4.5 miles leading left to the Black Rock Mine.

Continue on the main road to a junction with a trail to Champion Lakes at 4.7 miles (9,360 feet). This trail climbs 700 feet over the side of Washington Peak, then descends 1,419 feet to Upper Champion Lake, which is 1.8 miles from here. From the junction, continue on the road to the ruins of the highest cabin beside a meadow at 4.8 miles. The lower end of the meadow is a pond formed by an earthen dam. It was built by a black miner, George Washington Blackman, who lived in the highest cabin beginning in the 1880s. Washington and Blackman peaks were named for him. The narrow green pond and Castle Peak are visible from the cabin.

61 Germania Creek Trail to Chamberlain Creek

Maps 24, 25, 26

round trip: 12.6 miles
elevation gain: 380 feet
elevation loss (return climb): 1,210 feet
highest point: 7,880 feet
maps: Horton Peak, Galena Peak, Boulder Chain Lakes
time: 8 1/2 hours
difficulty: strenuous
access: From Highway 75, turn east 36 miles north of Ketchum onto the Pole Creek–Germania Creek Road and drive 4.6 miles on gravel and 7.5 miles on a primitive surface to the Three Cabins Creek trailhead at 12.1 miles.

In this canyon, Germania Creek changes from a tiny mountain stream to a large creek roaring through gorges and swirling through meadows. Charcoal

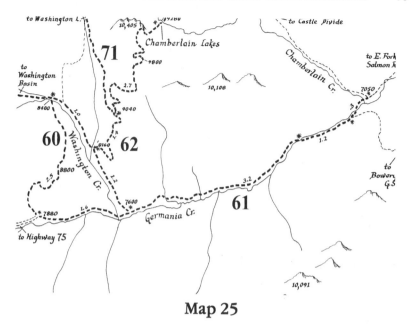

Map 25

gray scalloped cliffs overlook the lower canyon, especially at Chamberlain Creek. As the trail descends, it crosses several meadows and sagebrush slopes and the trees change from lodgepole and spruce to Douglas fir and cottonwood. Reaching the trailhead may require 4-wheel drive.

To reach the trailhead (7,880 feet), follow the access directions above. At 12.1 miles, the road turns left (north) at a "narrow steep road" sign and becomes the Washington Basin jeep trail. At this turn, look to the right (east) to find the register box for the Germania Creek Trail, which begins on the left (north) side of the creek. Within 100 yards, this trail fords a side stream, Three Cabins Creek.

At .8 mile, Deer Creek joins Germania Creek from the south side of the canyon. The trail climbs an open sagebrush area across from a double-humped gray mountain at 1.2 miles. It drops 100 feet off this slope through trees to a log crossing of Washington Creek at 1.5 miles (7,600 feet).

Beyond a small open area at 1.6 miles there is a signed junction with a trail up Washington Creek. It is 1.2 miles and a 560-foot climb on this trail to a junction (8,160 feet) with the trail to Chamberlain Lakes. From this junction, it is 4.1 more miles and 1,640 feet more elevation gain to the lakes, for a total distance of 6.9 miles and a total elevation gain of 2,100 feet. (Driving the Washington Basin jeep trail to the ford of Washington Creek shortens the distance to Chamberlain Lakes by 1.8 miles and the climb by 600 feet.)

Castle Peak from Chamberlain Lakes Trail

Below this junction, the Germania Creek Trail climbs onto a sagebrush hillside, and goes over a volcanic knoll at 2.2 miles. Next it drops down a wooded ravine to cross Jack Creek at 2.5 miles on rocks onto another sagebrush hillside. At 3 miles, the path descends to level woods at the upper end of a mile-long meadow. It threads clumps of trees, and almost disappears in grass and willows at the edge of the creek at 3.5 miles. At 3.8 miles, the path skirts rock ledges close to the creek, and at 4 miles, woods close in again.

The trail runs along a gravel bar and climbs a bank which has slid away. Here it has been rerouted. Across from a rock nubbin, the trail drops to ford the creek to the right (south) side in gravel at 4.8 miles.

For the next mile, the way is through a thick Douglas fir forest below dark gray cliffs. It is treacherous where the trail climbs and descends a 30-foot high rocky bluff at 5.5 miles. Level woods beside mossy outcrops and a narrow slot between cliffs and creek are followed by a meadow.

The trail climbs a steep bank at a sign for Bowery Guard Station Cutoff, and disappears in the meadow. This route to Bowery Guard Station turns away from the creek 90 degrees and leads 4.5 miles in a 1,660-foot climb and 2,000-foot descent to that guard station.

Those continuing down Germania Creek to the East Fork of the Salmon or planning to take the Chamberlain Creek route to Chamberlain Lakes need to cross Germania Creek in this meadow. However, it is hard to find where the trail crosses the creek. The easiest route is at the upper end of the meadow, where the creek widens over gravel. In early summer, this ford is hazardous. Across the canyon, cliffs tower above Chamberlain Creek.

Once across Germania Creek, cow paths join on a steep sagebrush hillside where gray rock knolls edge the creek. Behind these knolls, Germania Creek leaps down in hidden falls and cascades.

Next the trail fords Chamberlain Creek at 6.2 miles. Across the creek, only a cairn (7,050 feet) marks a trail to the left up Chamberlain Creek. This trail climbs 2,190 feet in 3.7 miles to the Castle Divide Trail .5 mile east of the lowest Chamberlain Lake. Reaching the lakes by this trail is 2.8 miles longer than the route via Washington Creek. From this junction, it is 5 miles of sagebrush and a 690-foot descent to the East Fork of the Salmon River Road.

62 Chamberlain Lakes from Three Cabins Creek

Maps 24, 25 and 26

round trip: 14.8 miles, additional 1.5 miles one-way to see the upper lakes
elevation gain: 2,200 feet, additional 652 feet for the upper lakes
elevation loss (return climb): 800 feet
highest point: 9,800 feet
maps: Horton Peak, Washington Peak, Galena Peak, Boulder Chain Lakes
time: 11 hours
difficulty: strenuous
access: From Highway 75, turn east 36 miles north of Ketchum onto the gravel and primitive Pole Creek–Germania Creek Road. Drive over Pole Creek Summit to the Three Cabins Creek trailhead at 12.1 miles. This may re-quire four-wheel drive. It is 2.4 miles farther to a junction of the Washington Basin jeep trail with the Washington Creek Trail.

The orange and white 2,500-foot wall of Castle Peak, cut with avalanche chutes, dwarfs the blue-green lakes in Chamberlain Basin, making them look like puddles. From a 9,800-foot divide on the trail, a grassy basin, sprinkled with trees and lakes, rolls toward this pinnacle-topped wall. The burnt orange of the left side of the wall turns to white on the right, and the white continues in a sharp-pointed shoulder. Rerouting of the trail over Chamberlain Divide since the last edition of this book has lengthened the round trip by 2.2 miles.

Above the lowest lake, three gullies branch to the skyline from the single gully separating Castle Peak from its shoulder. The left (west) gully is the route for scrambling up the peak. Across this green lake from the peak, stands a doubled humped white mountain with gray stripes.

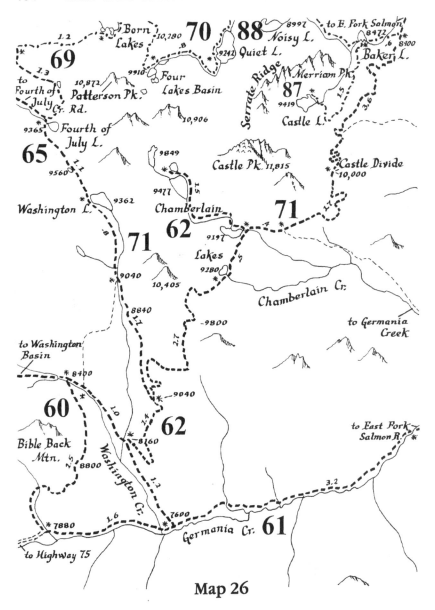

Map 26

The three upper lakes make a beautiful side trip. Hummocks of turf covered with wildflowers surround the turquoise water of the first of these. Above, a maze of orange needles hides the white part of Castle Peak.

To reach the trailhead, follow the access directions above. Hike from the register box at Three Cabins Creek (7,880 feet) down the Germania Creek Trail. At 1.6 miles, .2 mile beyond a log crossing of Washington Creek (7,600

Lowest Chamberlain Lake

feet), turn left on a signed trail up Washington Creek. This trail climbs 1.2 miles to a junction with a trail to Chamberlain Lakes and one going 1 mile to the Washington Basin jeep trail. (With four-wheel drive, you can drive the Washington Basin jeep trail to a ford 2.4 miles from the Three Cabins trailhead, and then hike the 1-mile trail to reach this junction.) By the main trail, the junction is 2.6 miles from the Three Cabins trailhead.

From the junction at the confluence of Washington Lake Creek with Washington Creek, the trail to Chamberlain Lakes makes a .2 mile switchback to the right and then turns back to the left toward ledges. It makes a shorter switchback to the right and then left among small hills to a junction (9,040 feet) with a trail from Washington and Fourth of July lakes at 4.2 miles.

The trail on to Chamberlain Lakes switchbacks up a ridge and goes east along the side of it for .5 mile. Then it goes straight uphill for .5 mile. Two more switchbacks lead to 9,800-foot Chamberlain Divide with the view of Castle Peak at 6 miles. On the other side, the trail cuts northwest through scree and wildflowers, and turns northeast. It follows a tiny inlet down to the first lake (9,280 feet) at 6.9 miles, which has campsites in the trees above it.

Below this lake, the route threads two round meadows to the lowest lake (9,197 feet) near its outlet at 7.4 miles. This point is 6.4 miles from the ford on the Washington Basin jeep trail. Campsites are off-trail on the south shore. At the outlet is a junction with the trail over Castle Divide to Little Boulder

Creek. From here, it is 6.4 miles and a 800-foot climb and 1,840-foot descent to the Little Boulder Creek Trail.

You can continue to the upper lakes from this junction by going along the north side of the lowest lake and then through woods into a meadow with a large campsite on the left. Then cross the creek and climb the right (east) side of a ravine lined with white rocks. Above this is a round green pond in the trees.

From the pond, follow the stream between the lakes on the right (east) side to the long turquoise lake (9,477 feet). Campsites are on the east shore of the lake. Just above the north lobe of the large lake is a small round lake. The highest lake (9,849 feet), 1.5 miles from the lowest lake, can be reached cross-country from the round lake by a gully to the left (west) of the cliffs above it.

63 Horton Peak
Map 27

round trip: 6.2 miles
elevation gain: 2,746 feet
maps: Alturas Lake, Horton Peak
time: 6 1/2 hours
difficulty: strenuous
access: From Highway 75, 45 miles north of Ketchum (just south of the turns for the Fourth of July Creek and Decker Flat roads) turn east on the Valley Road #194 and drive south 4.6 miles. Then turn left onto a spur road signed Horton Peak and go 1 mile to the end of the road. Passenger cars can drive this mile with caution. It is also possible to reach the spur road by turning east on the Pole Creek Road 36 miles north of Ketchum and going north on the Valley Road at 2.3 miles. By this rougher route, it is 7 miles to the spur road.

Horton Peak gives a relief-map view of Alturas, Perkins, Pettit, and Yellow Belly lakes and a 360-degree view of mountains. The mountains include the whole escarpment of the Sawtooths, the pink and gray summits of the Salmon River Mountains, and Castle Peak and the white peaks of the White Clouds. You also see parts of the Boulder and Smoky Mountains, and glimpse a bit of the Lost River Range. From Horton Peak, Castle Peak is an immense flat-topped triangle etched with gullies and streaks of snow.

To reach the trailhead, see the access directions above. The first 1.5 miles have no shade, so an early start will help. Note that the climb is nearly 3,000 feet in only 3 miles. Only a "no motor vehicles" sign marks the beginning of the trail. The trail heads northeast through an aspen grove and then comes out into sagebrush and grass. At .2 mile it switchbacks to the northwest, and at .3

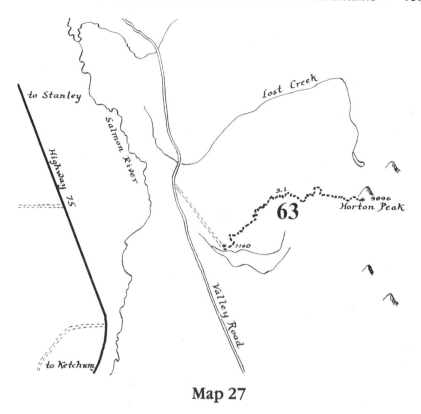

Map 27

mile back to the northeast. Then the path winds back and forth in smaller switchbacks past small outcrops.

At .5 mile the trail reaches the crest of the ridge and follows it up on the right (southeast) side of granite outcrops. At 1 mile is a long switchback to the north into a patch of forest. From the end of the switchback, there is an excellent view of Alturas Lake and the Salmon River. Next, the trail passes wooden poles from the former lookout telephone line. At 1.4 miles the path enters the first section of a Douglas fir forest, still on the ridge crest. From 1.8 to 2.2 miles, the route is in open sagebrush above the last of the aspens. At about 2.3 miles, the trail starts crossing back and forth over a dry creek bed, once again in forest, now of lodgepole pines. It stays in the forest the rest of the way, but the trees gradually thin out to scattered subalpine firs and whitebark pines.

At 2.5 miles is a ridgetop like a false summit. The trail goes straight up this gentle slope for 200 yards. The next section is the steepest, climbing 500 feet in .3 mile. At 2.9 miles the trail flattens out again in a little notch. Then it climbs a bare rocky slope another 100 vertical feet to the lookout at 3.1 miles. The lookout is no longer used regularly, but is still maintained for temporary use in emergencies. It is a historic building, so please treat it with respect.

Looking north from the lookout, down at the head of Lost Creek is a .2 mile-long turquoise sliver of lake with a hook on the end. To the east is a view of meadows along the South Fork of Champion Creek. Castle Peak and the cream-colored White Clouds Peaks section of the White Clouds dominate the view to the northeast. To the west are the jagged Sawtooths and the blue ovals of Alturas, Perkins, and Pettit lakes.

(*Researched with the help of John Moe and Neal Jareczek*)

FOURTH OF JULY CREEK AREA

64 Champion Creek
Maps 24 and 28

round trip: 16 miles
elevation gain: 1,460 feet
elevation loss: 480 feet
highest point: 8,500 feet at Lower Champion Lake
maps: Obsidian, Washington Peak
time: 2 to 3 days
difficulty: strenuous
access: Turn east off Highway 75, 45.7 miles north of Ketchum and go 4.6 miles up the Fourth of July Creek Road. Turn right at a sign for the Champion Creek trailhead and drive .1 mile to a parking area.
warning: This trail is closed to mountain bikes.

The first three miles of this trail are new, constructed to allow use of the Champion Creek Trail to Champion Lakes, a trail that had been blocked by posted private land. The new trail has excellent views of the southern end of the Sawtooths: such as McDonald and Snowyside peaks and the dinosaur-like mountains behind Alice Lake. A wildflower meadow at 1 mile, a view-point to the south at 2 miles, and a beaver pond at 3.5 miles make good destinations for day hikes.

This trail is a safer route to Champion Lakes for horses than the two-mile trail from Pole Creek–Germania Creek Road because it avoids the dangerous slippery section on the north side of the divide. That much shorter trail is still the easiest way for hikers to reach the lakes in spite of the poor access road and the slippery trail section. However, the new trail makes possible a 10-mile through trip from the Pole Creek–Germania Creek Road with a car shuttle, and 8 of those miles are downhill.

From the trailhead mentioned above (7,520 feet), the trail climbs west in subalpine firs. At .5 mile it passes below two long talus slopes of the white

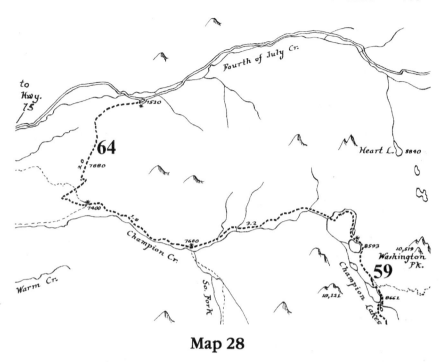

Map 28

rock typical of the White Clouds. At .7 mile, the route turns southwest and at
1 mile reaches the top of a spur ridge and a wildflower meadow that blends
into a sagebrush slope. The view from here is of McDonald Peak, Pettit Lake,
and the mountains above it.

In the next mile, the trail climbs only 40 feet through Douglas fir and
lodgepole underlain by short grasses. At 1.9 miles, the trail switchbacks northeast for .1 mile. Here the view opens up of the mountains and lakes to the
south and west, including Horton Peak, Abes Chair, McDonald Peak,
Snowyside Peak, and Pettit and Alturas Lakes.

At 2 miles, the trail switchbacks southwest, then at 2.2 miles crosses an
old trail connecting with a jeep trail to a ranch on Milky Creek. This old trail
crosses the main trail here and intersects it again at the 3-mile point. The
Forest Service blocked off this old trail to make finding the correct route less
confusing. From the first intersection with the old trail, the main trail descends to the northwest and then cuts back to the east at 2.5 miles. For this
mile, the trail is mostly in sagebrush with occasional stands of aspen, Douglas fir and lodgepole. A signed junction is at 3 miles with the trail down to
the old, closed Champion Creek trailhead.

The trail on up the creek stays out of the creek bottom a few feet to avoid
mud, but in this first mile of the canyon, only wooded ridges are visible. At

3.2 miles, the route descends closer to the creek in Douglas fir and lodgepole. A beaver pond of about one acre appears to the right of the trail at 3.5 miles. At 3.7 miles, the trail wanders through a grassy meadow with willows.

At 4.8 miles is a junction with the South Fork of Champion Creek Trail, and a view up that drainage. Between 5.3 and 7.2 miles, the trail fords four side creeks. At about 7 miles, you can look across the canyon at the wrinkled face of the 10,121-foot mountain that dominates the lower lake. A small teardrop-shaped pond is at 7.9 miles, and at 8 miles, the trail reaches Lower Champion Lake. Before July 15, the last mile below the lakes is usually snow-covered and muddy and therefore not recommended. Trying to travel this section too soon will damage the trail and may be dangerous.

(Researched with the help of Neal and Susan Jareczek)

65 Fourth of July and Washington Lakes
Maps 24 and 26

round trip: 5.8 miles
elevation gain: 800 feet
elevation loss (return climb): 200 feet
highest point: 9,560 feet
maps: Washington Peak, Boulder Chain Lakes
time: 5 hours
difficulty: easy
access: Drive 46.7 miles north of Ketchum and turn right (east) onto the gravel
    Fourth of July Creek Road and go 10.1 miles to the trailhead transfer camp.
warning: This trail is heavily used. For solitude, choose another.

Triangular gray cliffs flank the gray and orange sliced-off face of Patterson Peak. Below the peak, wildflowers color the meadows around shallow, green Fourth of July Lake. Over a ridge, an orange wall of crumbled cliffs and scree turns to white at the lower end of blue-green Washington Lake. Meadows on the trail side of this lake thrust two grassy peninsulas into the water. Since the last edition of this book, the road has been reconstructed to a gravel surface suitable for passenger cars.

To reach the trailhead (8,760 feet), follow the access directions above. Although the road continues beyond the trailhead, which has parking for about 30 cars, no parking is allowed beyond it, and about .2 mile farther is a locked gate.

From the trailhead, the trail crosses Fourth of July Creek on a log bridge to the right (south) at 100 yards and climbs along the creek in the trees. It crosses the Phyllis Lake jeep road at .2 mile and a side creek a few yards beyond it. Old mine buildings are across the canyon at .4 mile, as are meadows full of willows.

At .7 mile, the route joins the closed trail from the old trailhead, although it has been blocked off at a sign for the correct trail. From here on, the route of the trail and the creeks it crosses vary from those shown on the topographic map.

At .7 mile, the trail crosses the main creek on a flattened log to the left (north) side, then bridges a side creek at .8 mile only 20 feet from the main creek. The trail crosses to the left side of another creek at 1 mile, but there is still another creek in a meadow to the left of the trail.

The ground flattens out in forest as you approach a junction with a trail to Ants Basin and Warm Springs Creek at 1.4 miles. Turn right (south) here and walk over to the outlet just below the lake (9,365 feet) at 1.5 miles. There are campsites back in the trees across the outlet and on the north side of the lake.

After fording the outlet, the trail to Washington Lake climbs a ridge among lodgepoles with glimpses of the Sawtooths. At the flat, sandy top of the divide (9,560 feet) at 2.6 miles is a tiny snow pond. From here, the route descends an open slope to Washington Lake (9,362 feet) at 2.9 miles, crossing an inlet on the way. There are a few campsites in trees at the south end of the lake. From a pond in a meadow above the west shore of the lake, it is possible to climb south-southwest between ledges to a tiny unnamed lake at 9,480 feet.

66 Phyllis Lake
Map 24

round trip: 4 miles
elevation gain: 700 feet
elevation loss (return climb): 240 feet
highest point: 9,240 feet
map: Washington Peak
time: 6 1/2 hours
difficulty: moderate
access: On Highway 75, 45.7 miles north of Ketchum, turn right (east) on the gravel Fourth of July Creek Road and drive 10.1 miles to the new trailhead.

At Phyllis Lake, a white peak with slanting brown stripes contrasts with water so green it appears to have a light inside it. From this peak, cliffs with ribbon stripes of orange and brown extend to a rounded burnt orange shoulder of Washington Peak. Under this summit, a rocky peninsula guards a lime-green meadow where buttercups and marsh marigolds appear the minute the snow melts.

This hike description begins at the Fourth of July Creek trailhead. From the trailhead, walk up the new trail .2 mile to where it crosses the Phyllis Lake jeep trail and turn right (south) on the jeep trail. (If you have four-wheel drive, you can drive this track to within .2 mile of Phyllis Lake.) As you walk along the track, avoid roads downhill to the right and uphill to a prospect. The main road descends gently to a stream (8,980 feet) at 1.3 miles. The slopes are wooded with some open areas.

Across the stream, the road climbs through thick woods and over tiny streams to a junction at 1.7 miles. (The right (west) fork which goes to mines at the head of the canyon gives access to Lightning Lake.) Take the left (southeast) fork of the road (not shown on the topographic map), which ends in 300 yards. From its end, a path climbs left of a creek, then crosses it in a meadow at 1.8 miles and ascends a ravine, where the trail tread fades. At 1.9 miles, a path reappears and turns gradually right (south) over a low saddle to the lake (9,200 feet) at 2 miles.

67 Lightning Lake
Map 24

round trip: 5.8 miles (1.6 miles cross country)
elevation gain: 1,100 feet
elevation loss (return climb): 240 feet
this section one way: 1.2 miles, 640-foot gain, 40-foot loss
highest point: 9,600 feet
map: Washington Peak
time: 7 hours
difficulty: moderate
access: On Highway 75, 45.7 miles north of Ketchum, turn right (east) on the Fourth of July Creek Road and drive 10.1 miles to the new trailhead. Walk along the new trail to where it crosses the Phyllis Lake jeep trail at .2 mile and then walk 1.5 miles up the jeep trail to a split in the track. If you have four-wheel drive, you can drive to this point.

A furrowed mountain and a scalloped ridge enclose Lightning Lake in a cup of rocks. A few whitebark pines guard the natural rock dam which prevents the blue green water from spilling in wet years, but in dry years, the lake will be only a pool in the rocks. Wildflower meadows, the small green rectangle of Thunder Lake, and the pale amber saucer of a pond make the route colorful.

This hike description begins on the old jeep road to Phyllis Lake at the point where it branches (8,980 feet) 1.7 miles from the Fourth of July Creek trailhead. To reach this point, see the directions given above. The left fork of the jeep road goes a few yards toward Phyllis Lake and ends.

Walk down the right branch of the road through a gate .2 mile from the junction. The log cabin and mine diggings are beyond. This is private prop-

Lightning Lake

erty, so stay well away from the cabin and mine. Where a side road goes up to a tunnel, keep right (northwest) on the jeep trail down into a meadow.

Turn left (west) off the road at .4 mile at the creek in the meadow and climb a small stream to a bog. Circle the wet area on the right (north) and go over a small ridge (9,320 feet) to the outlet of Thunder Lake. Ascend the outlet on the left (east) side to the small green lake (9,200 feet) at .7 mile. Walk along the left (east) side of it and its inlet through rocks and grass. Cross grass and dead logs to reach an amber pond at 1 mile. Go right (west) around the pond and up the right side of its inlet through rocks to Lightning Lake (9,600 feet) at 1.2 miles.

68 Heart and Six Lakes
Map 24

round trip: 4 miles
elevation gain: 1,030 feet
elevation loss (return climb): 40 feet
highest point: 9,240 feet
map: Washington Peak
time: 4 hours
difficulty: cross-country
access: On Highway 75, 45.7 miles north of Ketchum, turn right (east) on the gravel Fourth of July Creek Road and drive 8.7 miles to an unmarked but graveled pullout about .5 mile above a big campsite in the trees. At the right spot, a chocolate brown mountain looms ahead up the canyon of Fourth of July Creek.
caution: This hike climbs 600 feet in a mile with slippery slopes, downed timber, and a difficult ford at the beginning.

At the upper end of Heart Lake, the reflections of a charcoal gray lava knoll color the green water inky blue. In the distance behind it, a pearl gray peak spreads into a triangle. East of Heart Lake, the second of the six lakes huddles under a corrugated wall that bristles with gray, brown and orange needles. Below the wall, blobs of chocolate brown rock melt into the talus edging the lake. The turquoise water of the highest lake mirrors whitebark pines and gentler, gray peaks at the head of the canyon.

To reach the beginning of this hike at 8,250 feet, follow the access directions given above. Drop south from the road pullout down to Fourth of July Creek. Carefully ford the creek. This ford will be hazardous in early summer and until August in wet years. Then climb south up the west (right) side of the outlet of Heart Lake. At an open area, climb the side of the gorge the creek runs in to less steep ground.

At .5 mile descend the hillside to a flat meadow. For the easiest walking, cross to the left (east) side of the creek for 150 yards and then back to the west side. At the lower end of a second meadow, go over to the east side of the creek and back again a second time. For the last .2 mile, climb along the right (west) side of the creek through forest to the lake (8,840 feet) at 1 mile. Although the hike is short, it is not recommended for small children or the elderly because of the ford, downed timber, and steep slopes.

To reach the higher lakes, go left (east) around Heart Lake to a creek east of the charcoal cliffs. Climb the meadow on the right (south) of the inlet along a 15-foot high ridge. Where the meadow turns into talus, turn right (south) to the lake at 1.5 miles.

Circle this lake on the right (west) along a wooded slope. At the southwest corner of the lake, climb a gully leading up the wooded knoll separating the lakes. From it, descend to a peninsula on the north edge of the highest lake (9,020 feet) at 2 miles. The other three lakes are small ponds west of the second lake.

69 Born Lakes
Maps 24, 26, and 33

round trip: 9.8 miles to the highest lake
elevation gain: 1,360 feet
elevation loss (return climb): 500 feet
this section one way: 3.4 miles, 825-foot gain, 500-foot loss
highest point: 9,900 feet
maps: Washington Peak, Boulder Chain Lakes
time: 8 hours
difficulty: partly cross-country
access: Using the directions for Hike 65 (Fourth of July and Washington Lakes), hike to the junction just below that lake.

Talus, wildflower meadows, subalpine firs and whitebark pines enclose the seven tiny ponds of the Born Lakes below orange and gray splintered crags. The largest lake is only 200 yards across, so these lakes seem newborn, but they are actually named for a prospector named Boren. Above the highest lake, a large gray pinnacle on a fractured ridge guards a notch called the Devils Staircase. At sunset, the alpenglow paints the ridge salmon pink. On the way to Born Lakes, the green velvet bench of Ants Basin gives a view across the abyss of Warm Springs Canyon to some of the White Cloud Peaks gleaming like white chalk. This entire range of mountains is called the White Clouds, but among them is a single chain known as the "White Cloud Peaks" for its color and the lack of individual names. It is mostly white rock, a metamorphosed limestone similar to marble but containing silica, too.

Pass between Born Lakes and Four Lakes Basin

To reach the beginning of this hike description, follow directions in Hike 65 to hike to the junction just below Fourth of July Lake, 1.4 miles and a 525-foot climb above the trailhead. At the junction, take the left branch of the trail northeast. The right one goes a few yards to Fourth of July Lake and then on to Washington Lake.

The trail that give access to Born Lakes heads northeast and then north. At .2 mile, it crosses a meadow where a side path comes up from Fourth of July Lake. The route continues northeast with fine views of this lake and the Sawtooths, then at .3 mile cuts back to the northwest. At .5 mile, it passes a small green pond in talus. The trail climbs west along the side of the ridge and zigzags to a saddle (9,900 feet) with the view of the white peaks at 1.1 miles.

The path parallels the saddle for 100 yards, then switchbacks down to Ants Basin (9,560 feet) at 1.3 miles, where it disappears. The trail from Ants Basin down into the Warm Springs Canyon is so seldom used there is no trail tread for it across the basin. This trail descends 1,100 feet in 1.5 miles to the Warm Springs Creek Trail, joining it 4.8 miles above the upper end of The Meadows. From that junction, the Warm Springs Creek Trail continues up the canyon to the third Born Lake.

Most hikers go directly to Born Lakes from Ants Basin without descending into the canyon. To do this, go east from the bottom of the steep slope to the southeast corner of Ants Basin at 1.7 miles. Descend a gully to the northeast and then go east across the lower edge of a talus slope, above the trees. Below the talus slope at the bottom of the valley is a meadow with a pond in it. The first Born Lake (9,420 feet) is at 2.5 miles. Go along the right (south) edge of the lake and over a small ridge to the second lake at 4 miles. To reach the third lake, climb either side of the inlet past a small pond or cut over a wooded hillside directly to it. Above the north side of the third lake (9,555 feet), traces of the trail coming up from Warm Springs Canyon can be found on the left (west) side of the creek between the third and fourth lakes. Climb along that creek through open country with clumps of whitebark pines to the fourth lake, which is set in the rocks (9,700 feet) 3.4 miles from Fourth of July Lake.

70 Born Lakes to Quiet Lake Through Four Lakes Basin
Maps 26 and 33

round trip: 13.4 miles
elevation gain: 2,085 feet
elevation loss (return climb): 1,538 feet
this section one-way: 1.8 miles, 725-foot gain, 1,038-foot loss
highest point: 10,280 feet
maps: Washington Peak, Boulder Chain Lakes
time: 3 to 4 days
difficulty: expert (all cross-country)
access: Hike to the third Born Lake at 9,555 feet. For directions see Hike 65 (Fourth of July Lake and Washington Lakes) and Hike 69 (Born Lakes).
caution: Cornices above Four Lakes Basin on this route can be hazardous until mid-August, but this divide is a much safer way of making a loop trip in the White Clouds than crossing from Born Lakes to the Boulder Chain Lakes over the hazardous pass sometimes called the Devils Staircase.

From the off-trail pass between Born Lakes and Four Lakes Basin, hikers see the crinkled ridges of Patterson Peak, the snow-patched, dark blue Sawtooths, and the great gabled wall of Castle Peak. At the four turquoise lakes in Four Lakes Basin, the few stunted whitebark pines grow only above the lakes on talus mounds where it is a little warmer than at lake level.

To reach the beginning of this cross-country route, hike to the third Born Lake at 9,555 feet, following the directions in the hikes listed above. From the east end of the lake, go south up a ravine to a big grassy basin on the side of the upper canyon. From the basin, zigzag up the greener parts of the scree toward the low point on the skyline (10,280 feet).

On the other side, descend a few feet to the large flat area (10,200 feet) shown on the map at .5 mile. To reach the lakes from here, you must first get around a big snowbank with a cornice at the southeast edge of the flat area. It is easiest to go to the right (southwest) about .2 mile along a ledge above cliffs until the slope lessens enough to walk down to Emerald Lake (9,910 feet) 1 mile from the third Born Lake. Late in the season, you can go to the left (east) end of the cornice and drop southeast to the creek between Emerald and Cornice Lakes. You can't drop directly to Cornice Lake from the saddle because of cliffs. The other two lakes, Rock and Glacier, are south of Emerald Lake.

To descend to Quiet Lake, go along the north side of Cornice Lake and its outlet, threading through boulders when the creek disappears. Trees and earth between the rocks begin again at about 1.4 miles. At 1.6 miles, leave the outlet at a flat area at 9,400 feet and descend a ravine east-northeast to the upper end of the lake (9,242 feet) at 1.8 miles.

71 Washington Lake to Castle Divide and Baker Lake Junction

Maps 24, 25, 26, and 33

round trip: 28 miles
elevation gain: 2,555 feet
elevation loss (return climb): 1,926 feet
this section one way: 11.8 miles, 1,835-foot gain, 1,725-foot loss
highest point: 10,000 feet
map: Boulder Chain Lakes
time: 3 to 4 days
difficulty: strenuous
access: Follow directions for Hike 65 (Fourth of July and Washington Lakes) to hike to Washington Lake, 2.6 miles from the trailhead.
caution: Castle Divide is usually closed by snow until early to mid-August. To avoid danger and to avoid damaging soils, wait until the snow melts from the trail before traveling it.

From Castle Divide, the view east is of Castle Peak and its white shoulders, jagged towers on Serrate Ridge,and the orange wall behind the Boulder Chain Lakes. Farther east the swirled stripes of Granite Peak near Frog Lake lead to the red rocks of Red Ridge. Closer to the divide, the white scree ridge above Castle Lake joins the white section of Castle Peak. The rerouting of the trail at Fourth of July Creek and over Chamberlain and Castle divides since the last edition of the book has lengthened the round trip by 5.4 miles.

To reach the beginning of this hike description, follow directions in the hikes listed above to hike to Washington Lake (9,362 feet). From the lower

Quiet Lake and Merriam Peak

end of the lake, the trail descends to a flat meadow at .5 mile, and at .8 mile in
a larger meadow, it crosses Washington Lake Creek to the left (east). There are

campsites on a knoll above the crossing. In the meadow is a junction with a section of the Washington Lake Trail not shown on the topographic map. This section descends Washington Lake Creek and climbs over a ridge to Washington Creek, .2 mile downstream from the Washington Basin jeep trail.

Just before the crossing of Washington Creek at .8 mile (9,040 feet), a dry gorge to the right (west) divides a pink hump of rock from a white hump. Up this gorge is an unnamed lake at 9,480 feet, but it is more easily reached from the pond just west of Washington Lake.

Beyond the ford, the trail to Chamberlain Lakes descends through lodgepoles, sagebrush and meadows to 8,840 feet, and then begins to climb the side of the canyon. It turns east to join the Livingston-Castle Divide Trail at 2.5 miles (9,040 feet).

From here the route is identical for 3.2 miles to the one described under Chamberlain Lakes. It climbs over a 9,800-foot divide and passes two of the lakes. For detailed directions, see Hike 62 (Chamberlain Lakes from Three Cabins Creek). This description resumes at the lowest of the Chamberlain Lakes (9,197 feet) directly under Castle Peak, at a point 5.7 miles from Washington Lake.

From the lowest Chamberlain Lake, the Castle Divide Trail climbs through rolling meadows to a junction (9,240 feet) at 6.1 miles with a trail down Chamberlain Creek. This little-used trail drops 2,180 feet in 3.5 miles to Germania Creek, meeting it 6.2 miles from Three Cabins Creek.

The main trail climbs over a ridge spur in the trees and crosses meadows with a view of the Boulder Mountains. The path then ascends scree and talus under red-orange rock walls. It circles to the right of a small hill marked 9,643 on the topographic map, and makes a big switchback to the right and then left below the summit pitch. Just below the top, the trail becomes steeper. At 7.8 miles is the summit of the divide (10,000 feet) between pink outcrops and the white shoulders of Castle Peak.

On the other side, the trail zigzags down in four switchbacks through grassy scree to the trees. Then it winds and zigzags down through forest to a junction (8,400 feet) at 11.4 miles with a .6 mile path to Baker Lake. The round trip for this hike is figured from this junction. The Livingston-Castle Divide Trail continues to a junction with the Little Boulder Creek Trail at 12.1 miles. This section is covered in Hike 86 (Boulder Chain to Baker Lakes). There is no water on the trail between Chamberlain Lakes and a stream one mile north of the divide.

OBSIDIAN AREA

72 The Meadows on Warm Springs Creek
Map 29

round trip: 7.4 miles to the meadows, 11.4 miles to a view up the canyon
elevation gain: 267 feet
elevation loss (return climb): 717 feet
highest point: 8,000 feet
map: Washington Peak
time: 5 1/2 to 7 1/2 hours
difficulty: moderate to strenuous
access: On Highway 75, 47.4 miles north of Ketchum, turn right (east) on the primitive Fisher Creek Road, and drive 6.8 miles to the Aztec Mine.
caution: The Fisher Creek Road and the first mile of the trail are part of a popular loop for mountain bicyclists and motorcyclists, so trail users need to watch for this traffic.

More than three miles of wide green meadows stretch along Warm Springs Creek half way between Robinson Bar and Born Lakes. The meadows carpeting the bottom of the canyon and the green wooded ridges hedging it in form an all-green world. From the upper end of The Meadows, an open hillside above a marshy pond gives a view of the gray and white crumbly peaks of the upper canyon. A shady downhill access trail begins at the old brown Aztec Mine buildings, which are roofed in warped rusty tin.

To reach the trailhead, follow the access directions above. The road can be very muddy in early season. The Aztec Mine buildings are picturesque, historic, and on private property, so respect them. From 8,000 feet, the trail winds down through woods as an old road, passing granite outcrops. At 1 mile is a junction (7,600 feet) with the Pigtail Creek Trail from the west. This two-mile trail connects with the Williams Creek Trail which goes west to Highway 75 near Obsidian.

The main trail continues through open grass and sagebrush, and enters woods and a meadow. At 2.4 miles, it circles the base of a granite knoll, then fords the creek to the east. At 2.8 miles, the path crosses back over the creek in a sandy place. It continues in woods, flattening out near a junction at 3.5 miles with another old road from the north. This road is the trail down Warm Springs Creek that goes 11.2 miles with a 1,360-foot elevation loss to a trailhead closed by private property at Robinson Bar.

At this junction, take the right branch southeast .2 mile to the edge of The Meadows (7,300 feet). This point makes a good day hike destination. Those

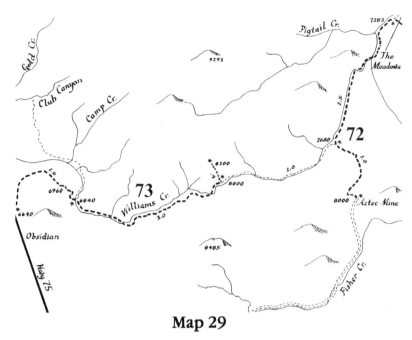

Map 29

eager to glimpse the upper canyon can turn right and continue south along the track at the west edge of The Meadows.

Now, the road turns to a trail and then comes close to the creek at 4 miles. Where there are gates, replace the gate poles or climb over them to keep the cows where they belong. As you follow the trail along the west edge of The Meadows at 4.8 miles, look for blazed posts which mark a route across it. There is no trail tread across the meadows.

Using the posts as a guide, find your way to the creek and ford it to the east. This will be difficult in early summer. The trail reappears at the edge of the woods at 5 miles. It turns east with the canyon, and at 5.7 miles, climbs 100 feet up the side of the canyon to an open area (7,550 feet). This spot gives a view of some of the peaks of the upper canyon and of a pond below. There is a campsite by the creek near the pond.

73 Williams Creek Trail
Map 29

round trip: 10 miles
elevation gain: 1,560 feet
elevation loss (return climb): 120 feet
highest point: 8,200 feet
map: Obsidian

time: 7 1/2 hours
difficulty: moderate
access: Park at the trailhead on the east side of Highway 75, 49.7 miles north of Ketchum.
caution: This trail is popular with bicyclists and motorcyclists. Therefore all trail users should watch carefully for traffic.

A ridge above this trail gives a close view of the white section of the White Clouds. In late afternoon, when the sun shines on this side of the peaks, they resemble mounds of vanilla ice cream. From the ridge, you also see a panorama of the Sawtooths that emphasizes the glacial sculpture below the teeth. The gradual, shady climb is pleasant on a warm day. Because the trail starts at the highway and the summit is only 8,000 feet, this route provides a way into the White Clouds when access roads and most trails are still closed by snow and mud.

To reach the trailhead, follow the directions above. At the beginning of the trail, keep well away from the house near it because it is private land. Have the courtesy to be as quiet as possible so as not to disturb the residents. Wheel motorcycles past the house before starting them up.

The trail angles along the side of a sagebrush hill and curves at .4 mile to the right (east) into lodgepoles. At .8 mile, it turns southeast at a small meadow. The path switchbacks over a 320-foot ridge and then descends 120 feet of sagebrush into a teardrop-shaped meadow at 1.5 miles. The trail crosses Williams Creek on a bridge at the lower end of the meadow at 1.6 miles (6,840 feet) and joins a trail from the Idaho Rocky Mountain Ranch. The Williams Creek Trail is not shown on the topographic map until it joins this trail.

The main trail goes east along the meadow, then at 1.8 miles, curves left (north). At 2.5 miles, it crosses to the right (south) of the creek on a culvert. Now the trail curves in and out of ravines across from sagebrush slopes dotted with splintered granite outcrops. At 4.4 miles, it goes back to the left (north) side of the creek. As it begins to climb a sagebrush slope, an old trail joins from the left. From this slope, Mt. Heyburn is visible.

Next, the way edges a basin of lodgepoles to the wooded 8,000-foot summit at 4.6 miles. There is no view from this point. The trail drops 400 feet on the other side in 2 miles to reach the trail from the Aztec Mine to The Meadows.

At the summit to view the Sawtooths and White Clouds, turn left (north) off the trail up a gentle ridge. The ridge becomes open and the Sawtooths appear at 4.8 miles and the White Clouds at 5 miles at about 8,200 feet.

74 Boundary Creek Trail, Casino Lakes and Big Casino Creek

Map 30

through trip: 11.4 miles
elevation gain: 2,760 feet
elevation loss: 3,300 feet
highest point: 9,560 feet
maps: Casino Lakes, East Basin Creek
time: 10 hours
difficulty: strenuous
access: From Highway 75, turn right (east) 54.7 miles north of Ketchum at a
sign for the Boundary Creek Trail. Drive .8 mile to the end of the dirt road.
Avoid the side roads to the cabins.

Wooded hills, talus ridges and white granite knolls shadow the marsh grass
that wreathes the shores of the three Casino Lakes. At the lower lake, asters,
gentians, elephant's head, and Jacob's ladder decorate a marshy garden. From
the highest point on the trail, the long blue ribbon of Redfish Lake glistens
below the overlapping zigzags of the Sawtooths. From here, the white peaks
of the White Clouds appear to the south and the pink and tan summits of the
Salmon River Mountains to the north. From the lakes, the Big Casino Trail
descends to the Salmon River beside the flowers and moss-covered rocks of a
shady canyon.

Making a through trip from Boundary Creek to the Salmon River instead of
returning to Boundary Creek avoids a 960-foot return climb. For this reason
the hike is described as a through trip.

To reach the Boundary Creek trailhead, follow the access directions above.
From the parking area (6,800 feet), the trail winds through sagebrush into
aspen, lodgepole and Douglas fir. At .5 mile, a trail joins from cabins across the
creek. Here, the main route turns north, zigzagging up a ridge. From an open
sagebrush area at 1.3 miles, there are views of Redfish Lake and the Sawtooths.

On a saddle (8,760 feet) at 2.8 miles at the top of the main ridge, the trail
returns to forest. Here, the unsigned Sunny Gulch Trail joins from the left. This
trail goes 5.2 miles with a 160-foot gain and 2,400-foot loss to the edge of the
Salmon River opposite the Sunny Gulch Campground, but it has no bridge
across the river. On the Sunny Gulch Trail, 3.5 miles west of its junction with
the Boundary Creek Trail, the Little Casino Creek Trail turns off to the north. It
goes 5.5 miles with a 1,200-foot loss to the Casino Creek Road. (The Sunny
Gulch Trail is not shown on the topographic map from its junction with the
Little Casino Creek Trail to the Salmon River.)

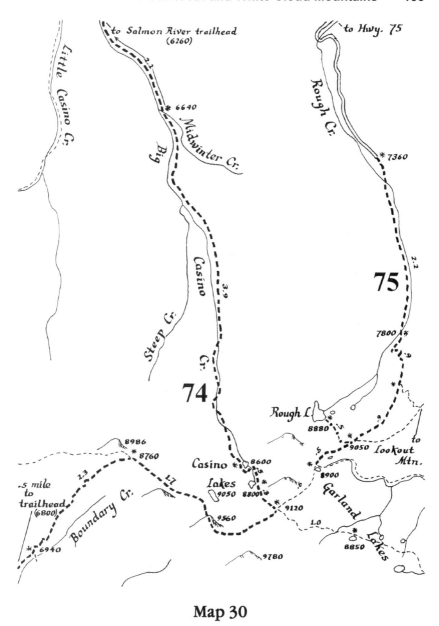

Map 30

From the saddle, continue on the Boundary Creek Trail to the right (southeast). It winds in trees on the right (west) side of the ridge through a narrow meadow, a dry grass flat, and a lush green meadow with springs. At 3.3 miles, the trail climbs onto and follows the crest of the ridge, reaching an elevation of 9,560 feet at 3.5 miles. From here, the view includes the Sawtooths, the Salmon River and White Cloud Mountains and the highest Casino Lake.

The path descends to a saddle (9,560 feet) and drops to the east along a spur ridge. This ridge is sprinkled with subalpine fir, lupine, and red mountain heather. At 4.2 miles, the route passes left of a large wet meadow with campsites and crosses a stream (not shown on the map) to the right (south). At 4.5 miles just east of a 9,120 foot-saddle is a junction with the Garland Creek and South Martin-Big Casino trails.

For your information, from this junction the Garland Creek Trail joins the Rough Creek Trail in a mile at one of the Garland Lakes, and then drops 2,240 feet in 5 miles down Garland Creek to Warm Springs Creek. The trail to the south passes near two of the Garland Lakes on the way to Martin Creek at 4.3 miles, 1,320 feet below.

From the junction, take the Big Casino Trail north. It crosses a stream to the west and then back to the east as it descends to the first of the marshy Casino Lakes (8,800 feet) at 4.8 miles. The trail continues to the lowest lake (8,600 feet), descending through forest on the right (east) of the creek, then crossing to the west just before the lake at 5.3 miles.

To reach the highest lake at 9,040 feet, cross-country hiking is needed. There are two possible routes. The simplest begins back at the 9,560-foot saddle. At that point, descend northeast and north 520 feet in .5 mile down a gully. The other route is to go west .5 mile from the first lake on the trail.

At the lowest lake, the main trail circles the south shore in woods, and goes downhill in a lodgepole forest to cross a small side stream. The path fords the main creek to the east at 5.9 miles. There are four more fords in the next mile before the route finally stays on the east (right) side of the creek. A talus slope at 7 miles is followed by Douglas firs and rocks. The trail hops a side stream well above the main creek at 7.8 miles. At 8.5 miles, it follows a stream bed for .5 mile in a level lodgepole forest between Big Casino and Midwinter Creeks, crossing tiny Midwinter Creek at 9.2 miles.

When the forest opens out and the valley widens, two rock outcrops resemble crocodiles. At 10.8 miles, the trail fords the creek to the left (west) to an old road and follows it. This track goes back over to the right side of the creek at 11 miles, and in 200 yards comes to a posted, locked gate. Here, ford the creek back to the left (west) at a crossing not shown on the topographic map. At 11.4 miles, the trail reaches the Big Casino Creek trailhead (6,260 feet). The bridge over the Salmon River to Highway 75 at Casino Creek is .2 mile away and Stanley is 3 miles west of the bridge.

ROUGH CREEK AREA

75 Rough and Garland Lakes
Map 30

round trip: 9 miles to Rough Lake with 1 mile cross-country, 9 miles for the first Garland Lake

elevation gain: 1,790 feet for Rough Lake; 1,690 feet for the first Garland Lake

elevation loss (return climb): 240 feet for Rough Lake, 150 feet for the first Garland Lake

side trip to other Garland Lakes: 2.4 miles one way, 320-foot gain, 240-foot loss

highest point: 9,160 feet

map: Casino Lakes

time: 7 1/2 hours for Rough Lake, 10 hours for all the Garland Lakes

difficulty: strenuous; expert ability for Rough Lake

access: Drive 10 miles northeast of Stanley on Highway 75. Just beyond Basin Creek, turn right (south) on a bridge over the Salmon River and drive 4.2 miles on the dirt Rough Creek Road to a signed trailhead.

Near the moss and wildflowers of the inlet, a round-topped 100-foot cliff falls into the blue-green water of Rough Lake. Along the shores grow whitebark pine, subalpine fir, Labrador tea, red mountain heather, and yellow monkey flower. The first amber-colored Garland Lake sits in a basin of grasses, kalmia, alpine buttercup, tiny firs, and red and white mountain heather. Water pipits sometimes fly along the shore and nest in the heather. From a saddle on the trail, there is a distant view of the high peaks of the White Clouds.

To reach the trailhead (7,360 feet), follow the access directions above. A logging road heads to the right at the trailhead, but the trail goes left (south) through shady woods. The trail crosses the creek on a log to the right (west) side at .3 mile. It climbs above the creek, but then returns to it and crosses back to the left (east) at 2.2 miles. The path makes a big switchback to the left (east) at 2.5 miles and then ascends steeply to a turnoff for Lookout Mountain at 3.1 miles. This side trail climbs 400 feet in 2 miles to the 9,984-foot summit.

Continue on the main trail, which curves west around the head of the canyon. There are several creek crossings on the way to a saddle (9,050 feet) at 4 miles. Just before the saddle, another trail to Lookout Mountain comes in from the east.

To reach Rough Lake from the saddle, leave the trail and climb west up the ridge until the slope lessens at about 9,160 feet. Then turn right (north) and descend 240 feet to the lake (8,880 feet) at 4.5 miles.

To reach the Garland Lakes, stay on the trail at the saddle, and descend it to the southwest. The Garland Creek Trail turns off part way down, not at the first lake as shown on the map. This trail descends Garland Creek 2,040 feet in 6.8 miles to the Warm Springs Creek Trail near the mouth of Swimm Creek, 3.5 miles below The Meadows.

Continue on the main trail past a pond. The first tiny Garland Lake (8,900 feet) is at 4.5 miles. To reach the other lakes, go southwest on the same trail for .6 mile. At a four-way junction, turn left (east) onto the Martin Creek Trail. Two additional Garland Lakes are along this trail. The first (8,850 feet) is 1 mile from the junction. To reach the second (8,800 feet), turn south off the trail 1.6 miles from the junction and walk .2 mile.

SLATE CREEK AREA

76 Hoodoo Lake
Map 31

round trip: 5 miles
elevation gain: 1,727 feet
highest point: 8,677 feet
map: Robinson Bar
time: 4 to 5 hours
difficulty: moderate, but the old road that serves as the trail has many confusing spurs and varies from what the topographic map shows.
access: Highway 75 crosses the Salmon River to the south side 23.7 miles northeast of Stanley. Just across the bridge, turn right (west) on a dirt road along the river. At .8 mile, turn left (south) on a rocky dirt road up Slate Creek and drive to a gate at 7.1 miles. The last 1.2 miles of the road are rough, rocky, and not maintained.

At the head of emerald-green Hoodoo Lake, a C-shaped groove, often filled with snow, indents the face of a gray mountain, which is one of the White Cloud Peaks. A burnt orange ridge bristling with trees and rock towers extends from it along the east side of the lake. Behind this, a wide triangle summit with one scalloped side stands across the canyon of Slate Creek. Creeping common juniper, marsh grass and shrubby cinquefoil line the shores of this lake, whose level was raised years ago by a small earthen dam.

To reach the trailhead, follow the access directions above. Park before reaching the gate, which is at about 6,950 feet. Walk through the gate, passing a "no motorized vehicles" sign, a hot spring, an inactive mine, and the high sandy rim of an old tailings pond. Do not enter any of the buildings. They are private property and contain dangerous mine shafts. Follow the dirt road around

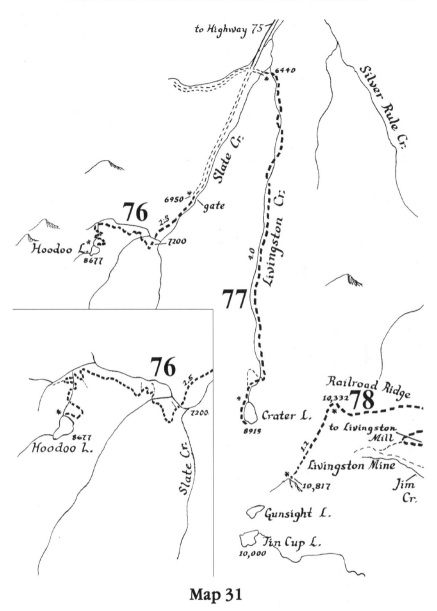

Map 31

the tailings pond and cross to the south side of the outlet of the lake on a culvert. Here at .5 mile the road splits. There are no signs.

Take the right (west) fork of the old road. Right away there is a spur track to the right, which you must avoid. Instead, head southwest on the large switchback shown on the topographic map. The road switches back to the right (northwest) toward the creek at .9 mile. At 1.2 miles the track crosses a

Hikers on the Hoodoo Lake Trail

side branch of the creek on a culvert and curves to the right. At the next switchback, the first of the three or four little switchbacks shown on the map between 7,600 and 7,800 feet, a road goes off to the right over big fallen rocks. Below this switchback, there is a waterfall on the creek.

Avoid the rock-covered road, and switchback to the left on the original road. It soon switchbacks to the right then left again. Part way along this switchback, avoid another road that goes off to the right. Finally, at 1.4 miles, the road turns straight up the canyon, passing to the right (north) of a talus slope at 1.5 miles. The track continues west along the side of the canyon above the creek into the trees.

At 1.8 miles, the road switchbacks left and then right at 8,200 feet. For the next half mile, the road is much different than it is shown on the topographic map. Where it switchbacks to the right, it runs under a high gravel bank. At this corner, a track goes off to the left (southeast) for 100 yards and ends. Keep to the right on the main road under the gravel bank to where the road crosses a side creek that falls north into the east-west running main creek. Do not go straight ahead on the road here because it ends.

Instead, turn left (south) and walk up the little side creek for 50 yards, which will not be a problem after mid-July. You soon see a road going off to the right at 2 miles. Walk along it and in a few yards, it switchbacks to the left and ends at the creek. Cross the creek here to the left (east) bank and climb along the creek on a path for 100 yards or so until you see the road going off to the right across the creek once more.

Follow the road to the right (west). It soon turns straight uphill. After 150 yards, it turns back to the left and crosses the creek to the east bank again. Now it is the same once more as is shown on the topographic map. Continue east on the road which soon has a good view of Slate Creek Canyon. Then the route curves back to the right (west), climbing steeply and comes out on a little knoll above the lake at 2.5 miles.

77 Crater Lake
Map 31

round trip: 8 miles
elevation gain: 2,479 feet
highest point: 8,919 feet
map: Livingston Creek
time: 7 1/2 hours
difficulty: strenuous
access: Drive northeast of Stanley on Highway 75 for 23.7 miles to the south
    side of a bridge over the Salmon River. Turn right (west) on a dirt road
    along the river. At .8 mile, turn right (west) on the dirt Slate Creek Road
    and drive to an unsigned four-way intersection at 5.9 miles. Because there is

little parking at the trailhead and it is on private land, park at this intersection. Then turn left and walk 200 yards across the private land to the beginning of the trail at Slate Creek.

Above the gray talus and cloudy blue water of Crater Lake, three small teeth, joined at the base, block passage across a saddle. To the left of the teeth, mining roads slash the round gravelly end of Railroad Ridge. To the right of the teeth, layers of white rock striped with dark gray tip up at each end, resembling a warped pile of weathered plywood. This mountain is called the Chinese Wall.

To reach the trailhead (6,440 feet), follow the access directions above. Be sure to park at the main road, possibly on an old spur road to the right. The trail is an old mining road beginning at Slate Creek. It is no longer open to motor vehicles and is not shown on the topographic map. First the trail crosses Slate Creek on a wooden footbridge, and goes past a cabin to a gate. Leave the gate as you found it and respect the private property. Beyond the gate, the track crosses Livingston Creek to the left (east) and climbs gently under Douglas firs.

At .5 mile, the track fords two sections of the creek to the right (west), and then returns to the east in 200 yards. Ignore old mining roads which join this track from time to time. Keep on the one nearest to the creek. At about 1 mile, the route fords to the west again, and returns to the left (east) at 1.2 miles. There are logs or rocks at some of the crossings.

The track passes an old log cabin and side stream, and levels out at 2.7 miles across from talus. The route reaches a basin of talus and grass at 3.5 miles. At an old mine tunnel at the head of this basin, the road crosses the creek again to the right (north) and makes a .3 mile-long switchback. To save distance, turn left and climb talus and ledges on the right (north) side of the creek. At 3.8 miles, the creek turns south. At 4 miles, both routes come out on a grassy area above the gray gravel at the lake (8,919 feet).

EAST FORK OF THE SALMON RIVER AREA

78 Railroad Ridge
Maps 32 and 32

round trip: 14 miles
elevation gain: 3,737 feet
elevation loss (return climb): 80 feet
highest point: 10,817 feet

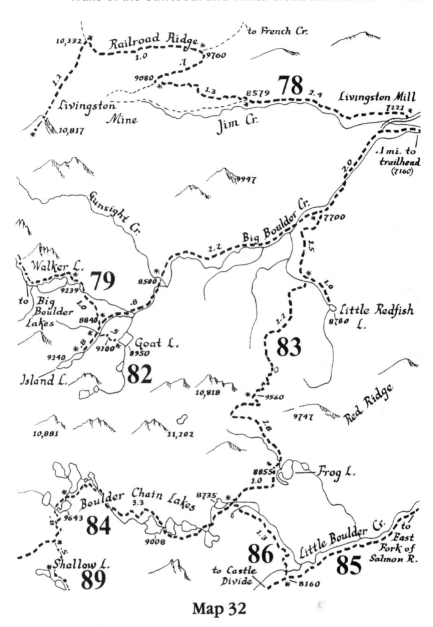

Map 32

map: Livingston Creek

time: 12 hours or 2 days

difficulty: strenuous; expert ability for the last .5 mile

access: On Highway 75, 36.5 miles east of Stanley, turn south on the East
Fork of the Salmon River Road. Drive 14.7 miles on pavement, and 2.9
miles on gravel. At 17.6 miles, turn northwest on the dirt Livingston Mill

Road and drive 4.8 miles. At a sign, turn left and go .2 mile to a parking area unless you have four-wheel drive.

caution: Stay well away from the mine buildings and houses. They are on private land. Before July 15 and in wet years until August 1 the track is too muddy and snow-covered for safe travel by car even with four-wheel drive. Before August 1, check with the SNRA first or plan to walk.

From the gables and avalanche chutes of Castle Peak to the fissured white wall of D.O. Lee Peak, the White Clouds seem to reach out toward the summit of Railroad Ridge. On the ridge grow fragile alpine flowers, such as alpine forget-me-not. From a knoll, southwest of this ridge, talus, ledges and whitebark pines emphasize the bleakness of the timberline sites of blue-green Tin Cup and Gunsight Lakes. North of the ridge, the gray talus setting of blue Crater Lake seems equally bleak. However, the dramatic mountains around Crater Lake make it beautiful. One of them, the Chinese Wall, is a textbook example of rock layers warped downward in the center.

East of Railroad Ridge near Livingston Mill stands a layer cake of strawberry and chocolate colored rock. Beyond it is the saddle-like summit of Mt. Borah. Far to the north stretches a panorama of the Salmon River Mountains, including the brown-striped towers of Cabin Creek Peak, the two sharp gray triangles of Twin Peaks, and the salmon-pink cap of Red Mountain.

To reach the trailhead, follow the access directions above. Leave your car at the transfer camp unless it has four-wheel drive because the road is much too steep for two-wheel drive. If you plan to drive up the ridge, check first with SNRA Headquarters for regulations and road conditions. The road crosses private property and can be impassable in early summer due to snow.

From the transfer camp (7,160 feet), walk back to the main road and up it through a gate to Livingston Mill and the junction at .4 mile (7,221 feet) with the road up Railroad Ridge. Leave the gate the way you find it. From the junction to the 2-mile point, the road climbs 1,000 feet up a sagebrush hillside, so this section can be hot.

At 2.9 miles where the road forks (8,579 feet), take the right (north) branch. A large campsite is at 3.5 miles in a grove of trees beside a stream. At 4.1 miles (9,090 feet), the road divides again. This is not shown on the topographic map. Take the right branch, which turns sharply to the right (northeast).

The road angles 600 feet up the ridge in .7 mile, crossing a washout half way up. At 4.8 miles, the track bends 180 degrees to the west. At this bend (9,760 feet), the French Creek jeep trail turns off to the north. The upper half of this jeep trail is still open to motor vehicles, but the lower half is open only to cycle, horse, and foot travel. However, there is no access across private land at the bottom of the jeep trail.

Tin Cup and Gunsight Lake from Railroad Ridge

From the jeep trail junction, keep west on the road along the top of the ridge. Now the high peaks begin to come into view. Soon the road splits to avoid a washout, and comes together again in 200 yards. At 5.8 miles (10,320 feet), the road divides. Turn left (southwest) on a faint track along the crest of the ridge. This track is not shown on the topographic map. Descend to a notch at 6.1 miles. Crater Lake may be seen from the ridge by walking downhill to the west for a short distance.

To see Tin Cup and Gunsight Lakes, climb from the notch south up a rocky knoll (10,817 feet). Stay near the left (east) edge of the cliffs at first, then move toward the right to the flat summit of the knoll at 7 miles. Descend 100 yards to the west toward a notch to see Tin Cup and Gunsight Lakes. Climbing down to these lakes from the sandy saddle (10,400 feet) east of the knoll is dangerous, but possible for experts carrying only day packs. You can drop from the knoll 500 vertical feet in .1 mile down a trough of scree to a talus basin .3 mile east of Gunsight Lake, but it is much safer to reach Tin Cup and Gunsight Lakes from Quicksand Meadows by way of Gunsight Creek.

79 **Walker Lake**
Map 32, 33, and 34

round trip: 12.2 miles
elevation gain: 2,079 feet
highest point: 9,239 feet

maps: Livingston Creek, Boulder Chain Lakes
time: 10 hours
difficulty: strenuous
access: On Highway 75, 36.5 miles east of Stanley, turn south on the East
    Fork of the Salmon River Road. Drive 14.7 miles on pavement and 2.9
    miles on gravel, then turn northwest on the dirt Livingston Mill Road and
    drive 4.8 miles. At a sign, turn left and go .2 mile to a parking area.
caution: Stay away from the buildings and cabins. They are on private land.

A village of weathered brown cabins surrounds the dilapidated Livingston
Mill near the trailhead. From the lower part of the trail, brown and white rock
layers on Railroad Ridge resemble melting vanilla ice cream on chocolate cake.
Bordering Quicksand Meadows farther up the trail, the pink, brown, rust and
white stripes and patches of Granite Peak form a patchwork crazy quilt. North
of aqua-green Walker Lake, triangular towers crown the double summit of an
orange and white peak. Above the upper end of the lake, the tips of two of the
White Cloud Peaks appear to float over the cliffs early on sunny mornings,
like icebergs.

To reach the trailhead (7,160 feet) near Livingston Mill, follow the access
directions above. From the transfer camp, the trail skirts Big Boulder Creek as
it goes through sagebrush flats to the register box at .5 mile. From here on, the
way at first follows an old road with a view of red rock towers across Big
Boulder Creek. At 1.5 miles, the route bridges the creek. The turnoff to Frog
Lakes is at 2.1 miles (7,700 feet). This trail, the Livingston–Castle Divide Trail,
goes all the way to Chamberlain Lakes. Frog Lake is reached in 5.5 miles with
a 1,840-foot elevation gain and 700-foot loss.

From the junction, the trail to Walker and Island Lakes crosses Big Boulder
Creek in two sections, first on a log bridge and then on rocks. The second
section of this may be difficult in early summer. The path climbs through
sagebrush, lodgepoles and aspens and at 3.1 miles, it is above a large meadow.
It climbs a steep grade, and goes through burnt trees above a 100-foot gorge.
Next the path drops into Quicksand Meadows, crosses a creek (8,500 feet), and
turns left (south).

Quicksand Meadows is shown as a flat, wooded area on the topographic
map, with a pond where two creeks join. Out in the meadows, the trail is
marked with posts and fords Gunsight Creek on logs at 4.3 miles. It then turns
right towards the forest. The lower meadows located off the trail are dangerous to stock because of quicksand.

Quicksand is caused by water upwelling underneath sand with such force
that it equals the weight of the sand, and thus separates the sand grains making
it possible for an object to sink. A person floats more easily in quicksand than
in water because it is denser, so the old tales of people drowning in quicksand

are exaggerated. The only way a person's head would sink is in a violent struggle to get free. To get out of quicksand, a person need only lie down and swim slowly, but a horse would have to be pulled out.

Beyond the meadows, cross the creek on a log and then return within a few feet to the right (west). The trail switchbacks up a talus slope, then climbs gently through trees, with views of the striped peak on the left. Across cascades in the canyon at 4.8 miles, the outlet of Goat Lake rushes down. The trail makes a switchback beside this cascade, then crosses a side creek. At 5.1 miles, the Walker and Island Lake trails diverge.

The trail from this junction to Walker Lake is not shown on the topographic map although it is an official trail. In addition, the lake is wrongly labeled Walter Lake. The trail winds up through trees left of a low granite knoll. Beyond the knoll, it descends to a meadow, then skirts a pond on the left (south). The path fords the creek between this pond and another, and then turns away from the creek over granite benches to the 9,239-foot lake at 6.1 miles.

80 Big Boulder Lakes
Maps 32 and 33

round trip: 16.2 miles
elevation gain: 2,880 feet
this section one way: 2 miles, 801-foot gain
highest point: 10,040 feet
map: Boulder Chain Lakes
time: 2 days
difficulty: cross-country
access: Follow directions in Hike 79 (Walker Lake) to hike to Walker Lake, where this hike description begins.

From above, the three Big Boulder Lakes resemble three sapphire blue platters with rims of dark green pines, turquoise bays and white outcrops. In the distance to the southeast, the gray, orange and cream-colored stripes of Granite Peak paint a backdrop. Above the lakes to the west, a scalloped, fluted ridge of white rock gleams like vanilla ice cream in the morning when the sun shines on it. In the afternoon, when the sun shines on the other side, it turns pearl gray. Recent glacial moraines surround the upper lake, Cirque Lake, but the glacier above has stopped moving so it is no longer a glacier.

The lower end of Walker Lake, where this hike description begins, is 6.1 miles and a 2,079-foot climb from Livingston Mill. To get there, follow the directions given above. Take the trail along the north shore of Walker Lake and go .5 mile to the upper end of the lake.

Cirque Lake, the highest of the Big Boulder Lakes

Turn right (east) and go up the right (north) branch of the inlet, which is called Bighorn Creek. Where a stream joins it from the left at .7 mile, cross the inlet and go west up the left side of the side stream, which is not shown on the map. Cross to the right, then back to the left of this stream just before the flat area shown at 9,600 feet on the topographic map. In this area, turn left (south) and climb between ledges.

Beyond the top of the ledges at 1 mile, drop to the east end of a narrow pond called Hook Lake. To reach Cove Lake, go around this pond and head south between granite benches. From the upper end of Cove Lake (9,842 feet) at 1.5 miles, ascend the right (north) side of the inlet to Sapphire Lake (9,888 feet) at 1.6 miles. Cross rock benches on the north side of its inlet to Cirque Lake (10,040 feet) at 2 miles.

It is easier to reach Cove Lake from Island Lake but the route is less obvious. To do this, go north 300 feet up a gully or ramp from the north corner of that lake to the top of a ridge at 9,600 feet. Turn left (west) along the ridge to a tiny pond (shown only as an open area on the map) under the summit of the ridge. Follow the 9,800-foot contour line west and northwest to Cove Lake, 1 mile from Island Lake.

This route is difficult to find on the return from Cove Lake, unless you have reached the lake by it. Don't descend the canyon between Cove and Island Lakes because it is full of boulders and cliffs. Also, getting around Island Lake is difficult from this canyon. That is because boulders and rock benches

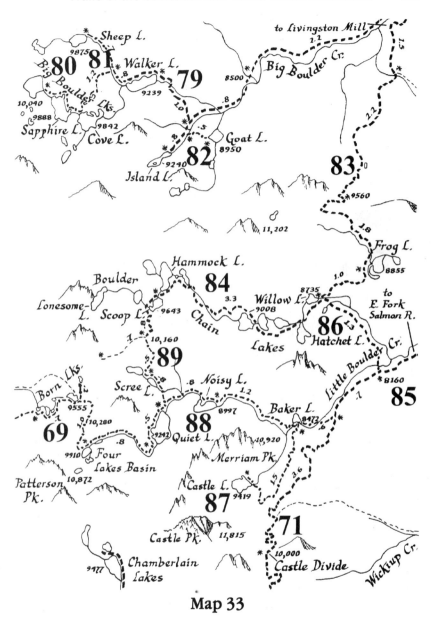

Map 33

edge the upper end and south side of the lake and a big cliff drops into the
water on the north side, preventing passage altogether.

81 Sheep Lake
Maps 32 and 33

round trip: 15.2 miles
elevation gain: 2,715 feet
this section one way: 1.5 miles, 636-foot gain
highest point: 9,875 feet
map: Boulder Chain Lakes
time: 2 to 3 days
difficulty: cross-country
access: Using directions in Hike 79 (Walker Lake), hike from Livingston Mill
to Walker Lake.

Granite benches and ledges softened by bits of wildflower meadow surround Sheep Lake. In the distance below, patchwork designs decorate the wall
of Granite Peak. The pinnacles and jumbled cliffs of a peach-colored mountain
rise 1,200 feet above the east side of the lake. Across the blue water, a row of
blunt, dark gray summits faces this peak. Two matching rock triangles stand at
the head of the canyon above the granite shelves holding Neck and Slide
Lakes.

To reach the beginning of this hike description, hike to the lower end of
Walker Lake, using the directions for Hike 79. It is 6.1 miles and a 2,079-foot
climb to this point from the trailhead. Go .5 mile to the upper end of Walker
Lake on the right (north) side, and climb along the right (east) side of the right
(north) branch of the inlet. This branch is called Bighorn Creek.

Keep straight ahead at .7 mile where a side stream comes in from the flat
place on the left (west) that marks the easiest route to the Big Boulder Lakes.
Continue along the east side of Bighorn Creek to Sheep Lake (9,875 feet) at 1.5
miles. There are only one or two small campsites. To reach Neck Lake (a
narrow pond) and Slide Lake (10,200 feet), 320 feet above Sheep Lake, walk .5
mile up beside the creek connecting the lakes.

82 Island and Goat Lakes
Maps 32 and 33

round trip: 11.8 miles to Island Lake
elevation gain: 2,080 feet
this section one way: .8 mile, 400-foot gain; additional .5 mile and 100-foot
gain and 200-foot loss for Goat Lake
highest point: 9,240 feet
maps: Boulder Chain Lakes, Livingston Creek
time: 9 1/2 to 11 hours or 2 days
difficulty: strenuous

access: Follow directions in Hike 79 (Walker Lake) to hike to the junction of the Island Lake Trail with the Walker Lake Trail.

The aquamarine water of Island Lake holds two islands, one big enough for whitebark pines and the other just a granite pancake. Granite benches surround the lake except for a narrow boulder-dotted meadow at the upper end and a 200-foot cliff beside it. From the lower end of the lake, a natural ramp gives access to the Big Boulder Lakes. Above the green water of Goat Lake, chocolate, gray, and buff stripes wander east across Granite Peak to a jumble of pinnacles.

To reach the beginning of this hike description, use the directions in Hike 79 (Walker Lake) to reach the Walker–Island Lake junction (8,840 feet), 5.1 miles and a 1,700-foot climb from Livingston Mill. From the junction, the Island Lake Trail at first climbs the canyon at a distance from the gorge containing the lake's outlet. At a bog beyond the gorge at .4 mile, it is possible to climb to the left (east) cross-country over a 100-foot ridge to Goat Lake.

To do this, at the bog look east and notice a saddle between a rock knoll and a ridge. Head for this saddle .1 mile from the trail. From the saddle, descend 200 feet through the trees to Goat Lake (8,950 feet), .5 mile from the trail.

From the bog, the main trail runs along above a second gorge, crosses a side creek and reaches Island Lake (9,240 feet) at a campsite .8 mile from the Walker Lake junction. To reach the Big Boulder Lakes from Island Lake, see directions under Hike 80 (Big Boulder Lakes).

83 Livingston Mill to Frog Lake
Maps 32, 33, and 34

round trip: 15 miles
elevation gain: 2,400 feet
elevation loss (return climb): 705 feet
highest point: 9,560 feet
maps: Livingston Creek, Boulder Chain Lakes
time: 2 to 3 days
difficulty: strenuous
access: On Highway 75, 36.5 miles east of Stanley, turn south on the East Fork of the Salmon River Road. Drive 14.7 miles on pavement and 2.9 miles on gravel. Then turn right (northwest) on the dirt Livingston Mill Road and drive 4.8 miles. At a sign, turn left and go .2 mile to the parking area.
caution: Avoid the buildings and cabins. They are private property.

Hatchet Lake

Southwest of the summit of the Livingston Mill to Frog Lake Trail, two snow-filled ravines in the distance gouge the face of Castle Peak, which is char-coal gray on this side. To the right of the peak, the view includes the orange needles of Serrate Ridge parading to the cathedral of Merriam Peak. Closer to the divide on the west, burnt orange patches and stripes pattern the white face of Granite Peak. South of the divide, yellow water lilies float on Frog and Little Frog Lakes. These lakes sit in a wide marshy basin with a view of Castle Peak.

To reach the trailhead (7,160 feet), follow the access directions above. From the parking area and transfer camp, the trail goes along the creek through sagebrush flats to the register box near the old brown cottages of Livingston Mill at .5 mile. Now for a time, the trail is an old road across the creek from red towers. It bridges Big Boulder Creek in a small meadow at 1.6 miles.

At 2.1 miles, the Frog Lake Trail turns south. It makes switchbacks not shown on the topographic map in a forest underlain by the jackstraws of dead trees. The trail climbs gently because it was constructed for trail bike riders. Even small streams have bridges. At 3.6 miles is a junction with a 1-mile side trail to Little Redfish Lake (8,780 feet), 400 feet above. This lake in marsh grass and water lilies is surrounded by wooded ridges.

The main trail continues up in big switchbacks, crossing and recrossing streams. Across Big Boulder Creek from an open grassy area are colorful orange mountains. At a corner at 4 miles, white limestone peaks appear behind the Big Boulder Lakes. The trail climbs through open grassy areas, flattens out in lodgepoles, and passes a pond at 5.1 miles.

Above the pond, long switchbacks in the open lead to a divide (9,560 feet) at 5.7 miles. On the other side of it at 5.8 miles is a close-up view of Granite Peak. Now the path turns west for .2 mile, then zips back to the east the same distance. At 6.5 miles, it turns southeast down a small creek through meadows. The trail reaches a tiny pond beside Frog Lake (8,855 feet) at 7.5 miles. Little Frog Lake is .2 mile to the east in a marshy meadow.

84 Boulder Chain Lakes
Maps 32 and 33

round trip: 23.6 miles to Scoop Lake
elevation gain: 3,308 feet
elevation loss (return climb): 825 feet
this section one way: 4.3 miles, 908-foot gain, 120-foot loss (.7 mile additional one way cross-country and 990 feet additional gain to see the highest two lakes)
highest point: 9,643 feet
map: Boulder Chain Lakes
time: 3 to 4 days
difficulty: strenuous
access: Hike to Frog Lake from Livingston Mill (see Hike 88, Livingston Mill to Frog Lake for directions), or hike to the first Boulder Chain Lake following

directions in Hike 85, Little Boulder Creek Trail and Hike 86, Boulder Chain Lakes to Baker Lake.

A glacier strung these eleven lakes on a creek like sparkling blue beads on a necklace. A ridge of orange slabs and pinnacles links the first five of the lakes. From the trail between Frog Lake and the first Boulder Chain Lake you see the dark snow-slashed face of Castle Peak peering over the orange ridge. On this ridge, a tower with owl-like ears overlooks the second lake, Hatchet Lake. Surrounding the upper lakes are splintered white peaks, rock benches, whitebark pines, and small meadows brimming with wildflowers.

This trail section begins at Frog Lake (8,855 feet), 7.5 miles and 2,400 feet above Livingston Mill. To reach this point, see Hike 83 (Livingston Mill to Frog Lake). Below Frog Lake, the trail drops through trees to a view of Castle Peak, and then turns west along a sagebrush ridge.

At 1 mile, the route crosses the outlet of Willow Lake (8,735 feet) on a footbridge. Here, the orange ridge peers over granite knolls above marsh grass and woods. The trail goes around the lake on the left (south) side near campsites. Sites are also 200 yards southeast off-trail at a pond called Waterdog Lake.

The trail climbs through trees to Hatchet Lake (8,884 feet) at 1.5 miles. Blue-green water, marsh grass and the tower with ears distinguish this lake. Campsites are off-trail on the northeast side.

The trail comes close to this lake only at the outlet, which it fords. In .2 mile, the way crosses the inlet from the third lake, 8,939-foot Shelf Lake. Then it climbs above the lake. Forest, bluffs and rock shelves stand on the north side of this lake and the eared mountain behind woods on the south.

As the trail passes Shelf Lake, it climbs next to the cliffs of the orange mountain. It goes through trees under the eared tower to boulders and turf on the south shore of the fourth lake, Sliderock Lake (8,978 feet), at 2 miles. Rock peninsulas decorated with trees distinguish this lake. Campsites are located behind the peninsulas.

The trail circles the head of the lake, then crosses the inlet to the north side on rocks. The path then goes along the north shore of the fifth lake, Lodgepole Lake (9,008 feet). Here the orange ridge sheds talus into the water on the south, and on the north, a clear inlet not shown on the topographic map flows into the lake in a tongue of golden sand.

Now there is a one-mile gap in the chain of lakes, and the route stays away from Boulder Chain Lakes Creek, climbing steeply over rock benches and through forest. At 3.4 miles, the trail crosses to the west side of the creek, then east and west again just below Hourglass Lake at 3.7 miles.

This upper basin holds three lakes: Hidden (9,517 feet), Hammock (9,514 feet) and Hourglass (9,731 feet), which sit below splintered off-white peaks. Campsites are abundant off-trail. The trail continues up a shelf to the ninth lake, Scoop Lake (9,643 feet) at 4.3 miles. This lake, the last lake on the trail, is in a hollow of solid rock with a few stunted whitebark pines and no good campsites.

The trail keeps ascending through a pass called Windy Devil (10,000 feet) at 4.9 miles. The two upper lakes, Headwall (9,755 feet) and Lonesome (10,435 feet) are above timberline. They can be reached by going around the west side of Scoop Lake on the trail, and up the inlet 990 feet cross-country for .7 mile.

From the pass, the trail climbs out onto a shelf (10,200 feet) and ends at 5.6 miles. The end of the trail is 557 feet and 1.3 miles above Scoop Lake. It is dangerous to try to go from here to Born Lakes over the off-trail pass sometimes called the Devils Staircase.

85 Little Boulder Creek Trail
Maps 32, 33 and 34

round trip: 13 miles
elevation gain: 1,940 feet
highest point: 8,160 feet
maps: Bowery Creek, Boulder Chain Lakes
time: 9 1/2 hours
difficulty: strenuous
access: On Highway 75, 36.5 miles east of Stanley, turn south on the East Fork of the Salmon River Road. Drive 14.4 miles on pavement, and 6 miles on gravel to a parking area and hikers transfer camp for the Little Boulder Creek Trail, 19.4 miles from the highway. From here walk .3 mile south along the road to reach the trailhead. (There is no room at all to park at the trailhead.) Horse users should park at the corrals .7 mile farther up the East Fork at the mouths of Sheep and Wickiup creeks.

The Little Boulder Creek Trail is the shortest route to the Boulder Chain Lakes and Baker Lake. This trail was reopened in 1991 after the Forest Service built a 3-mile road around the property of a private landowner who had blocked access to this trail and others at the upper end of the East Fork of the Salmon River Road for about 13 years. From this trail, there are two fine views of Castle Peak. One is from a meadow at 3.4 miles and another is from the large meadow at the junction with the Livingston Mill–Castle Divide Trail at 6 miles. Photographs of the view from this meadow showing the furrowed dark face of Castle Peak and its burnt orange companion, Merriam Peak, have

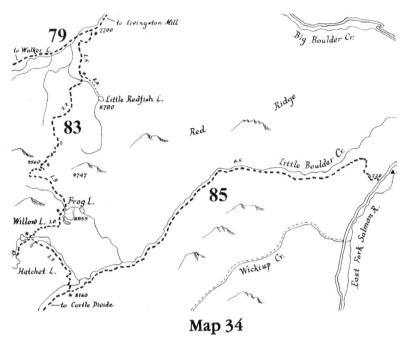

Map 34

appeared in many books and national magazines, especially during the controversy over mining in the White Clouds in the early 1970s.

From the road at 6,200 feet, the first 1.8 miles of the trail climb 1,000 feet through sagebrush. There are only two groves of trees and no water. The trail is the southernmost of the three trails the topographic map shows joining to form the Little Boulder Creek Trail. (The other two branches are closed.)

The trail first angles down the canyon as it climbs above the road. At .1 mile, it runs left toward the hillside. At .5 mile, the path descends into a grassy area where a trace of the middle one of the three trails joins. From here the main trail climbs through a grove of aspens where high peaks can be seen up the canyon. Then it angles uphill to the right in the sagebrush again. At .7 mile, the third trail, all overgrown, joins. Ahead is more sagebrush with a few Douglas firs scattered on rocky bluffs to the left. At .9 mile, the route parallels the red rock formations of Red Ridge on a flat area and passes through a tongue of trees at 1.1 mile.

The path enters forest at last at 1.8 miles and comes close to Little Boulder Creek for the first time at 2.8 miles. A meadow choked with willows at 3.4 miles offers the first view of Castle Peak. The trail then climbs along the creek to the second large meadow at 6 miles. At the upper end of this meadow at 6.5 miles (8,160 feet), it joins the Livingston Mill-Castle Divide Trail.

Hammock Lake

86 Boulder Chain Lakes to Baker Lake
Maps 32 and 33

round trip: 22.2 miles from Livingston Mill; 15.6 miles from the Little Boulder
Creek trailhead without going to the first Boulder Chain Lake
elevation gain: 2,712 feet
elevation loss (return climb): 1,280 feet
this section one way: 2.6 miles, 312-foot gain, 575-foot loss
highest point: 9,560 feet on the Livingston–Frog Lake Divide
map: Boulder Chain Lakes
time: 3 to 4 days
difficulty: strenuous
access: Follow directions in Hike 83 (Livingston Mill to Frog Lake) and Hike
84 (Boulder Chain Lakes) to hike from Livingston Mill to the first Boulder
Chain Lake (Willow Lake).

Marsh grass nibbles at shallow, green Baker Lake beneath pearl gray granite
ridges. Northwest of the lake, cylindrical orange towers corrugate the wall of
Merriam Peak, the highest point on Serrate Ridge. To the left of it, the furrowed dark gray face of Castle Peak peers over a wooded ridge. If the Sawtooth National Recreation Area hadn't been formed in 1972, this ridge now
probably would be an open pit molybdenum mine.

Follow access directions in the hikes listed above to hike to the first Boulder Chain Lake (Willow Lake) at 8,735 feet, where this hike description begins. Willow Lake is 8.5 miles with a 2,400-foot climb and 825-foot descent from Livingston Mill.

The trail leads down the wooded canyon of the outlet of the Boulder Chain Lakes, and crosses the outlet of Waterdog Lake at .2 mile. At .8 mile, the path is on an open sagebrush slope decorated with aspens. The way fords Little Boulder Creek at 1.2 miles to the south side and at 1.3 miles, meets the Little Boulder Creek Trail (8,160 feet). This trail descends 6.5 miles and 1,940 feet to the East Fork of the Salmon River Road.

Turn right (southwest) on the Castle Divide Trail and hike up wooded slopes to an unsigned path 2 miles from Willow Lake (.7 mile above the Little Boulder Creek junction). Turn right (west) on this path and drop down to a prospect. Cross the outlet and climb a few feet to the lake (8,472 feet) at 2.6 miles. There are several campsites now that the mine buildings have been removed.

87 Castle Lake
Map 33 or 26

round trip: 23.4 miles via Livingston Mill, 22 miles from Three Cabins Creek, 18.6 miles via Little Boulder Creek
elevation gain: 3,699 feet via Livingston
elevation loss (return climb): 1,320 feet
this section one way: 1.5 miles, 947-foot gain, 40-foot loss from Baker Lake
highest point: 9,419 feet
map: Boulder Chain Lakes
time: 3 to 4 days
difficulty: cross-country for experts
access: Using directions in Hike 83 (Livingston to Frog Lake) or Hike 85 (Little Boulder Creek) and Hike 86 (Boulder Chain Lakes to Baker Lake), hike to Baker Lake; or using directions in Hike 62 and Hike 71, hike over Castle Divide to a point .5 mile north of it at the bottom of the switchbacks.
caution: The route to Castle Lake is slippery and has a dropoff of several hundred feet. Avoid camping in the lake basin because it is a fragile alpine area.

Two snow-filled chimneys form a "V" on the charcoal gray face of Castle Peak above Castle Lake. The lake is so deep and the mountain so dark that the color of the water changes from blue green around the edges to navy blue in the middle. Talus surrounds the lake except for the ledges, benches and

Castle Lake

whitebark pines across the lower end. At the north corner of the lake below the orange sawteeth of Merriam Peak and Serrate Ridge, a solid-rock peninsula sprinkled with bonsai-sized trees encloses a small turquoise bay.

To reach the beginning of this hike description, hike to Baker Lake, following the directions in the hikes listed above. It is 11.1 miles and a 2,712-foot climb and 1,280-foot descent from Livingston Mill or 13.7 miles and a 2,105-foot climb and 2,513-foot descent from Three Cabins Creek.

From Baker Lake (8,472 feet) take the right (west) of two mining roads which leave the lake from the west side of a log bridge over the outlet. The road crosses a stream at .1 mile. At .4 mile, just past a clearcut area, the main trail over Castle Divide is close enough to see its blazes. Continue on the road across another stream, and around two switchbacks to a split at .5 mile. Take the left branch up the right (west) side of the center of a ridge (9,204 feet). Where the road splits again at 1 mile, take the right (west) branch downhill, and then go up across a ravine.

Beyond the ravine, turn left (south) off the road up a sandy ridge to a spring and old log cabin. Go straight up the ridge above the cabin to a .4 mile-long narrow flat area of grass and talus shown on the topographic map as an open area at 1.2 miles (9,300 feet). Note that there is no water in or near the flat. You can also reach this flat by descending 500 feet in .5 mile from Castle Divide, cutting west along the south edge of the timber, and walking north from a higher flat at 9,400 feet.

From the lower (north) end of the 9,300-foot flat, the route to the lake is difficult and should only be attempted by experts. First, angle up the ridge of white gravel to the right (north-northwest) toward Baker Lake. Where gravel covers solid rock, use extreme caution. At the top of the ridge, circle the end of it and then drop west to the lake (9,419 feet) at 1.5 miles.

88 Baker Lake to Quiet and Noisy Lakes
Map 33 and 26

round trip: 20.6 miles from the Little Boulder Creek trailhead
elevation gain: 3,482 feet
elevation loss (return climb): 1,280 feet
this section one way: 2 to 2.5 miles, 770-foot gain
highest point: 9,242 feet
map: Boulder Chain Lakes
time: 3 to 4 days
difficulty: cross-country for experts
access: Using directions in Hike 85 (Little Boulder Creek) or Hike 83 (Livingston Mill to Frog Lake) and Hike 86 (Boulder Chain to Baker Lake), hike to Baker Lake.

caution: The climb up the ledges above Baker Lake can be hazardous for those with backpacks.

A pointed orange and gray peak guards the upper end of jade green Noisy Lake. From the south side of the lake, apricot and gray cliffs climb the splintery side of Serrate Ridge. In these cliffs, a waterfall splashes down in a niche most of the summer. Above Quiet Lake, Castle Peak spreads out into an orange and gray face covered with a network of avalanche troughs and outcrops resembling roof gables. From the upper end of this lake, the orange pleats and sawteeth of Serrate Ridge zigzag along from Castle Peak to Merriam Peak.

To reach Baker Lake, hike in from one of the trailheads suggested above. It is 11.1 miles and a 2,712-foot climb and 1,280-foot descent from Livingston Mill and 13.7 miles with a 2,105-foot climb and 2,513-foot descent from Three Cabins Creek to Baker Lake. From the Little Boulder Creek trailhead, it is 7.8 miles with a 2,260-foot elevation gain.

At the lake, cross the log bridge over the outlet. Go around the south side of the lake and ignore the mine road toward Castle Lake. Ford the inlet in a marsh and walk up its right (west) side to a talus slope with grass below it. A waterfall appears to the right. The falls are on Slickenside Creek, which joins the inlet here. Zigzag northwest up ledges beside this creek, staying well to the right of it. Descending these ledges with a pack is more difficult than going up.

At the top of the ledges 400 feet above Baker Lake, continue along the right (north) side of the creek through forest and granite benches to Noisy Lake (8,997 feet) at 1.2 miles.

Then edge the north side of the lake in woods, cross the inlet on slippery logs and climb along the left (south) side of this inlet to the lower end of Quiet Lake (9,242 feet) at 2 miles. To continue to the upper end at 2.5 miles, ford the outlet and go along the west shore of the lake across grass and talus.

89 Shallow and Scree Lakes
Maps 32 and 33

round trip: 21.2 miles from the Little Boulder Creek trailhead, 27.8 miles
    from Livingston Mill
elevation gain: 3,825 feet
elevation loss (return climb): 1,743 feet
this section one way: 2.1 miles, 397-foot gain, 918-foot loss
highest point: 10,160 feet
map: Boulder Chain Lakes
time: 4 to 5 days
difficulty: expert

access: Hike to the ninth Boulder Chain Lake, Scoop Lake, using directions in Hike 85 (Little Boulder Creek) or Hike 83 (Livingston to Frog Lake) and Hike 84 (Boulder Chain Lakes)

The triangular towers of Serrate Ridge form a zigzag wall across the canyon from the turquoise water, whitebark pines, and pale orange granite ledges of Scree Lake. Shallow Lake is .2 mile above Scree Lake, where large blocks of granite create pale green rectangles underwater and white islands above. A ridge with a gray tower that guards the Devils Staircase stands to the west above the head of the lake.

Less than a mile north of Shallow Lake is the ninth Boulder Chain Lake, Scoop Lake, which is shaped like the scoop of a diesel shovel. From this lake, the trail climbs south through a notch called Windy Devil. It goes out onto a shelf and ends near the Devils Staircase, a dangerous divide between the Boulder Chain Lakes and Born Lakes. From the end of the trail, hikers can reach Shallow and Scree Lakes cross-country. They can also hike up from Quiet Lake through a slot in the rocks which is like a secret staircase.

This hike description begins at Scoop Lake (9,643 feet) 11.8 miles from Livingston Mill. To reach it, follow the instructions in the hikes listed above. From Scoop Lake, the trail switchbacks across talus to the notch in the ridge called Windy Devil at .7 mile. From the trail, the tenth lake, Headwall Lake, can be seen on a rocky shelf to the west. Snow may be on the trail here as late as mid-August. Beyond the notch, the trail turns right (west) and climbs an additional 150 feet to a flat, rocky basin where it ends 1.5 miles from Scoop Lake. Taking the pass sometimes called the Devils Staircase to Born Lakes from here is not recommended.

To go to Shallow Lake (9,635 feet), turn left (south) off the trail where it turns west .8 mile from the lower end of Scoop Lake. Descend a ridge and the side of it to Shallow Lake at 1.3 miles. From Shallow Lake, continue down the north side of the creek to Scree Lake. A few campsites lie along this creek.

To descend from here to Quiet Lake, go around the north side of Scree Lake (9,550 feet) and then down its outlet on the left (northeast). Angle east away from the creek a few yards to find the slot in the cliffs. Descend the slot and follow the canyon of the outlet until it bends to the left (east) and the pink granite ledges stop. Here, ford the creek to the south side and go south .2 mile to the lower end of Quiet Lake (9,242 feet) at 2.1 miles.

trails in the
SMOKY
MOUNTAINS

Titus Lake

GALENA AREA

90 Headwaters of the Salmon River

Map 35 or 1

round trip: 5 miles
elevation gain: 700 feet
highest point: 8,300 feet
maps: Frenchman Creek, Galena
time: 4 hours
difficulty: easy
access: From Highway 75 at the bottom of the Galena Summit grade in Sawtooth Valley 33.8 miles north of Ketchum, turn left (south) at a sign for the Salmon River Road. Two branches join to form this road. At .9 mile, turn right at a sign for Chemetkan Campground. At 3.2 miles, just before the campground, ford a creek. Continue 1.7 miles beyond the campground on a primitive road to a ford of the river 4.9 miles from the highway. Park before the ford because driving across the river here damages salmon spawning habitat.

This easy hike leads you to the place where a branch of the main Salmon River begins in a wildflower meadow. This meadow is just below the divide between Sawtooth Valley and the canyon of Big Smoky Creek. In it, rivulets collect into a three-foot wide stream which rushes down a ravine to begin one of the two branches that make up the headwaters of the Salmon. To the east, two lumpy gray shoulders of 10,225-foot Bromaghin Peak overlook the infant river. Across a divide from the meadow, tiers of cliffs decorate the canyon wall of Big Smoky Creek, which flows into the Boise River. The headwaters of the Salmon River divide the Sawtooth Mountains on the west and north from the Smoky Mountains on the east and south.

To reach the beginning of the hike, follow the directions above. The road fords the river or a branch of it four times in the first .5 mile. There are no logs for hikers, so it is easiest to wade the river once to the right (west) side and walk south cross-country through sagebrush along the east side of the river to the beginning of the jeep trail shown on the map at 1.5 miles.

Walk up the jeep trail as it climbs gently up and down in forest. At 1.3 miles, the track fords the river, which is only six feet wide, to the left (east) where there are some campsites in a grassy area. From here, the road switchbacks left up a wooded hillside to a gate at 1.5 miles.

Take a path around the gate and continue up the road, which makes two switchbacks and then winds south along the edge of a 60-foot gorge. Just above the meadow at 2.2 miles, turn left (east) off the jeep trail onto a pack trail. This

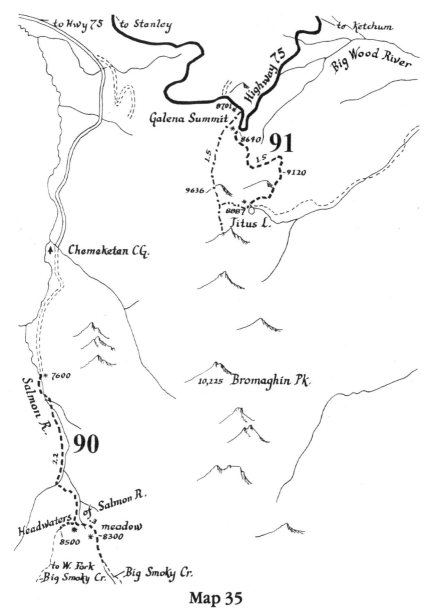

Map 35

trail drops into the lower end of a meadow and fords the three-foot wide river at 2.3 miles. Springs in the meadow begin the river. The trail goes around the northeast side of the meadow to the divide (8,300 feet) at 2.5 miles. From here, the Big Smoky Creek Trail descends 2,920 feet in 18.5 miles to Canyon Campground, which can be reached by road from Fairfield or Featherville. To see the rugged canyon wall of Big Smoky Creek continue downhill .5 mile.

Back on the jeep trail, a 200-foot climb gives you a view of Bromaghin Peak and of a second branch of the river. It is more valid to say the second branch of the river is the headwaters because it is longer, but it is much easier to visit the branch on the trail. To reach the head of the second branch, take the jeep trail 1.3 miles south of the turn off to the meadow and go along the side of the ridge to a saddle. Then leave the track, follow the ridge west, and cut down to the center stream about .7 mile from the saddle.

91 Titus Lake
Map 35

round trip: 3 miles
elevation gain: 480 feet
elevation loss (return climb): 233 feet
highest point: 9,120 feet
map: Galena
time: 3 1/2 hours
difficulty: easy except for slippery sections, expert for cross-country side trip
  to peak
access: On Highway 75, 28.8 miles north of Ketchum, park .3 mile south of
  Galena Summit in a large turnout on the east side of the road.
caution: Keep off the meadows at the lower end of the lake to avoid damaging
  the plants and grasses.

In July once the snow melts, blue flax, shooting star, phlox and arrowleaf balsamroot color the slopes along the trail to Titus Lake. Willows and mountain bluebells separate the cloudy emerald green water of the lake from a marshy meadow. Overlooking the miniature lake is a gray and orange ridge of crumbled ledges. Southeast across Titus Creek from the lake, grooves divide the scalloped cliffs of the canyon wall into lobes. Southwest behind a saddle, cliffs and snowbanks slope up to the pointed top of Bromaghin Peak.

From the summits of either of two unnamed peaks north of the lake, the jagged mountains of six ranges stretch in every direction. The ranges are the Sawtooth, White Cloud, Boulder, Pioneer, Smoky, and Salmon River mountains.

To reach the trailhead (8,640 feet), follow the access directions given above. Watching for traffic, go west across the highway to a dirt road leading south from the end of the highest big hairpin south of Galena Summit. Walk south along this dirt road for 100 yards to a register box.

From the box, the trail heads to the left (southeast), crossing a small creek at .1 mile and another at .5 mile. Then it turns left (east) in forest and runs along the side of a ridge, gradually climbing to the top of a wrinkle in the ridge (9,000 feet) at .8 mile. The path climbs south over another wrinkle at 1 mile (9,120 feet). From here, it dips southwest into the canyon of the north branch of Titus Creek. At 1.2 miles, the trail turns west and descends 233 feet to the lake (8,887 feet) at 1.5 miles.

Expert hikers can climb west .3 mile cross-country above the lake onto a saddle between Peaks 9,921 and 9,636 and walk up either peak for a view. It is also possible to walk north from Peak 9,636 down the ridge to Galena Summit. By this route, it is 1.5 miles from the lake to the highway. Another possible route descends the outlet of the lake and Titus Creek (1,598 feet in 3.5 miles) to the highway across from Galena Lodge.

trails in the
BOULDER
MOUNTAINS

Boulder Mountains from Galena Gulch Trail

POLE CREEK AREA

92 Grand Prize Gulch
Maps 36 and 23

round trip: 8.4 miles to the top of the Galena Gulch-Grand Prize Divide; an extra 1 mile (cross-country) to a pond

elevation gain: 1,860 feet to the top of the divide, an additional 100 feet to the pond

highest point: 9,560 feet

map: Horton Peak

time: 7 1/2 hours

difficulty: expert

access: Go north on Highway 75 from Ketchum for 36 miles. Turn right (east) onto the Pole Creek-Germania Creek Road. Keep right at the Pole Creek-Valley Road junction at 2.3 miles. At 6.5 miles, turn right (east) at a sign for Grand Prize Gulch and drive down to the creek at 6.7 miles. Because of a 30-inch vertical bank, it is impossible to drive across the creek.

From the destination of this hike, the divide between the Grand Prize Gulch and Galena Gulch trails, hikers see to the south high orange and charcoal gray peaks and crumbly cliffs typical of the Boulder Mountains. To the north rise the creamy summits of the White Clouds. Near the divide, four rounded towers overlook a tiny amber pond. For directions for seeing Deer Lakes from a viewpoint on a ridge above the divide, see Hike 93 (Galena Gulch).

To reach the trailhead (7,700 feet), follow the access directions given above. Cross the creek on a log and walk up the old road through small lodgepoles, avoiding side roads. The road angles to the right, then goes back to the left.

At 1.5 miles, the road fords the creek to the east and switchbacks above it. Small trees are sprinkled over an old avalanche area across the creek. At a meadow where a road branches to the right, keep straight ahead. At 2.3 miles, the road turns left uphill to a prospect. Turn off the road onto a trail to the right (signed "trail") that continues up the canyon.

The trail crosses a flat meadow, then climbs gently to the low point on the skyline ahead, reaching it at 3.3 miles. At 3.5 miles, a rock cairn at 9,040 feet marks a junction with the Gladiator Creek Divide Trail which crosses the Boulder Mountains to a trailhead near Galena Lodge on Highway 75.

Continue 100 yards on the main trail down the West Fork of the East Fork of the Salmon River. Then turn left onto the sketchy Galena Gulch Trail shown on the topographic map. There is no path or sign for the trail. (The main trail descends the West Fork of the East Fork and the East Fork to Bow-

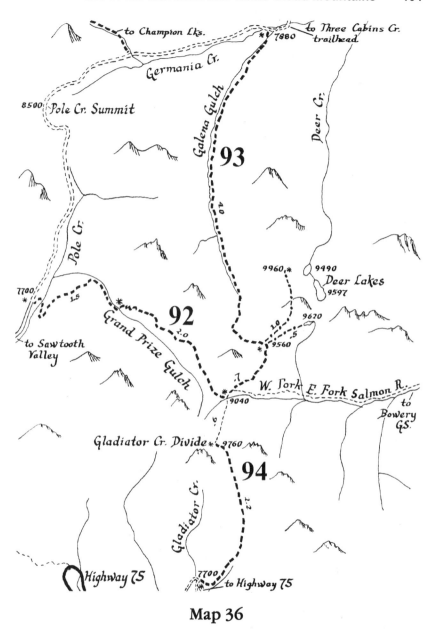

Map 36

ery Guard Station at the end of the East Fork of the Salmon River Road. It loses 2,240 feet of elevation in this 9.5 miles.)

As you follow the route of the Galena Gulch Trail towards the divide, there are bits of paths which don't connect, so it can be hard to follow. Generally, the route angles northeast below a spring, which dries up in late season.

Then it circles below a rock knoll and heads straight up to the saddle (9,560 feet) at 4.2 miles.

To reach the amber pond (9,620 feet) from the saddle, walk northeast between rock benches. This tarn at 4.7 miles makes a fine destination, especially for those with children. Those with more energy will want to climb from the divide on up its ridge northeast and then north to look down on Deer Lakes from 9,960 feet. (See the detailed description for reaching this viewpoint in Hike 93, Galena Gulch.)

93 Galena Gulch
Map 36

round trip: 8 miles
elevation gain: 1,680 feet
side trip to view Deer Lakes: 1 mile cross-country one way, additional 600-foot gain
highest point: 9,560 feet
map: Horton Peak
time: 7 hours
difficulty: expert
access: From Highway 75, turn east 36 miles north of Ketchum onto the gravel and primitive Pole Creek–Germania Creek Road. Drive over Pole Creek Summit to a ford of Germania Creek at 11.8 miles, which is .2 mile before another ford and .3 mile before the Three Cabins Creek trailhead.

In Galena Gulch, lumpy ridges banded with gray and apricot overlook avalanche slopes crowded with tiny lodgepoles. The trail offers a view of the white, gold and red peaks around Washington Basin in the White Clouds. From the divide at the head of the canyon, a dark gray tooth, crumbly cliffs, and orange mountains near Bowery Guard Station are seen to the south. From a ridge above the divide, Deer Lakes spread out below hidden cliffs in a basin of gray rock and whitebark pines. Streaks of black sand show through the water of the lower lake, and the upper lake resembles a melting green guitar.

This trail allows backpackers to make a loop trip from Three Cabins Creek to Bowery Guard Station by returning over the Bowery Cutoff and Germania Creek trails and 300 yards of road. To reach the trailhead (7,860 feet), follow the access directions given above. Two fords near the end of the road are not shown on the topographic map. The unsigned trail begins just beyond (east) of the first ford where a sign says "no motorized vehicles." (Earlier fords at 7.3 miles may require 4-wheel drive.)

The trail crosses a tiny stream in moss, and at 150 yards goes left (east) on a footlog over Galena Gulch Creek. Next it leads uphill away from the creek

Grand Prize Gulch

through Douglas firs, and then returns to the creek which runs in a ravine here. At 1 mile is an avalanche area with small lodgepoles. As the trail crosses a second grass-covered avalanche area at 1.3 miles, it disappears, and then reappears in the woods beyond.

There are three more avalanche areas with open grassy slopes and downed timber before the 2-mile point and another three between 2 and 3 miles. Use the topographic map to find the trail in the woods beyond each avalanche area. Below a meadow at 3.2 miles, the trail fords the creek back to the right (west) side.

Now the path curves up into forest beneath outcrops, and over a rock knoll. Above a little meadow, the trail turns 90 degrees to the right (southwest). Walk along the right (west) side of the meadow to its upper end, then at 3.5 miles, cross its tiny stream to the south side. Be sure not to cross the stream too soon or you'll lose the trail.

Here watch for blazes to distinguish the trail from animal paths. The route stays at the edge of the forest below the rocky headwall until it crosses a scree slope just before the saddle (9,560 feet) at 4 miles.

To see Deer Lakes, go northeast up the sandy ridge, which levels out at 9,960 feet, where the summit of an unnamed peak is ahead. From the level area, turn left and walk north until you are about 1 mile from the saddle and the lakes appear below, under hidden cliffs. To the left (north) of these cliffs are steep scree slopes, which experts could descend to the lakes (9,490 and 9,597 feet).

GALENA AREA

94 Gladiator Creek Divide
Map 36

round trip: 4.4 miles
elevation gain: 2,060 feet
highest point: 9,760 feet
maps: Galena, Horton Peak
time: 5 hours
difficulty: strenuous
access: On Highway 75, turn north at Galena Lodge, 23 miles north of Ketchum. Drive 1.7 miles on a dirt road to the register box.

This trail climbs so steeply and shows so many of the Boulder and White Cloud Mountains that it seems like a slow glass elevator. You climb past two grassy basins that stairstep up the headwall of the canyon. Ahead, dark green whitebark pines and dark gray and burnt orange towers stand out against a pale gray and pale green background.

East of where the trail crosses the headwall, knobby gray and orange ridges line canyons in the Boulder Mountains. To the north rise the white peaks of the White Clouds, streaked pink and gold, and accented by the fluted white and orange-gray wall of Castle Peak.

Wood River from Gladiator Creek Divide

To reach the trailhead, turn north at the Gladiator Creek sign just west of Galena Lodge. Drive 1.7 miles, past Westernhome Gulch and Senate Creek, to a register box at 7,700 feet.

The trail starts southeast as an old road. The road gradually turns north, steepens and ends in trees at .5 mile. From here, the trail leads northeast through forest onto a sagebrush slope.

The path climbs steeply, with few switchbacks. At .8 mile, where a gray peak with a brown summit is visible ahead, it crosses talus. The trail passes a grove of trees, and goes between tiny whitebark pines opposite orange mine tailings at 1.5 miles. Then it crosses to the right (east) of the creek, which is dry most of the summer.

At 1.7 miles, the way reaches the lower of two grassy basins. At the head of the lower basin, where the creek trickles down a gray outcrop, it climbs to the right to a second, smaller basin at 2 miles. Then the path goes up through whitebark pines to the divide (9,760 feet) at 2.2 miles.

The trail turns east for 100 feet along the crest of the divide, and then drops down talus. After a 520-foot descent in .6 mile, it joins the Grand Prize Gulch Trail. This junction is 100 yards south of the junction with the West Fork of the East Fork and Galena Gulch trails, and the Gladiator Divide Trail has no trail tread at the junction.

EASLEY AREA

95 Silver Lake
Map 37

round trip: 3 miles (2 miles cross-country)
elevation gain: 1,242 feet
highest point: 9,642 feet
map: Easley Hot Springs
time: 5 to 6 hours
difficulty: expert
access: On Highway 75, 15.2 miles north of Ketchum, turn right (east) at a sign for Silver Creek. Drive across the bridge and up a steep primitive road on sagebrush and grass-covered hills. Avoid two roads turning left near the bottom. Leave passenger cars at 2 miles. At 2.3 miles, where the road enters a gully, four-wheel drive is needed. Eventually, the road may be closed to motor vehicles here. At 3 miles where the road splits, park and walk up the right branch to its end in an aspen grove at 3.4 miles, just below a steep bluff where the road ends.
caution: The route is difficult to find, and rocks hidden in the plants make footing hazardous.

Rock benches, whitebark pines and subalpine firs ring the clear green water of Silver Lake below silver-gray mountains sided with talus and broken cliffs. Between the lake and the rim of mountains, ponds, and meadows fill dents in gray and orange talus. Near the beginning of the hike, white rock between gray layers resembles dripping icing.

To reach the end of the jeep road (8,400 feet), follow the access directions above. From the aspen grove, the road climbs a short, steep bluff and ends. From here, go north across a grassy slope blanketed with blue-violet whorled penstemon in season. At .2 mile, enter the forest. Pass a sandstone bluff at .3

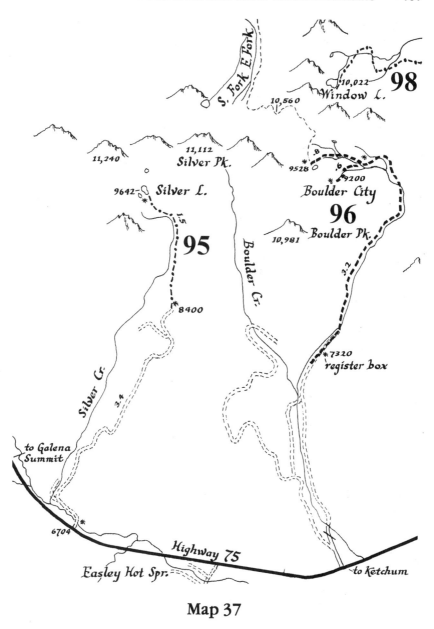

Map 37

mile by dropping 50 vertical feet to the left below it. Continue in trees to a ravine and cross it.

Beyond the ravine, continue to stay on the east side of the main creek and well above it. At .7 mile, the route crosses talus and then goes through stick-seed which covers hidden rocks.

At 1 mile in wildflowers, the creek splits into two cascades. Using the topographic map, climb up beside the cascades, then turn left (west) across the right stream and climb the right (north) side of the left stream. In 100 yards, a third creek goes off to the right. Go up this creek along the right side of it. This is the middle creek shown on the map. The route goes left of a pale orange knoll at 1.3 miles, then comes to a point where the creek splashes over a bluff.

Cross the creek to the left and follow a faint path to the top of this wall. Walk along rock benches left (west) of a bog to the lake (9,642 feet) at 1.5 miles. Two of the three ponds are located 200 yards to the southwest.

96 Boulder Basin
Map 37

round trip: 8.6 miles from the first ford to Boulder City; an additional .8 mile
  one way to the largest lake
elevation gain: 2,000 feet from the register box to the city, 360 feet additional
  to the lake
highest point: 9,528 feet
maps: Easley Hot Springs, Amber Lakes
time: 7 1/2 hours
difficulty: strenuous
access: On Highway 75, 12.2 miles north of Ketchum, turn east on the Boulder Creek Road. For further directions, see the description below.

A rusty boiler, tumbled mill building and cabins of silvered logs leaning at odd angles mark the location of Boulder City. Above the mill, a rusted tramway stretches up the mountain to a mine under crinkled peaks. Nearby, below rock buttresses, meadows sprinkled with gentians in season fringe a small aquamarine lake. Above the lake, curving stripes of pink, white and orange swirl across the gray face of Boulder Peak.

A jeep trail leads to Boulder City and the lake, but the upper section is rough enough to damage four-wheel drive vehicles. To reach the trailhead take the Boulder Creek Road. At 1.2 miles, where the Left Fork of Boulder Creek Road turns uphill, keep straight ahead. The road fords the creek at 1.7 miles. Leave passenger cars before the ford.

The hike mileage starts at this ford. It is .5 mile to a campsite and registration box in the forest. Those with pickups can continue to a log cabin at 1.0 mile. (7,560 feet). The road crosses the creek to the west at 1.4 miles. This ford and the road beyond it require four-wheel drive, but there is no parking between the log cabin and the ford. It is safest to take four-wheel drive vehicles

Cabin at Boulder City

only as far as a branch road at the "mine dump" shown on the map at 1.8 miles (7,920 feet).

From here, walk along the main road which skirts the base of a talus slope for .4 mile. In the trees beyond this, the road splits. There are several more splits in the next mile. Most of these soon rejoin, so it doesn't matter which you take. Water runs over all of them and some have mud holes. By the time the track fords the creek in a big mudhole to the north at 3.1 miles, the roads have all rejoined.

In a basin of little trees at 3.3 miles, the road makes a sharp left (west) turn. At 3.5 miles, it crosses a branch of the creek to the left (south) in sand in a big meadow. At 3.7 miles (9,100 feet), the road splits again. The right fork leads to tiny lakes at the head of the canyon, while the left fork leads to Boulder City.

To see Boulder City, follow the left branch, which crosses to the south side of the main creek in a ravine at 3.9 miles. The road fords another creek at 4.2 miles and goes out into a grassy basin below talus and crags. Two leaning cabins are on the left and the hill to the right holds the old mill and tramway at 4.3 miles (9,200 feet).

To see the lakes, back at the road junction, take the right branch through woods north of the creek, which runs in a gorge here. At 4.2 miles, the creek comes out into a meadow which the road skirts on the right. In the meadow, the track fords the creek to the left (south). At a T-intersection at 4.3 miles, take the left fork around a hairpin turn to the largest lake (9,528 feet). This lake is 4.5 miles from the ford of Boulder Creek at the beginning.

The right branch at the "T" intersection climbs 1 mile over talus and past tiny ponds to a divide at 10,560 feet. From here an unmaintained trail descends the South Fork of the East Fork of the Salmon River 3,400 feet in 7.5 miles to the trail along the East Fork 4.5 miles above Bowery Guard Station.

NORTH FORK AREA

97 East Fork North Fork Big Wood River
Map 38

round trip: 7 miles
elevation gain: 1,460 feet
highest point: 8,300 feet at the end of the official trail
maps: Amber Lakes, Rock Roll Canyon
time: 8 1/2 hours
difficulty: expert
access: From Highway 75 at SNRA Headquarters 7.4 miles north of Ketchum, drive 3.9 miles on the gravel and dirt North Fork Road to a side road .3 mile past Camp Manapu. Turn right on this road. When it branches, drive up its north branch, avoiding a road on the left to an aspen grove. Park passenger cars before the road drops down a small hill. High wheelbase vehicles can continue to a split in the road below the hill. Leave vehicles at the bottom of the hill and walk along the right fork of the road until it becomes a trail.

This trail is a pleasant walk below crumbly apricot and gray peaks. Half way up, an enormous snowbank covered with the pine needles of many avalanches usually spans the creek. Beyond this point, the trail dwindles, disappearing before the canyon forks at 3.5 miles. Because few hikers take this trail, it is a good place to see wildlife early in the morning.

To reach the trailhead, follow the access directions above. At first, grassy slopes alternate with groves of Douglas fir. At .7 mile, there is forest and at 1 mile, an open area across from talus cross-hatched with animal paths. Then the trail goes through 200 yards of timber close to the creek, and at 1.2 miles, climbs above the creek below talus.

The path ascends an open hillside at 1.3 miles. It reaches the needle-covered snowbank at 1.9 miles, where it fords a side creek at 7,650 feet. Keeping away from the East Fork, the sketchy trail returns to forest that has three narrow

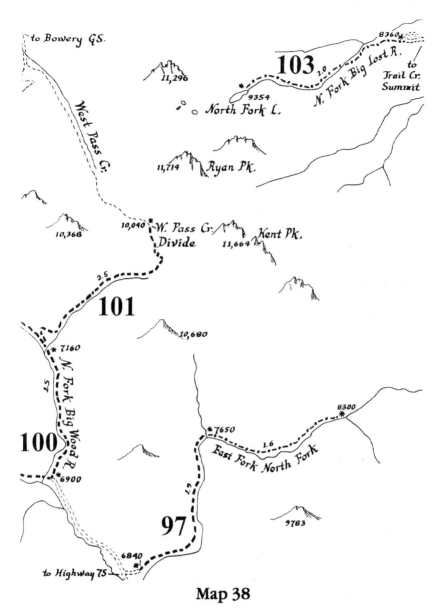

Map 38

open areas between 2 and 2.5 miles. At 2.5 miles below a pinkish-gray mountain, willows line the canyon bottom and the canyon gradually curves left.

Beyond a strip of trees, the path reaches another long open area. Now the trail is hard to find in thick timber, and after crossing two small side creeks, it ends. A few yards farther is a fork in the canyon at 3.5 miles (8,300 feet), which gives a view of a wide peak of apricot talus farther up the canyon.

From the end of the trail, you can climb cross-country over a 10,000-foot divide to a trail connecting Trail Creek with the West Fork of Trail Creek. The East Fork of the North Fork Trail is maintained only by volunteers.

98 West Fork North Fork Big Wood River and Window Lake

Maps 39 and 37

round trip: 9 miles (3.4 miles cross-country) to Window Lake, 7.6 miles to the end of the West Fork North Fork Big Wood River Trail
elevation gain: 3,122 feet to Window Lake, 2,260 feet to the end of the trail
highest point: 10,022 feet
maps: Amber Lakes, Easley Hot Springs
time: 10 hours
difficulty: expert
access: On Highway 75, turn right (east) 7.4 miles north of Ketchum at the SNRA Headquarters onto the gravel and dirt North Fork Big Wood River Road and drive to the end of the road at 5 miles.
caution: The route to Window Lake is steep, hazardous, and hard to find. Because the lake is in a fragile alpine area, avoid camping at it.

At the end of the West Fork North Fork Wood River Trail is a valley of wildflowers below sheer-walled peaks. At the head of this valley, a feathery waterfall glides down a niche in a black cliff. Along the lower parts of the trail, other waterfalls hide in mossy gorges.

If you choose the rough cross-country route to blue-green Window Lake instead, you will find an alpine garden. In it, red and white mountain heather, marsh marigold, alpine buttercup and dwarf lupine grow among pink, orange and gray rocks. On a knoll below crumbling gray peaks, stand the only trees, dwarfed and flattened whitebark pines.

To reach the trailhead, follow the access directions above. Park at the end of the road (6,900 feet). Start the hike by fording the North Fork of the Big Wood River to the west bank. This ford can be hazardous in early summer and until early August in wet years. On the far side of the ford, the trail starts as an old road in the woods. Beyond a register box at 150 yards, the trail turns left off the road and begins to climb above the creek within 200 yards. In an avalanche area full of little trees, it returns to the creek. At Amber Gulch at 1 mile, the trail angles up to the right onto a wooded bench.

In meadows at 1.5 miles, the tread becomes faint or non-existant for 1.2 miles. Here there is a view ahead of peaks above Window Lake. A path close to a waterfall at the head of the open area is not the trail; the correct route is uphill. At 2.3 miles, the trail reappears in the trees 100 feet above the creek and

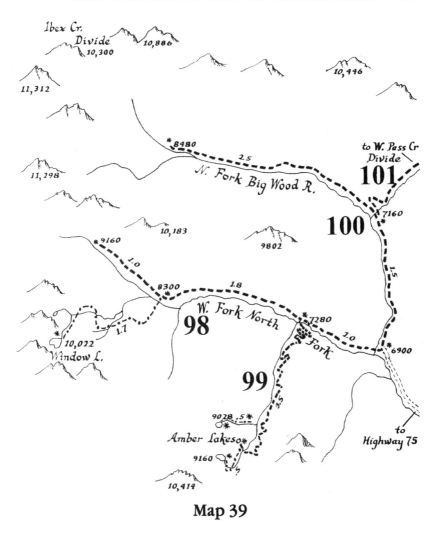

Map 39

climbs along in woods with occasional switchbacks. When the path descends 100 feet at 2.6 miles, a wooded side canyon appears across the creek, but it is not the canyon of Window Lake.

At 2.8 miles, a narrow open area of grass and tiny trees extends southwest up the ridge that is across the main creek. This open strip is the easiest route to Window Lake. To climb this slope, leave the trail at 2.8 miles (8,300 feet) and cross the creek. The total climb to Window Lake from the trailhead is 3,122 feet, so it will take longer than usual for a 4.5 mile hike. At 3.5 miles, where the hillside becomes less steep for a short distance 600 vertical feet above the creek, turn right (west) to two streams. The right (north) one of these is the outlet of Window Lake.

Keep left of both streams at first. In .1 mile where the left stream splits, climb the right branch of this split, which is usually dry, in a ravine. This leads to a large flat grassy area at 9,400 feet, which is shown on the topographic map as a wide interval between contour lines.

From the flat area, go right (north) to the outlet of Window Lake and cross it to the north side below a waterfall at 3.8 miles. Climb away from the creek around a rock bench, and return to it at 4.1 miles where it meets a creek from a pond. Ford back to the left (south) of the creek and walk over rock benches to the lake (10,022 feet) at 4.5 miles.

If you want to go to the end of the trail instead of the lake, do not turn off at 2.8 miles. Stay on the trail, which gradually turns northwest into an open valley of grass and rocks at 3 miles where a feathery waterfall is seen in the distance. The trail ends below the waterfall at 3.8 miles (9,160 feet).

99 Amber Lakes
Map 39

round trip: 9 miles to the end of the trail; 1 mile additional to see the upper
 lake; 2 miles additional for both lakes
elevation gain: 2,260 feet
highest point: 9,160 feet
map: Amber Lakes
time: 10 hours to see both lakes
difficulty: strenuous to the end of the trail; expert for the lakes
access: Turn north off of Highway 75 at the SNRA Headquarters 7.4 miles
 north of Ketchum. Drive 5 miles on the gravel and dirt North Fork Big
 Wood River Road to the end of the road.
caution: Avoid camping in the fragile alpine lake basin.

In some lights, the two tiny Amber Lakes reflect the amber color of the peaks above, but in others, they reflect the blue of the sky. Jumbled silver wood from old avalanches line the edges of both shallow lakes and debris from a recent avalanche has flattened the trees at the upper lake. The climb provides excellent views of the colorfully striped Boulder Mountains. To reach the lakes from the end of the trail, which was reconstructed in 1995, cross-country travel is required.

To reach the trailhead, follow the access directions above. The ford of the West Fork of the Big Wood River at the beginning of the hike can be hazardous or impassable in early summer. To begin the hike, wade across the West Fork here and follow the trail along it for 1 mile. The Amber Lakes turnoff (7,280 feet) is on a bench in the woods. The trail begins by dropping to a ford of the West Fork of the North Fork that can be difficult in early summer. Just

North Fork Big Wood River

before the ford, a sign directs you to it. There is a footlog high above the West Fork, but many hikers will feel safer wading across.

On the other side of the West Fork, the trail switchbacks up through the woods in six long switchbacks. At 2 miles from the trailhead, it goes below a boulder field. The new trail stays out of the gorge of the creek, now and then making short switchbacks. At 3 miles it runs along the left side of a grassy bowl sprinkled with little trees. The trail continues up a wooded ridge to another grassy valley at 3.5 miles, where the outlet of the lower lake cascades into the main creek. From here the path switchbacks along the left side of the outlet of the upper lake, then crosses it to the right side. It ends at a small pond at 4.5 miles.

To reach the lower lake from the second grassy valley, climb .5 mile up the ledges and grass on the right (north) of its outlet to the lake (9,028 feet). To reach the upper lake from the pond where the trail ends, walk up grassy slopes on the right (west) side of the main creek with woods above on both sides. At 5.2 miles the woods end and the creek curves west and north around a knoll. The lake is at 5.5 miles (9,160 feet). From either lake, hikers can reach the other by climbing over the 250-foot saddle between them.

100 North Fork Big Wood River
Map 38 and 39

round trip: 8 miles
elevation gain: 1,620 feet
elevation loss (return climb): 40 feet
highest point: 8,480 feet
maps: Amber Lakes, Ryan Peak
time: 6 1/2 to 7 hours
difficulty: moderate
access: On Highway 75, 7.4 miles north of Ketchum, turn north at the SNRA
Headquarters. Drive 5 miles on the gravel and dirt road to the trailhead.

On this hike through wildflower meadows under orange and gray crags,
waterfalls hide in chasms. The meadows are avalanche areas that extend up the
canyon walls. Some are beginning to be filled with tiny subalpine firs. From
the upper trail, the pleated, jagged top of Kent Peak bars the canyon. At 4
miles, the trail disappears in downed timber, but energetic experts can hike
cross-country another 1.5 miles and 1,800 vertical feet to a 10,300-foot divide
overlooking Ibex Creek.

To reach the trailhead (6,900 feet), follow the access directions above. The
trail first climbs 80 feet up a wooded ridge, then drops to the edge of the creek.
Next, it goes along the side of the canyon to avoid a washout, then returns to
the creek at a grassy flat at .4 mile. Here the official trail fords the river to the
west bank for .4 mile, but most hikers climb a steep path on an open hillside to
a sagebrush flat at .6 mile. After a stretch of woods at .8 mile, the path rejoins
the main trail which has returned to the east side of the river.

The trail crosses talus and two or three side creeks. It turns 90 degrees to the
right in forest, makes a hairpin turn, and goes straight up the canyon again on
a smaller sagebrush flat. In this flat at 1.5 miles, cairns and a path mark the
turnoff for the trail to the West Pass Creek Divide.

Keep on the main trail, which returns to the edge of the creek in willows.
The first of the wildflower-sagebrush meadows is at 2 miles, where the creek
runs in cascades and then in a gorge. To avoid confusion, watch for cairns
marking the trail through the meadows.

At 2.4 miles, the route crosses a side stream and climbs an outcrop. Beyond
a gully full of rye grass, the trail ascends a bluff to the left. At 2.6 miles, the
trail returns to forest beside waterfalls in a gorge. The way levels at a campsite,
and at 2.7 miles, enters another long meadow. At the far end at 3.6 miles, the
trail climbs another bluff into more woods. A third, much shorter open area
with downed trees is at 3.7 miles. Here, the route fords a side creek, but it does
not go back and forth across the river at 3.6 and 3.7 miles as shown on the

map. Beyond where the river splits into a "Y" at 3.8 miles, the trail enters woods and at 4 miles (8,480 feet), disappears in downed timber.

101 West Pass Creek Divide
Maps 38 and 39

round trip: 8 miles
elevation gain: 3,140 feet
highest point: 10,040 feet
maps: Amber Lakes, Ryan Peak
time: 8 hours
difficulty: strenuous
access: On Highway 75, 7.4 miles north of Ketchum, turn north on the North Fork Big Wood River Road at SNRA Headquarters. Drive 5 miles on the gravel and dirt road to the trailhead.

Across West Pass Creek from this divide, Glassford Peak and the peaks around it are tinted red, gold and orange. East of these peaks float the white peaks of the White Clouds. Above the divide, the orange-streaked cliffs of Ryan Peak merge with the crinkled wall and towers of Kent Peak. This trail climbs almost 2,880 feet in 2.5 miles, so you need to plan for the steep ascent.

To reach the trailhead, follow the access directions above. For the first 1.5 miles of the trail along the North Fork of the Wood River, detailed directions are given in Hike 100 (North Fork Wood River). On this trail at 1.5 miles just beyond a long sagebrush area, the trail turns 90 degrees to the right for 100 yards. Then it makes a hairpin turn to the left and goes straight up the canyon into another sagebrush flat. In the flat (7,160 feet) cairns mark an unsigned trail to the right (east). This is the trail to the West Pass Creek Divide.

Turn off onto it, looking for blazes in the forest to find the right route. The trail angles up the canyon for 200 yards, and then makes two switchbacks, each 400 yards long. At 2 miles, the way comes to the edge of a side canyon of the North Fork above a waterfall. From here, the trail turns up the side canyon on an open slope. It hops two small side creeks, which are dry in late season, and goes below a grove of Douglas firs.

At the head of a gorge at 2.8 miles, the trail comes close to the branch of the North Fork. After crossing a third side creek, it climbs scree and talus. At 3 miles, the main creek splits in a basin of tiny subalpine firs. Across the basin to the south, rock ledges stairstep up an unnamed gray triangular peak.

The route curves west up the left branch of the creek in whitebark pines near a lumpy campsite at 3.2 miles. The trail edges the creek at 3.4 miles, and disappears in moss. It winds northwest up a steep rocky slope onto a talus ridge dotted with whitebark pines. At 3.7 miles, the path runs along on the left of a gully across from a burnt orange outcrop. It goes into a grass and talus basin at 3.8 miles. After climbing above this basin, the trail disappears in turf and reaches the divide at 4 miles. On the other side, it descends 2,000 feet in 2.5 miles into the canyon of West Pass Creek to an old road up that creek from Bowery Guard Station. This road is closed to motor vehicles at a ford 5 miles below the pass.

EAST FORK OF SALMON RIVER AREA

102 East Fork Salmon River Trail
Map 40

round trip: 9 miles
elevation gain: 440 feet
highest point: 7,200 feet
maps: Ryan Peak, Galena Peak
time: 6 1/2 hours
difficulty: moderate
access: On Highway 75, 36.5 miles east of Stanley, turn south on the East Fork of the Salmon River Road. Drive 14.7 miles on pavement, 6.3 miles on gravel, and 7.3 miles on dirt to the end of the road at a gate .2 mile before the Bowery Guard Station. A new trailhead from near West Pass Creek .3 mile before the gate is planned.

This hike leads toward an alpine headwall of the highest Boulder Mountains. You can see the headwall from the trailhead, but it is much more impressive from close up. In early to mid-summer, the headwall holds streaks and patches of snow. With triangular gray peaks flanking it, the rectangular top of Galena Peak marks the center. Cool weather is best for this hike, as the trail follows the blue-green curves of the East Fork in sagebrush with no shade. A ford of the East Fork at one mile limits this route at present to midsummer and later. The Forest Service plans to build a new trailhead and a new trail for this first mile that will cross the river on a bridge. Both the present trail and the route of the proposed new section are described here.

To begin the hike, follow the access directions above. From the gate on the road 28.3 miles from Highway 75, the present trail starts off up a slope to the left (east) of the gate. From here to the junction at the head of the canyon, the trail follows an old road closed so long ago to motor vehicles that two tracks are seldom found. The topographic map wrongly shows it as a road. At .2 mile, the trail turns right (west) and goes through a gate, and soon the guard station is seen across the river.

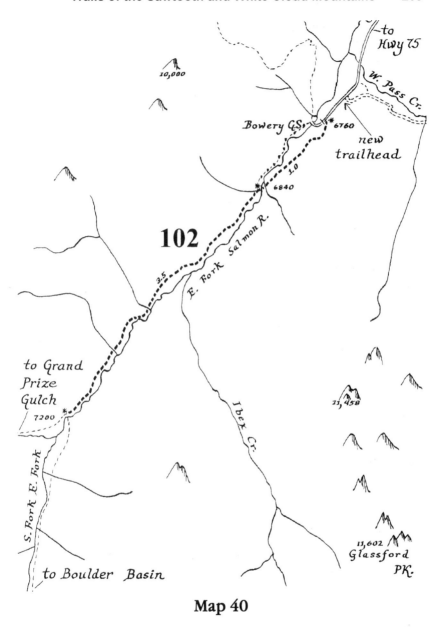

Map 40

The trail continues on a sagebrush bench above the river, then goes between two small sagebrush hills and through a second gate. At .7 mile the route drops into a meadow, crosses a side stream at 1 mile and fords the river a few yards farther on. This ford is impassable to hikers until mid- or late-

Boulder Mountains from East Fork Salmon River Trail

August in wet years and until August 1 in dry years because the river is swift here and more than knee deep. It is too wide for logs to span it.

The proposed new trail will begin where a road turns off up West Pass Creek 28 miles from Highway 93 and will lead up the main road .3 mile to the guard station fence. Then it will probably follow the road across a bridge over the river to meet the Bowery Cutoff Trail. This trail has come 4.5 miles with a 1,660-foot elevation gain and 2,000-foot loss from the Germania Creek Trail 6.7 miles east of the Three Cabins Creek trailhead.

From the junction with the Bowery Cutoff Trail, the trail up the East Fork will roughly follow the route of an existing path along the west side of the river. This first leads up onto a sagebrush bench 50 feet above the river, passing a rounded gray knoll on the opposite bank 1 mile from the proposed trailhead. Then it will drop to the river and run along next to it between rock outcrops on a steep slope and willows edging the river bank. The route will skirt the edge of a marshy area at 1.4 miles and join the main trail just beyond the existing ford at 1.5 miles, 1 mile from the trailhead by way of the current trail. At present the path that avoids the ford has treacherous footing and disappears in the marsh.

On the current trail, if you are unable to wade the ford, and prefer not to cross the bridge and take the path, hike cross-country 2 miles up the east side of the river to a better ford. Much of this 2 miles is across grass and willow flats and gentle sagebrush slopes.

There are two main obstacles on this route. First, the river flows right under a steep wooded slope from 1.5 through 1.8 miles. Here you must climb 30 to 50 feet up the slope and edge along it. The second obstacle is a ford of Ibex Creek at 2.3 miles. The creek is two-thirds the size of the river. Ibex Creek can be forded most easily where it spreads out 100 yards above the river. To ford the river itself, at 3.1 miles look for a place where it curves 90 degrees to the right (west) for .1 mile and then splits into several sections.

If the ford on the trail at 1 mile is passable, the trail from there to the 3-mile point runs along open sagebrush slopes, skirting a patch of forest at 2 miles. Willows, cottonwoods, small meadows, Douglas firs, and lodgepoles edge the river. Wooded ridges form the left side of the canyon and on the right side, sagebrush, scattered Douglas firs, and outcrops rise to four pinkish-gray summits. At 2.3 miles, there is a view of cliffs, a rounded mountain, and a prominent dark gray tooth up Ibex Creek. At 3.1 miles, the path crosses a side creek and drops to a meadow beside the wide section of the river that provides a better ford than the one on the trail.

Beyond the meadow, the trail jogs up to the right 30 vertical feet, then turns back up the canyon, keeping well above the river most of the time. At 3.7 miles, the trail fords a small side creek in a strip of trees that frame the best view of the headwall.

At 3.9 miles, the trail drops to the edge of the riverside willows and then climbs back up onto sagebrush slopes. It hops a small side stream that may be dry at 4 miles, and then flattens out. At 4.5 miles the path is beside a curve of the river at 7,200 feet.

Beyond here the canyons of the South Fork of the East Fork and the West Fork of the East Fork divide, and trails lead up both. However, there is no sign or trail tread for the South Fork Trail on this side of the river. To find it, go 30 yards west and look across the river for a "closed to motorized travel" sign on a tree. This trail leads over a 10,600-foot pass to Boulder Basin, 13 miles from the Bowery trailhead, but it is seldom maintained.

From the unmarked junction, the West Fork of East Fork Trail climbs sagebrush slopes into forest below two prominent wooded peaks with summits of gray rock. This trail goes 5 miles with a 1,840-foot climb to connect with the Galena Gulch and Grand Prize Gulch trails. It gives access 6 miles from the Bowery Guard Station to an unnamed lake at 9,550 feet, 1.5 miles south of the trail.

TRAIL CREEK AREA

103 North Fork Lake

Map 38

round trip: 4 miles
elevation gain: 994 feet
highest point: 9,354 feet
maps: Meridian Peak, Ryan Peak
time: 6 1/2 hours
difficulty: expert
access: From Main Street in Ketchum, go east on the paved and gravel Trail Creek Road over Trail Creek Summit. At 20.6 miles, turn left (west) on the dirt North Fork of the Big Lost River Road and drive along it to Blind Creek at 30.8 miles. Turn left and cross the North Fork on a bridge. Continue on a primitive road, taking the right branch at 32 miles. Where the road makes a small loop at 32.9 miles, go left and park in aspens at 33.3 miles.

The narrow strip of aquamarine North Fork Lake separates a gray mountain wall from an orange one. At the head of the lake, orange rock meets gray in a row of orange cylinders divided by strips of gray. The gray talus on the south side of the lake rises to a sheer gray wall, and the orange talus on the north slopes to a mottled orange mountain. This hike, which is corss-country at present, is just outside the Sawtooth National Recreation Area but within the same scenic high country.

To reach the beginning of this hike, follow the access directions above. Above the parking area, red, orange, gray and cream stripes twist and curve across the high peaks of the Boulder Mountains. From it, walk southwest up the ridge for only 200 yards. (Continuing up the ridge is a much more difficult route than ascending the creek because of downed timber and steep talus.)

Turn right and gradually descend to the North Fork at .5 mile, where a side branch joins from the west. Climb south away from the creek a few yards onto a wrinkle to stay out of the creek's ravine. At a meadow at 1 mile, ford the creek to the right (north). Long ago a trail led to the lake, but it disappeared. Volunteers are repairing it. Now the route climbs a steep slope with ledges and then goes above a 100-foot gorge. Be careful.

Above this, the slope lessens and the gorge widens opposite a slope of tiny firs and downed timber. At 1.3 miles, descend to the creek and walk along the grass beside it. Keep well away from the creek at 1.5 miles on a steep grassy hillside. After the ground flattens at 1.7 miles, walk through the grass to the lower end of the lake at 2 miles.

APPENDIX
TRAILS NOT COVERED IN TEXT

SAWTOOTHS

BENCH CREEK: Access: Highway 21. From Highway 21, .4 mile south of road to Bull Trout Lake, southeast to Swamp Creek Trail .1 mile north of Marten Lake. Only .7 mile of this trail is in the SNRA. 5.5 miles, 1,280 feet gain, 644 feet loss. Map: Banner Summit.

BENEDICT CREEK: Access: Grandjean. From South Fork of Payette River Trail 2.9 miles above Elk Lake, southwest to junction of Queens River Trail and trail to Benedict Lake. Trail from this junction to Spangle Lakes, considered a part of Benedict Creek Trail, is covered in text. 3.5 miles, 960 feet gain. Map: Mt. Everly.

BRAXON LAKE: Access: Grandjean or Redfish Inlet Transfer Camp. Originally from Baron Creek Trail 1.0 mile below Baron Lake to old trail crew camp below Braxon Lakes. Now peters out half way to lakes. Not maintained, not shown on maps. Mileage and elevation gain not available. Map: Warbonnet Peak.

BULL MOOSE: Access: Decker Flat. From Decker Flat to Redfish-Decker Lake Trail .2 mile southwest of junction with Redfish Ridge Trail. 4.5 miles, 1,020 feet gain. Map: Mt. Cramer.

DIAMOND LAKE: Access: Atlanta. From Little Queens River Trail .3 mile west of Browns Lake Junction to Diamond Lake. Old trail, no longer maintained and not on any maps. Fords river, steep. .9 mile, 640 feet gain. Map: Nahneke Mountain.

ELK CREEK: Access: Elk Meadows or Stanley Lake. From Elk Meadows-Elizabeth Lake Junction south up to Elk Summit and then east down to Stanley Lake Creek Trail. 9.5 miles, 1,780 feet gain, 1,520 feet loss. Maps: Banner Summit, Grandjean, Stanley Lake.

EUREKA GULCH (jeep trail): Access: Alturas Lake Road. From Alturas Lake Road .3 mile west of ford of Alpine Creek to mines of old mining settlement of Eureka. No buildings. Good view of Alpine Creek Canyon. 3 miles, 1,580 feet gain. Maps: Snowyside Peak, Marshall Peak.

FLAT TOP LAKES: Access: Queens River Road. From Scenic Lakes Trail 2.4 miles from Little Queens River to first of two Flat Top Lakes. No path, just a line of blazes. .7 mile, 800 feet gain. Map: Nahneke Mountain.

Galena Peak and Boulder Mountains from Governors Punchbowl

HIDDEN LAKE: (No trail) Access: Highway 75. Although a trail is shown on the topographic map, it does not exist. Only cow paths wander over the meadows in the area. The lake can be reached from a picnic area at the highway by walking up the chain of meadows along Meadow Creek, then at 1.5 miles climbing up on a ridge to the right (north) and following it to the lake at 2 miles. Reaching the lake is difficult and hazardous because of bogs, downed timber, and lack of landmarks. A compass is required.

HUCKLEBERRY CREEK: Access: Decker Flat. From Decker Flat southwest to Redfish-Decker Lake Trail .7 mile north of Hell Roaring Lake. 3.8 miles, 1,430 feet gain. Map: Mt. Cramer.

JOE DALEY: Access: Atlanta. From Queens River Trail south to roads near Atlanta airstrip that lead to bridge and Riverside Campground. 4.5 miles, 1,320 feet gain. Map: Atlanta West.

JOHNSON CREEK (near Graham): Access: road to Graham Guard Station. From Johnson Creek Campground east and north to Bayhouse Trail. Upper end covered in text. Four fords of creek. The area along the trail burned in the 1994 fires. 5 miles, 700 feet gain. Maps: Swanholm Peak, Nahneke Mountain.

JOHNSON CREEK (North Fork Ross Fork): Access: Alturas Creek Road. From Mattingly Creek Divide Trail south past a junction with the North Fork of Ross Fork Trail at .6 mile, then southeast to Ross Fork of Boise River.

Provides cross-country access to Johnson Lake and access to Ross Fork, Perkons and Bass Lakes without the need to drive around by Dollarhide Summit or Fairfield. 7.6 miles, 235 feet gain, 2,055 feet loss. Map: Marshall Peak.

LILY POND: Access: Redfish Lake boat or trail around lake. Take unsigned trail south toward Hell Roaring Lake from Redfish Inlet Transfer Camp across bridge over Redfish Creek and along shore of lake for .3 mile, then turn right on .2 mile path to pond. .5 mile, 100 feet gain from transfer camp. Map: Mt. Cramer.

MEADOW CREEK: Access: BLOCKED by posted private land. From pasture 3.0 miles southwest of Stanley to Alpine Way Trail 2.8 miles north of Marshall Lake. 1.2 miles, 450 feet gain. Map: Stanley Lake.

NEINMEYER CREEK: Access: Queens River Road or Graham Road. From Johnson Creek Trail .6 mile south of Bayhouse Trail Junction southeast over Grouse Creek Pass down into Black Warrior Creek, over another divide and down to the Little Queens River 6.2 miles from the trailhead. Much of the area along the trail burned in the 1994 fires. 7.6 miles, 2,320 feet gain, 2,080 feet loss. Map: Nahneke Mountain.

NORTH FORK BOISE RIVER: Access: Grandjean or Silver Creek trailhead on Graham Road. From South Fork Payette River Trail 3.8 miles from Grandjean south to Bayhouse Trail 1.0 mile east of Graham Road. North end begins with 120-foot ford of South Fork of Payette, which can be dangerous or impassable in early summer. South end connects with trail to Graham Road, a rough, primitive road recommended only for four-wheel drive vehicles. The area along the trail and road burned in the 1994 fires. 11.8 miles, 2,271 feet gain, 1,656 feet loss. Maps: Edaho Mountain, Nahneke Mountain, Swanholm Peak.

PICKET MOUNTAIN: Access: Grandjean. From North Fork Boise River Trail over Picket Mountain (within 100 feet of summit) and out of the SNRA to junction with Wapiti Creek Trail. The area along the trail burned in the 1994 fires. 4.5 miles, 1,404 feet gain, 280 feet loss. Map: Edaho Mountain.

REDFISH RIDGE: Access: Decker Flat Road. From Bull Moose Trail .2 mile from trailhead to Grand Mogul Trail 2.5 miles from Sockeye Campground. 3.0 miles, 740 feet gain. Maps: Mt. Cramer, Stanley.

SMILEY CREEK: Access: Smiley Creek Road. Unsigned trail from Vienna south to divide between Smiley Creek and West Fork Big Smoky Creek. To avoid posted land park at Vienna and walk up road to trail. Covered in *Trails of Western Idaho* by the author. 3.0 miles, 1,440 feet gain. Map: Frenchman Creek.

SWAMP CREEK: Access: Highway 21. From .7 mile south of Thatcher Creek Campground to Trap Creek Trail at Marten Lake. 6.0 miles, 910 feet gain. Map: Banner Summit.

THREE ISLAND LAKE: Access: From Atlanta or Grandjean or Yellow Belly Lake. From Benedict Creek Trail between Rock Slide and Benedict Lakes south to Three Island Lake. .6 mile, 200 feet gain. Map: Mt. Everly.

WHITE CLOUDS

BIG LAKE CREEK: Access: East Fork Salmon River Road. From end of 1.3-mile spur road up Big Lake Creek northwest past Jimmy Smith Lake at .2 mile and then west up Big Lake Creek to French Creek Jeep Trail. Joins 1.5 miles north of Railroad Ridge. Most of trail in sagebrush. No view of high peaks from lake. 10.5 miles, 3,020 feet gain. Maps: Potaman Peak, Livingston Creek.

BLUETT CREEK: Access: East Fork Salmon River. From East Fork Salmon River Road west and then north to Big Lake Creek Trail 5.8 miles from trailhead. Not signed, not maintained, not on topographic map. About 6 miles, 2,500 feet gain. Map: Potaman Peak.

CHAMBERLAIN CREEK: Access: Pole Creek - Germania Creek Road. From Germania Creek Trail to Livingston - Castle Divide Trail .5 mile east of the lowest Chamberlain Lake. 2.3 miles along trail, Chamberlain Creek Falls lies in chasm .2 mile south of trail. Provides loop to Chamberlain Lakes and back by way of Washington Creek. 3.7 miles, 2,190 feet gain. Map: Boulder Chain Lakes.

OLD CHAMPION CREEK: Access: BLOCKED by private land reached from the Valley Road. From spur road up Champion Creek east to new Champion Creek Trail from Fourth of July Creek. **Use new trail instead.** Maps: Washington Peak, Horton Peak.

FRENCH CREEK: Access: Highway 75 between Sunbeam and Clayton. From Highway 75, 1 mile east of Yankee Fork Guard Station south to Railroad Ridge. Top third still open to motor vehicles, bottom two-thirds closed to vehicles, but all but the bottom half mile is open to cycles. Access at bottom in the Salmon River Canyon presently is BLOCKED by posted private property. 11.5 miles, 4,160 feet gain. Maps: Clayton, Potaman Peak, Livingston Creek.

GARLAND CREEK: Access: Rough Creek or Boundary Creek. From Rough Creek Trail 4.5 miles from trailhead east to Warm Springs Creek 6.8 miles south of Robinson Bar. 5.5 miles, 2,020 feet loss. Maps: Casino Lakes, Robinson Bar.

GOVERNORS PUNCHBOWL: Access: Highway 75, 25.3 miles north of Ketchum. From parking area north of highway to small, greenish-gray pond. Trail is only a strip cleared of timber long ago for a stock driveway. Lower part marked with yellow stock driveway signs. Starts along branch road closest to highway leading west. Unsigned, no path after the first 200 yards, rough ground. Beautiful wildflowers and view of Boulder Mountains. 1.2 miles, 1,672 feet gain. Map: Horton Peak.

LITTLE CASINO CREEK: Access: From Highway 75, 3 miles east of Stanley by Big Casino Creek Bridge. From dirt road along river southwest to junction with Boundary Creek Trail. 9.0 miles, 2,800 feet gain. Maps: East Basin Creek, Casino Lakes.

LITTLE REDFISH LAKE: Access: Livingston Mill - Frog Lake Trail. From that trail 1.5 miles south of junction with Big Boulder Creek Trail southeast to Little Redfish Lake. 1.0 mile, 400 feet gain. Map: Boulder Chain Lakes.

LOOKOUT MOUNTAIN: Access: Rough Creek. From Rough Creek Trail 3.1 miles above trailhead northeast to summit of Lookout Mountain. Lookout no longer occupied but is being restored. 2.5 miles, 420 feet gain. Map: Casino Lakes.

MARTIN CREEK: Access: Rough Creek or Boundary Creek. From Big Casino - Boundary Creek Junction southeast to Martin Creek and east to Warm Springs Creek at north end The Meadows. 6.0 miles, 1,680 feet loss. Maps: Casino Lakes, Robinson Bar.

RED RIDGE: Trail on map no longer exists. Map: Bowery Creek.

SULLIVAN LAKE: Access: From Highway 75, 2.5 miles east of Yankee Fork Ranger Station. BLOCKED by posted private property of ranch at beginning of trail. Can best be reached by Corral Creek Trail from north end Jimmy Smith Lake. This route is 12 miles round trip, 1540 feet gain, and 80% in sagebrush with no shade. Route from Highway 75 covered in *Trails of Western Idaho* by the author. Mostly sagebrush, but colorful canyon. 2.6 miles, 1,170 feet gain. Maps: Clayton, Potaman Peak.

SUNNY GULCH: Access: Highway 75 at Sunny Gulch Campground. From Sunny Gulch Campground to Little Casino Creek Trail 3.5 miles northwest of Boundary Creek Junction. No bridge over Salmon River at beginning of trail. Not on topo map. About 1.5 miles, 1,040 feet gain. Map: Stanley.

WARM SPRINGS CREEK (lower): Access: From Highway 75 BLOCKED by posted private property and gate. Use access from Aztec Mine and Pigtail Creek Trail (see Hike 72, Warm Springs Meadows and Hike 73, Williams Creek). Four fords of Warm Springs Creek and five fords of large side creeks. Provides cross-country access to Swimm Lake via Swimm Creek. 11.2 miles from Salmon River to The Meadows, 1,360 feet gain. Map: Robinson Bar.

WASHINGTON BASIN TO CHAMPION LAKES: Access: Washington Basin Jeep Trail. From jeep trail to Champion Lakes Trail at Upper Champion Lake. 1.8 miles, 680 feet gain. Map: Washington Peak.

WICKIUP CREEK: Access: East Fork Salmon River Road. From East Fork Salmon River Road near the corrals at the mouth of Wickiup and Sheep Creeks, southwest and then northwest to Castle Divide Trail .6 mile north of divide. Not maintained. 7.0 miles, 3,140 feet gain. Maps: Bowery Creek, Boulder Chain Lakes.

BOULDERS

BOWERY CUTOFF: Access: East Fork of Salmon River Road to Bowery Guard Station. From trailhead 0.5 mile below Bowery Guard Station to Germania Creek Trail 6.7 miles east of Three Cabins Creek trailhead. 5.0 miles, 1,660 feet gain, 2,000 feet loss. Maps: Boulder Chain Lakes, Galena Peak, Ryan Peak.

KONRAD CREEK: Goes up only the lower 1.5 miles of Konrad Creek. Not on topographic map. Location of trail on forest map wrong. Goes up Konrad Creek on west side, crossing to the east at .7 mile. Does not connect with Amber Lakes Trail. Map: Amber Lakes.

SOUTH FORK EAST FORK SALMON RIVER: Access: East Fork of Salmon River Road to Bowery Guard Station. From junction on East Fork Salmon River Trail 4.0 miles above trailhead with trail up West Fork East Fork. Goes south to divide above Boulder Basin. No road access. East Fork Trail shown as road is not open to four-wheeled vehicles. Not maintained, hard to find. 7.6 miles, 3,360 feet gain. Maps: Easley Hot Springs, Galena Peak.

WEST FORK EAST FORK SALMON RIVER: Access: Grand Prize Gulch. From Grand Prize Gulch Trail at Gladiator Creek Junction to South Fork East Fork Trail. 5.0 miles, 1,840 feet loss. Maps: Horton Peak, Galena Peak.

SMOKIES

BAKER LAKE: Access: Baker Creek Road. From that road west to Baker Lake. Not in SNRA; administered by Ketchum Ranger District. Covered in *Trails of Western Idaho* by author. 1.0 mile, 870 feet gain. Map: Baker Peak.

MILL LAKE: Access: Prairie Creek Road. From Prairie Creek Road to Mill Lake. The road (not the trail and lake) is in the SNRA; the trail and lake are in the Ketchum Ranger District. Covered in *Trails of Western Idaho* by author. 2.0 miles, 1,020 feet gain. Map: Galena.

Hikers on the way to Boulder Basin

MINER LAKE: Access: Prairie Creek Road. From Prairie Creek Trail 2.5 miles south of trailhead to Miner Lake. The road (not the trail and lake) is in the SNRA; the trail and lake are in the Ketchum Ranger District. Covered in *Trails of Western Idaho.* 1.5 miles, 1,100 feet gain. Map: Galena.

NORTON LAKE: Access: Baker Creek Road. From 1-mile spur road up Norton Creek to Norton Lakes. Not in SNRA; in Ketchum Ranger District. Covered in *Trails of Western Idaho.* 2.2 miles, 1,460 feet gain. Map: Baker Peak

PRAIRIE LAKES: Access: Prairie Creek Road. From that road to Prairie Lakes. The road (not the trail and lakes) is in the SNRA; the trail and lakes are in the Ketchum Ranger District. Covered in *Trails of Western Idaho.* 5.0 miles, 1,500 feet gain. Map: Galena.

WEST FORK PRAIRIE CREEK: Access: Prairie Creek Road. From that road northwest up canyon to dead end. Originally it continued to the head of the canyon, over a divide and back down to Prairie Creek. In Ketchum Ranger District. Existing trail about 1.8 miles, 600 feet gain. Map: Galena.

SUGGESTIONS FOR LOOP OR THROUGH TRIPS

trailhead	points on the trail	miles	days
Grandjean	Baron, Alpine, Hidden and Elk lakes	43	4-6
Hell Roaring Creek	Imogene, Edith, Edna, Hidden, Cramer, Alpine, Baron, and Trail Creek lakes, Stanley Lake Creek, Alpine Way, Marshall, Redfish, Bench and Decker lakes, Hell Roaring Lake	92	11-14
Powerplant CG at Atlanta to Grandjean	Rock Creek, Spangle, Ardeth, Edna, Cramer, and Baron lakes, Grandjean.	74	7-10
Queens River to Grandjean	Queens River, Everly Lake, Benedict Creek, South Fork of the Payette, Grandjean	41	5
Livingston Mill to Little Boulder Cr.	Walker, Frog, Boulder Chain, and Baker lakes, Little Boulder Creek	35	5-7
Germania Creek	Germania Creek, Bowery Guard Station, East Fork Salmon River Trail, West Fork of East Fork Trail, Galena Gulch	26	3-4
Germania Creek to Little Boulder Creek	Germania Creek, Chamberlain Lakes, Castle Divide, Baker Lake Boulder Chain Lakes, Little Boulder Creek	21	3-5

GUIDE TO TRIPS

EASY TRIPS (not more than 7 miles; less than 1,000-foot elevation gain; no cross-country travel)

Elk Meadows (must ford creek), Farley Lake, Fishhook Creek, Fourth of July Lake, Headwaters of the Salmon River, Hell Roaring Lake, Phyllis Lake, Redfish Lake to Flatrock Junction.

MODERATE TRIPS (5 to 10 miles and 1,000 to 1,800-foot elevation gain, no cross-country travel)

Alpine Way (north), Bench Lakes, Mays Creek to McDonald Lake, Marten and Kelly Lakes, Sawtooth Lake, Warm Springs Meadows.

PARTLY CROSS COUNTRY (for experienced hikers only). To protect fragile soils and plants, do not camp at these lakes; take only small parties; in the cross-country part walk on rock where possible.

Alpine Creek Lakes, Amber Lakes, Bench Lakes 3,4, and 5, Big Boulder Lakes, Born Lakes, Castle Lake, Decker Lakes, Elizabeth Lake, Four Lakes Basin, Goat Lake (Sawtooths), Goat Lake (White Clouds), Hanson Lakes, Heart Lake (Sawtooths), Heart and Six Lakes (White Clouds), Leggit Lake (trail disappears), Lightning Lake, Lucille and Profile Lakes, North Fork Lake, Quiet and Noisy Lakes, Rainbow Lake, Rough Lake, Saddleback Lakes, Shallow and Scree Lakes, Sheep Lake, Silver Lake, Upper Redfish Lakes.

HIKES FOR EXPERTS (poor footing and/or route difficult to find). These areas are fragile; avoid camping in the lake basins.

Alpine Creek Lakes, Big Boulder Lakes, Castle Lake, East Fork North Fork, Elizabeth Lake, Four Lakes Basin, Galena Gulch, Goat Lake, Leggit Lake, Lucille and Profile Lakes, North Fork Lake, Quiet and Noisy Lakes, Rainbow Lake, Rough Lake, Saddleback Lakes, Scenic Lakes, Shallow and Scree Lakes, Silver Lake, Upper Redfish Lakes, West Fork North Fork Wood River.

LIKELY TO BE OVERCROWDED

Alice Lake, Alpine Lake (Redfish), Alpine Lake (Iron Creek), Baron Lakes, Bench Lakes, Boulder Chain Lakes, Cramer Lakes, Farley Lake, Fishhook Creek, Fourth of July Lake, Frog Lake, Hell Roaring Lake, Imogene Lake, Sawtooth Lake, Toxaway Lake, Twin Lakes, Walker Lake, Washington Lake, Williams Creek.

SELDOM VISITED

Benedict, Rock Slide, and Ingeborg Lakes, Hanson Lakes, Camp and Heart Lakes, Casino and Garland Lakes, Elizabeth Lake, Elk Lake to Hidden Lake Junction, Everly and Plummer Lakes, Frenchman Creek, Johnson Lake, Leggit Lake, Marten and Kelly Lakes, North Fork Wood River, Pats and Arrowhead

Lakes, Quiet and Noisy Lakes, Rock Creek to Spangle Lakes, Rough Lake, Scenic Lakes, Shallow and Scree Lakes, Washington Basin, West Pass Creek Divide

RARELY VISITED

Bayhouse and Johnson Creek Trail, Champion Creek, Decker Lakes to Redfish Inlet, East Fork North Fork Wood River, East Fork Salmon River, Ga-lena Gulch, Gladiator Creek Divide, Mays Creek, Timpa Lake

OVERNIGHT TRIPS

TWO OR THREE DAYS REQUIRED ON FOOT

Baker Lake, Baron Lakes, Boulder Chain Lakes, Browns Lake, Chamberlain Lakes, Edna Lake, Leggit Lake, Livingston Mill to Frog Lake, North Fork Baron Creek, Observation Peak, Sand Mountain Pass and the Imogene Divide, Scenic Lakes

THREE TO FIVE DAYS ON FOOT

Ardeth and Spangle Lakes, Arrowhead Lake, Everly and Plummer Lakes, Hidden Lake, Ingeborg, Rock Slide, and Benedict Lakes, Timpa Lake.

OPEN ABOUT JULY 1 IN AN AVERAGE YEAR (except that stream crossings will still be high and difficult)

Alpine Way Trail, Alpine Lake (near Sawtooth Lake), Alturas Shore, Bench Lakes, Bridalveil Falls, Champion Creek, Elk Lake, Farley Lake (from Pettit), Fishhook Creek, Frenchman Creek, Grand Prize Gulch, Marshall Lake, Mays Creek, Middle Fork Boise to Rock Creek, Williams Creek

OPEN EARLY OR MID-AUGUST

Alpine-Baron Divide, Ardeth-Spangle Divide, Big Boulder Lakes, Castle Divide, Cramer Divide, Divide just above Ingeborg Lake, Elizabeth Lake from Stanley Lake, Four Lakes Basin, High Pass, Imogene Divide, Windy Devil Pass above Scoop Lake, Pats Lake Divide (latest pass in the SNRA to open), Sand Mountain Pass, Snowyside Pass.

ACCESS ROADS FOR TOUGH VEHICLES AND EXPERIENCED DRIVERS

Graham Guard Station (four-wheel drive required)

Hell Roaring Creek (four-wheel drive required); will be closed as soon as new trailhead at Salmon River is completed.

Pole Creek-Germania Creek Road.

West Pass Creek from Bowery Guard Station; Yellow Belly Lake.

BIBLIOGRAPHY

Alt, David D. and Donald W. Hyndman, *Roadside Geology of Idaho*, Mountain Press, Missoula, 1989

Arno, Stephen and Ramona Hammerly, *Timberline: Mountain and Arctic Forest Frontiers*, The Mountaineers, Seattle, 1984

Bradley, Jim, *Environmental Outfitting*, Moose Creek Ranger District, Nez Perce National Forest, 1975

Brower, David, *Sierra Club Wilderness Handbook*, Sierra Club, Ballentine Books, New York, 1971

Craighead, John J. and Frank C., *Field Guide to Rocky Mountain Wildflowers*, Houghton Mifflin Co., Boston, 1963

Derig, Betty, *Roadside History of Idaho*, Mountain Press, Missoula, 1996

D'Easum, Dick, *Sawtooth Tales*, Caxton Printers, Caldwell, Idaho, 1977

Duft, Joseph, and Robert Moseley, *Alpine Wildflowers of the Rocky Mountains*, Mountain Press, Missoula, 1989.

Fuller, Margaret, *Mountains: A Natural History and Hiking Guide*, John Wiley & Sons, New York, 1989.

Fuller, Margaret, *Forest Fires: An Introduction to Wildland Fire Behavior, Management, Firefighting, and Prevention*, John Wiley & Sons, 1991.

Fuller, Margaret, *Trails of the Frank Church-River of No Return Wilderness*, Signpost Books, Edmonds, Washington, 1987.

Fuller, Margaret, *Trails of Western Idaho*, Signpost Books, 1982, revised 1992.

Godwin, Victor and John Hussey, *Sawtooth Mountain Area Study, Idaho: History*, U.S. Forest Service, National Park Service, 1965

Hart, John, *Walking Softly in the Wilderness*, Sierra Club, San Francisco, 1977

Johnson, Frederic D., *Wild Trees of Idaho*, University of Idaho Press, Moscow, Idaho, 1995

Little, Elbert L., *The Audubon Society Field Guide to North American Trees, Western Region*, Alfred A. Knopf, New York, 1980.

Lopez, Tom, *Exploring Idaho's Mountains: A Guide for Climbers, Scramblers and Hikers*, The Mountaineers, Seattle 1990

Maley, Terry, *Exploring Idaho Geology*, Mineral Land Publications, Boise, 1979

Manning, Harvey, *Backpacking, One Step at a Time*, Vintage Books, New York, 1980

Manning, Harvey, *Mountaineering, the Freedom of the Hills*, The Mountaineers, Seattle, 1974, updated regularly.

Miller, Robert W., *Guide for Using Horses in Mountain Country*, Montana, Montana Wilderness Association, 1974

Off Belay, Renton, Washington, February 1975
Bachman, Ben, "Sawtooth Prolog", page 4
Stur, Louis, "Sawtooth Pioneering", page 10
Bachman, Ben, and Smutek, Ray, "Sawtooth Mountaineering", page 18

Petzoldt, Paul, *The Wilderness Handbook*, W.W. Norton Co. New York, 1974

Preston, Richard Jr. *Rocky Mountain Trees*, Dover Publications, New New York, 1968

Rethmel, R.C., *Backpacking*, Burgess Publishing Co., Minneapolis 1974

Reynolds, Gray; Fournier, Edwin; and Hamre, Vern, *General Management Plan and Final Environmental Statement for the Sawtooth National Recreation Area*, United States Forest Service, Department of Agriculture, 1975

Schaefer, Vincent and John A. Day, *A Field Guide to the Atmosphere*, National Audubon Society and National Wildlife Federation, Houghton Mifflin Company, Boston 1981

Simer, Peter, *The National Outdoor Leadership School's Wilderness Guide*, Simon & Schuster, 1985

Sparling, Wayne, *Southern Idaho Ghost Towns*, Caxton Printers, Caldwell, Idaho, 1976

Spellenberg, Richard, *The Audubon Society's Field Guide to North American Wildflowers, Western Region*, Alfred A. Knopf, New York, 1979

Udvardy, Miklos, *The Audubon Society's Field Guide to North American Birds*, Western Region, Alfred A. Knopf, New York 1977

Whitaker, John O. Jr., *The Audubon Society's Field Guide to North American Mammals*, Alfred A. Knopf, New York, 1980

Wilkerson, James A., *Hypothermia, Frostbite, and Other Cold Injuries*, The Mountaineers, Seattle, Washington, 1986

Yarber, Esther and McGown, Edna, *Stanley-Sawtooth Country*, Publishers Press, Salt Lake City, 1976

BASIC BACKPACKING EQUIPMENT

CLOTHING

broken-in hiking boots
*long pants
sweater or fleece jacket
*wool hat
*rain poncho or jacket
*sunglasses
mosquito headnet

wool or acrylic boot socks
*long-sleeved shirt
*insulated jacket
sun hat
rain pants or chaps
complete change of clothes

GENERAL

comfortable backpack
*flashlight
extra batteries and bulbs
*compass
plastic bags

*topographic map
plastic trowel
toilet paper
20 feet of 1/8" nylon rope
mirror and whistle for signalling

COOKING

aluminum cooking pots
utensils
folding plastic washbasin
biodegradeable soap
pot scrubber, nylon filament
pot scrubber, metal mesh
*waterproof matches
*water filter or small kettle for boiling water

cup and spoon per person
backpacking stove
extra fuel
work gloves or pot grippers
*pocket knife
*firestarter
*extra food

SLEEPING

tent (breathable fabric with waterproof rainfly; single wall tents aren't warm
    enough)

down or synthetic fill three-season sleeping bag inside plastic bag <u>and</u> water-
    proof stuff sack

open or closed cell foam pad or <u>foam-filled</u> air mattress

FIRST AID

mosquito repellant   sunburn cream   lip salve

*minimum first aid kit:
    pain pills, moleskin, Bandaids, salt tablets, gauze, adhesive tape, antibiotic
    ointment, electrolyte balance restoring powder to treat shock and other
    items recommended by your doctor

* indicates essential items for every hiker (the "ten essentials")

ABOUT THE AUTHOR

Margaret Fuller was born and raised in Palo Alto, California. While growing up, she hiked extensively in California in the Tahoe and Mt. Lassen areas and on the Muir Trail. She received her B.A. in biology from Stanford University in 1956 and has lived in Idaho since 1957, first in Caldwell, and for the last twelve years in Weiser.

Margaret Fuller

The idea for a trail guide to the Sawtooths came when she, her husband, Wayne, and their five children found it difficult to find information about good short hikes suitable for families. She has hiked every trail and cross-country hike discussed in detail in this guide, 95% of them two or more times. For the second edition, published in 1988, she repeated 66 of the original 73 hikes and did 24 new ones. For this third edition she repeated 7 of the original hikes, added 5 new ones, and checked changes in the other trails with SNRA officials. In writing her guidebooks, she has hiked over 4,400 miles on Idaho's trails.

Trails of the Sawtooth and White Cloud Mountains was first published in 1979 by Signpost Books, Edmonds, Washington. Margaret is the author of four other books: *Trails of Western Idaho, Signpost Books,* 1982, revised 1992; *Trails of the Frank Church - River of No Return Wilderness,* Signpost Books, 1987; *Mountains: A Natural History and Hiking Guide,* John Wiley & Sons, New York, 1989; and *Forest Fires: An Introduction to Wildland Fire Behavior, Management, Firefighting, and Prevention,* John Wiley & Sons, New York, 1991.

Margaret has taught backpacking in community education courses, led backpacking treks for the Idaho Lung Association and taught workshops on mountain ecology. She has given over 200 slide shows about Idaho mountains.

In 1982 she received the Writer of the Year Award from the Idaho Writer's League. In 1990, the Idaho Centennial Commission designated her three trail guides as Centennial Books. In 1991 she received the Achievement Award from the Idaho Trails Council. In 1992, *Forest Fires* won first place in the Northwest Outdoor Writers Association annual contest and Library Journal mentioned the book as "one of the best sci-tech books of 1991."

Her hobbies are hiking, writing, photography, nature study, playing the flute, cross-country skiing and sewing. She and her husband, Wayne, a former district judge, live in Weiser. They have five grown children and three grandchildren.

INDEX

Titanium Pots - E-Bay → Bike racks, lenses
Fire Mgt
Cup Nood/Ram - Patty
Order Trail Book

Double Skeewer

Next Trip
New Bug Spray
Extra Large Skillet
Camp Fuel
Quinoa